Readers familiar with *Dracula* and *The Strange Case of Dr. Jekyll and Mr. Hyde* may not know that dozens of equally remarkable Gothic texts were written in Great Britain at the end of the nineteenth century. This book accounts for the resurgence of Gothic, and its immense popularity, during the British *fin de siècle*. Kelly Hurley explores a key scenario that haunts the genre: the loss of a unified and stable human identity, and the emergence of a chaotic and transformative "abhuman" identity in its place. She shows that such representations of Gothic bodies are strongly indebted to those found in nineteenth-century biology and social medicine, evolutionism, criminal anthropology and degeneration theory. Gothic is revealed as a highly productive and speculative genre, standing in opportunistic relation to nineteenth-century scientific and social theories.

CAMBRIDGE STUDIES IN
NINETEENTH-CENTURY LITERATURE
AND CULTURE 8

THE GOTHIC BODY

CAMBRIDGE STUDIES IN NINETEENTH-CENTURY
LITERATURE AND CULTURE 8

General editors
GILLIAN BEER, *University of Cambridge*
CATHERINE GALLAGHER, *University of California, Berkeley*

Editorial board
ISOBEL ARMSTRONG, *Birkbeck College, London*
TERRY EAGLETON, *University of Oxford*
LEONORE DAVIDOFF, *University of Essex*
D. A. MILLER, *Harvard University*
J. HILLIS MILLER, *University of California, Irvine*
MARY POOVEY, *The Johns Hopkins University*
ELAINE SHOWALTER, *Princeton University*

Nineteenth-century British literature and culture have been rich fields for interdisciplinary studies. Since the turn of the twentieth century, scholars and critics have tracked the intersections and tensions between Victorian literature and the visual arts, politics, social organization, economic life, technical innovations, scientific thought – in short, culture in its broadest sense. In recent years, theoretical challenges and histographical shifts have unsettled the assumptions of previous scholarly syntheses and called into question the terms of older debates. Whereas the tendency in much past literary critical interpretation was to use the metaphor of culture as "background," feminist, Foucauldian, and other analyses have employed more dynamic models that raise questions of power and of circulation. Such developments have reanimated the field.

This series aims to accomodate and promote the most interesting work being undertaken on the frontiers of the field of nineteenth-century literary studies: work which intersects fruitfully with other fields of study such as history, or literary theory, or the history of science. Comparative as well as interdisciplinary approaches are welcomed.

A complete list of titles published will be found at the end of the book.

THE GOTHIC BODY

Sexuality, materialism, and degeneration
at the fin de siècle

KELLY HURLEY

University of Colorado at Boulder

CAMBRIDGE
UNIVERSITY PRESS

PUBLISHED BY THE PRESS SYNDICATE OF THE UNIVERSITY OF CAMBRIDGE
The Pitt Building, Trumpington Street, Cambridge, United Kingdom

CAMBRIDGE UNIVERSITY PRESS
The Edinburgh Building, Cambridge CB2 2RU, UK
40 West 20th Street, New York NY 10011–4211, USA
477 Williamstown Road, Port Melbourne, VIC 3207, Australia
Ruiz de Alarcón 13, 28014 Madrid, Spain
Dock House, The Waterfront, Cape Town 8001, South Africa

http://www.cambridge.org

First published 1996
First paperback edition 2004

A catalogue record for this book is available from the British Library

Library of Congress cataloguing in publication data

Hurley, Kelly.
The Gothic body: sexuality, materialism, and degeneration at the
fin de siècle / Kelly Hurley.
p. cm. – (Cambridge studies in nineteenth-century literature
and culture; 8)
Includes bibliographical references and index.
ISBN 0 521 55259 1 (hardback)
1. English fiction – 19th century – History and criticism.
2. Gothic revival (Literature) – Great Britain – History –
19th century.   3. Literature and society – Great Britain – History –
19th century.   4. Literature and science – Great Britain – History –
19th century.   5. Horror tales, English – History and criticism.
6. Degeneration in literature.   7. Body, Human, in literature.
8. Materialism in literature.   9. Sex in literature.
II. Series.
PR878.T3H87   1997
823'.0872909–DC20   96–7337 CIP

ISBN 0 521 55259 1 hardback
ISBN 0 521 60711 6 paperback

Transferred to digital printing 2004

For Maree Hurley, with love

Contents

ix

Acknowledgments

This book had its beginnings in a Stanford University dissertation, which was partially funded by a Whiting Foundation Fellowship and a Jacob K. Javits Graduate Fellowship. My dissertation advisors, Barbara Charlesworth Gelpi, Regenia Gagnier, and Rob Polhemus, taught me rigor of thought, independence of mind, and pleasure in the absurdities, rich textures, and complexities of Victorian prose. I am grateful for their intellectual mentorship, and for the support and friendship they have continued to offer since I left Stanford.

I also wish to thank the Graduate Committee on the Arts and Humanities and the Council for Research and Creative Work at the University of Colorado at Boulder, both of which provided funding for research travel, and the Elizabeth Colwill Wiegers Fellowship, which provided a semester of leave time as well as research funding. I could not have undertaken this project without the use of the following collections: the British Library; the J. Lloyd Eaton Collection of Science Fiction and Fantasy, University of California at Riverside; Green Library and Lane Medical Library, Stanford University; the National Library of Medicine; and Norlin Library, University of Colorado at Boulder. Particular thanks are due to Skip Hamilton of Norlin, and the staffs of the interlibrary loan departments at Green and Norlin.

I am most grateful for the very thoughtful and valuable suggestions offered by my readers at the Press, Jonathan Dollimore and Catherine Gallagher. Many thanks to Josie Dixon who, along with Catherine Gallagher, brought this project into the series, and who helped me turn the manuscript into a book. I also wish to acknowledge the help of Linda Bree, who oversaw the book's production, and of my copy-editor Polly Richards.

Those persons who read chapters, shared references, and offered other kinds of intellectual, institutional, and personal support include Margaret Ferguson, Lydia Alix Fillingham, Sidney Goldfarb, Judith

Halberstam, Bruce Kawin, James Kincaid, Gerry Kinneavy, Lee Krauth, Ira Livingston, Tom Lutz, Charles Middleton, Susan Navarette, Michael Petit, Robert M. Philmus, Rubin Rabinowitz, Elizabeth Robertson, David Simpson, John Stevenson, Stacey Vallas, Sue Zemka, and the members of the CU Boulder Women Studies work-in-progress group. I especially appreciate the help of Jeffrey Robinson. I am grateful to all of the students who have discussed popular culture with me, particularly those students from the Fall 1991 graduate seminar "The Victorian Gothic" and the Spring 1994 senior seminar "Gothic Horror." I owe various debts of gratitude and friendship to Denise Albanese, Deb Azorsky, John, Valerie, and Zachary Brady, Sandy French, Carol Glowinsky, Victor Luftig, Hilary Schor, Tasha Spencer, and Harte Weiner. And I wish to take this opportunity to remember Tim Hurley, Bill Lankford, Gary Spear, and Keith Thomas, all of whom died much too young, and who are sadly missed.

Thanks to my sister Mary Hurley and my brother Paul Hurley for their love and support throughout the years. To Maree Hurley, best of mothers and wittiest of women, this book is dedicated.

Mary Klages has given me so much – as my reader and critic, as my interlocutor, as my dear friend – that I can never hope to repay her, except with bowling. And finally, my best love goes to Eric White, who read through countless pages of draft, engaged in endless conversations about the *fin-de-siècle* Gothic, and always encouraged me to write *this* book, rather than the one I sometimes thought I ought to write.

The jacket illustration, Franz von Stuck's "The Sphinx's Kiss" (1895), is reproduced from *Die Kunst* 9 (shelfmark pp 1931 dde) by permission of the British Library.

An earlier version of chapter 4.1 appeared in *Nineteenth-Century Contexts* 14.2 (1990), and is reprinted here by kind permission of *Nineteenth-Century Contexts*. An earlier version of chapter 6.1 appeared in *Virginal Sexuality and Textuality in Victorian Literature*, ed. Lloyd Davis (1993), and is reprinted here by kind permission of the State University of New York Press.

Introduction

The abhuman

A naked man was lying on the floor, his arms and legs stretched wide apart, and bound to pegs that had been hammered into the boards. The body was torn and mutilated in the most hideous fashion, scarred with the marks of red-hot irons, a shameful ruin of the human shape. But upon the middle of the body a fire of coals was smouldering; the flesh had been burnt through. The man was dead, but the smoke of his torment mounted still, a black vapour.
"The young man with spectacles," said Mr. Dyson.
Arthur Machen, The Three Imposters (p. 353)[1]

As the archaeology of our thought easily shows, man is an invention of recent date. And one perhaps nearing its end.
Michel Foucault, The Order of Things (p. 387)

The topic of this book is the ruination of the human subject. Such a ruination, figured in the most violent, absolute, and often repulsive terms, is practiced insistently, almost obsessively, in the pages of British Gothic fiction at the end of the nineteenth century and the beginning of the twentieth. Or perhaps it would be more precise to say that the topic of this book is the ruination of traditional constructs of human identity that accompanied the modeling of new ones at the turn of the century. In place of a human body stable and integral (at least, liable to no worse than the ravages of time and disease), the *fin-de-siècle* Gothic offers the spectacle of a body metamorphic and undifferentiated; in place of the possibility of human transcendence, the prospect of an existence circumscribed within the realities of gross corporeality; in place of a unitary and securely bounded human subjectivity, one that is both fragmented and permeable. Within this genre one may witness the relentless destruction of "the human" and the unfolding in its stead of what I will call, to borrow an evocative term from supernaturalist author William Hope Hodgson, the "abhuman."[2] The abhuman subject is a not-quite-human subject, characterized by its morphic variability, continually in danger of

3

becoming not-itself, becoming other. The prefix "ab-" signals a movement away from a site or condition, and thus a loss. But a movement away from is also a movement towards – towards a site or condition as yet unspecified – and thus entails both a threat and a promise.

The word "abhuman" may be seen as resonating with the psychoanalytic philosopher Julia Kristeva's formulation of "abjection" in *Powers of Horror: An Essay on Abjection*. Literally meaning "cast away" or "cast under, abased," "abjection" is shaded by Kristeva to describe the ambivalent status of a human subject who, on the one hand, labors to maintain (the illusion of) an autonomous and discrete self-identity, responding to any threat to that self-conception with emphatic, sometimes violent, denial, and who on the other hand welcomes the event or confrontation that breaches the boundaries of the ego and casts the self down into the vertiginous pleasures of indifferentiation. To be thus "outcast" is to suffer an anxiety often nauseating in its intensity, but to embrace abjection is to experience *jouissance*.[3] The *fin-de-siècle* Gothic is positioned within precisely such an ambivalence: convulsed by nostalgia for the "fully human" subject whose undoing it accomplishes so resolutely, and yet aroused by the prospect of a monstrous becoming. One may read its obsessive staging and restaging of the spectacle of abhumanness as a paralysis, a species of trauma, but one must also note the variety and sheer exuberance of the spectacle, as the human body collapses and is reshapen across an astonishing range of morphic possibilities: into slug-men, snake-women, ape-men, beast-people, octopus-seal-men, beetle-women, dog-men, fungus-people.

The last decades of the nineteenth century witnessed the reemergence of the Gothic as a significant literary form in Great Britain, after its virtual disappearance in the middle of the century. While certain broad narrative and thematic continuities link this form to the late eighteenth-century and Romantic Gothic novel, the *fin-de-siècle* Gothic rematerializes as a genre in many ways unrecognizable, transfigured, bespeaking an altered sensibility that resonates more closely with contemporary horrific representations than those generated at the far edge of the Enlightenment. More graphic than before, soliciting a more visceral readerly response than before, the *fin-de-siècle* Gothic manifests a new set of generic strategies, discussed below, which function maximally to enact the defamiliarization and violent reconstitution of the human subject.

In *Marxism and Literary Criticism*, Terry Eagleton argues that a new artistic mode, or a "significant development in literary form," may evolve out of a "collective psychological demand" having its roots in some massive social or ideological shift within a culture (pp. 20–7). Such an approach seems especially appropriate to the analysis of popular genres, of like-minded and -structured texts produced in quantity and consumed by a wide-ranging audience, since the very popularity of a genre speaks for its efficacy in interpreting and refiguring unmanageable realities for its audience. Gothic in particular has been theorized as an instrumental genre, reemerging cyclically, at periods of cultural stress, to negotiate the anxieties that accompany social and epistemological transformations and crises.

In the pages that follow I will situate the *fin-de-siècle* revival of the Gothic, in its new avatar as a genre centrally concerned with the horrific re-making of the human subject, within a general anxiety about the nature of human identity permeating late-Victorian and Edwardian culture, an anxiety generated by scientific discourses, biological and sociomedical, which served to dismantle conventional notions of "the human" as radically as did the Gothic which arose in response to them. Evolutionism, criminal anthropology, degeneration theory, sexology, pre-Freudian psychology – all articulated new models of the human as abhuman, as bodily ambiguated or otherwise discontinuous in identity. The end-of-century Gothic is a genre thoroughly imbricated with biology and social medicine: sometimes borrowing conceptual remodelings of human physical identity, as it did from criminal anthropology; sometimes borrowing narrative remodelings of human heredity and culture, as it did from the interrelated discourses of evolutionism, degeneration, and entropy; sometimes borrowing spatial remodelings of the human subject, as it did from the psychologies of the unconscious.[4]

As I have formulated my argument thus far, the *fin-de-siècle* Gothic might appear as purely reactive, emerging within late-Victorian culture as a symptom of a general malaise occasioned by the sciences. The relationship between scientific and Gothic literary discourses is, however, far more complex than the formulation of genre-as-symptom would indicate. In the first place, without arguing a direct influence on the sciences by the Gothic, I will be attentive throughout this study to the "gothicity" of a range of scientific discourses, to rhetoric, modes of imaging, and narrative structures which reveal the surprising compatibility of empiricism and supernaturalism at this historical moment. The province of the nineteenth-century human sciences was after all very like that of the earlier Gothic novel: the pre-Victorian Gothic provided a space wherein to explore phenomena at the borders of human identity and culture – insanity, criminality, barbarity, sexual perversion – precisely those phenomena that would come under the purview of social medicine in later decades. A number of critics have pointed out the ways in which the earlier Gothic's invention of a systematic discourse of the irrational was radically to complicate and reshape understandings of human subjectivity and the "realist" narrative forms increasingly concerned with the intricacies of human consciousness.[5] Understanding scientific inquiry as a culturally embedded rather than disengaged activity, one may speculate on its indebtedness, however subtle, to a "Gothic sensibility" newly available in the nineteenth century, despite the relative attenuation of the genre for fifty years.

One must as well emphasize the sheerly disruptive force of such new concepts as natural selection, or the human unconscious. Pre-Freudian modelings of the unconscious, to take one example, increasingly revealed a human subject fractured by discontinuity and profoundly alienated from itself. The implications of Darwinism,[6] to take another, were perceived as disastrous and traumatic – one might say "gothic" – by a majority of the population. Gothic fiction, working in the negative register of horror, brought this sense of trauma to vivid life, supernatural-izing both the specific content of scientific theories and scientific activity in general. In this sense it can be said to manage the anxieties engendered of scientific innovations by reframing these within the non-realistic, and thus more easily distanced, mode of gothicity.

The *fin-de-siècle* Gothic, however, did more than throw into relief and negotiate a crisis in the epistemology of human identity. For the Gothic served not only to manage anxieties about the shifting nature of "the human" but also to aggravate them. I mean this in no pejorative sense. A crucial strand of argument in this study identifies the Gothic as a *productive* genre: a highly speculative art form, one part of whose cultural work is the invention of new representational strategies by which to imagine human (or not-so-human) realities. Here it should be seen as in opportunistic relation to the sciences. To take one example, the Darwinian narrative of the evolution of species was a narrative within which any combination of morphic traits, any transfiguration of bodily form, was possible; species integrity was undone and remade according to the immediate, situational logic of adaptation to environment.[7] Gothic plotting seized upon this logic as a device by which to generate a seemingly infinite procession of admixed embodiments – monstrous embodiments to be sure, but nonetheless appealing in their audacious refusal to acknowledge any limitations to bodily plasticity. Darwinism opened up a space wherein hitherto unthinkable morphic structures could emerge; the *fin-de-siècle* Gothic occupied that space and pried it open further, attempting to give shape to the unthinkable. That the Gothic frequently concluded by checking its own movement towards innovation – its vampires staked, its beetle-women squashed, its anthropophagous trees dynamited – need not, I think, argue against its role as a fundamentally speculative, even theoretical, genre.

Argument and method

Hysterical utterance has been theorized as a vatic discourse, one which expresses, in "ephemeral and enigmatic" bodily signs that "constitute a language only by analogy," an alternate field of meaning that lies within the interstices of conventional symbolic structures, and thus points toward liberatory possibilities exceeding those allowed within the dominant cultural order.[8] In a roughly parallel argument, Rosemary Jackson posits that fantastic literature "traces the unsaid and the unseen of culture: that which has been silenced, made invisible, covered over and made 'absent'" (*Fantasy: The Literature of Subversion*, p. 4). Though the fantastic exists in "parasitical" relation to the dominant cultural order, bringing into view the forces of disorder and non-meaning against which this order constitutes itself (p. 20), when the fantastic text refuses closure and leaves these forces in view it disrupts conventional meaning systems and makes room for new ones to emerge. Both arguments are intriguing, for both characterize "out-of-control" discourses as oppositional and highly productive, rather than merely symptomatic.

A danger to which such an analysis is prone is an assumption of too great a coherence on the part of the dominant cultural order. Jackson argues that such orders are "closed systems," purveying "single, reductive 'truths'" and upholding a "unitary vision." Mainstream discourses, like the nineteenth-century realist novel, are said to partake of this univocality: "The fantastic exists as the inside, or underside, of realism, opposing the novel's closed, monological forms with open, dialogical structures, as if the novel had given rise to its own opposite, its unrecognizable reflection" (Jackson, p. 25).

In attempting to specify the Gothic's relationship (both contestatory and highly imbricated) to dominant ideologies of human identity found within the nineteenth century, I have taken a cue from Mary Poovey's *Uneven Developments: The Ideological Work of Gender in Mid-Victorian England.*

Here Poovey argues against an understanding of ideologies as monolithic or invulnerable: they are instead contradictory formations, formations in process, characterized simultaneously by "apparent coherence and authenticity" and "internal instability and artificiality." They are "both contested and always under construction . . . always open to revision, dispute, and the emergence of oppositional formations" (p. 3). Poovey focuses on salient points of stress and fracture within Victorian gender ideologies: what she calls "border cases," which serve to expose not only "the artificiality of the binary logic that governed the Victorian symbolic economy" (p. 12), but also the historical contingency of the ideology in question. Very many recent studies have attended to precisely such border cases, emphasizing the "uneven," if not utterly discontinuous and self-contradictory, nature of Victorian ideological formations.

Since my argument is in general concerned with the *fin-de-siècle* Gothic's contestation of the meanings of human identity, it does assume that there was during the nineteenth century such a thing as a dominant understanding of the subject. But this is not to imply that human identity was uniformly and unproblematically conceived as unitary, discrete, and immutable. Critics like Nancy Armstrong and Regenia Gagnier have demonstrated the immense cultural labor required to produce and maintain that entity variously known as the liberal humanist subject, the modern bourgeois subject, and the autonomous individual, whose features include self-sufficiency, self-continuity, a complex yet self-contained interiority, and the potential for full self-knowledge.[9]

A crucial part of that cultural labor was the Victorian impulse toward scientific classification and a subsequent normalization of the possibilities – bodily, subjective, sexual – of human identity. But ideologies of normative sexual identity, to take one instance, were not only fluctuable, self-contradictory, and highly contested during the nineteenth century. The concept of a "self" whose essential nature was intimately linked to something called sexual identity was very much under construction during the period. Michel Foucault has demonstrated this famously in his first volume of *The History of Sexuality*, where he also argues that hegemonic discourses *produce* the very oppositional possibilities they are designed to preempt.[10] Thus Victorian *scientia sexualis*, in building up a profile of "the homosexual," on the one hand served to stigmatize same-sex desires and erotic practices, but on the other made newly or differently available a homosexual ontology of sorts, which could be appropriated in any number of ways. Moreover, its elaboration of theories of a "third sex" would destabilize the very project sexology seemed to be embarked on: the consolidation of a model of human identity based on a rigidly binaristic understanding of male and female, masculine and feminine.[11] As Lawrence Birkin describes it, sexology undermined its own attempts to normativize sexuality by foregrounding the "multiplicity" of human sexual practices, and the "radically idiosyncratic character of desire itself."[12]

In other words, I am positing the *fin-de-siècle* Gothic as a highly innovative genre which is at the same time deeply imbricated within its cultural moment. Jacques Derrida argues that there can be no such thing as absolute discursive originality in any case; even the most inventive of discourses borrows its "concepts from the text of a heritage which is more or less coherent or ruined" ("Structure, Sign and Play in the Discourse of the Human Sciences," p. 285). Understandings of human identity underwent a radical transfiguration at the *fin de siècle* as new modes of imaging and narrativizing the (ab)human subject became available. Those scientific disciplines like sexology, which sought to fix the meanings of human identity, were capable of fracturing it beyond recognition; the "heritage" they made available for discourses like the Gothic was sometimes "more or less coherent," sometimes more or less in ruins. I will not go so far as to say that the sciences bodied forth a "shameful ruin of the human shape," to recur to the Machen quote which began this chapter. That would be left for the Gothic to accomplish. This study will trace the outlines of this "shameful ruin," and explore the vexing question of why and how the ruination of the human subject can afford such pleasure to those who witness it.

I have divided my argument into three sections, corresponding to three broad topical themes: "The Gothic Material World," "Gothic Bodies," and "Gothic Sexualities." Part I theorizes the exemplary abhuman body – liminal, admixed, nauseating, abominable – represented by the *fin-de-siècle* Gothic in relation to materialist science and philosophy of the later nineteenth century and, retrospectively, the twentieth. Within a materialist reality, no transcendent meaningfulness anchors the chaotic fluctuability of the material universe. Matter is no longer subordinate to form, because attempts formally to classify matter, such as the attempt to stabilize the meanings of "human identity," are provisional and stop-gap measures at best. Within such a reality, in other words, bodies are without integrity or stability; they are instead composite and changeful. Nothing is left but Things: forms rent from within by their own heterogeneity, and always in the process of becoming-Other. Part I both traces "Thing-ness" as a thematic preoccupation of the *fin-de-siècle* Gothic, and considers the ontological and affective position of the reader asked to share this preoccupation.

Part II situates the Gothic's making-abhuman of the human body within a range of evolutionist discourses: Darwinism, criminal anthropology, and degeneration theory. Besides positing a too intimate continuity between humans and the "lower" species, Darwinism described the natural order as a disorder, within which species identity was characterized by admixture and flux rather than integrity and fixity. Similarly, the Gothic represents human bodies as between species: always-already in a state of indifferentiation, or undergoing metamorphoses into a bizarre assortment of human/not-human configurations. The Gothic also mapped out alternate trajectories of evolution than the one set forth by Darwin, imagining monstrous modifications of known species, or the emergence of horrific new ones, in accordance with the logics of specific ecosystems.

Whereas the Darwinian narrative was a non-telic one, governed by natural processes that worked in no particular direction and towards no particular end, the nineteenth-century imagination was preoccupied with the prospect of the reversal of evolution, insofar as this was understood as a synonym for "progress." Of relevance here are the sociomedical discourses of degeneration theory and criminal anthropology. The former described the disastrous effects of the inheritance of undesirable traits within a familial line and, more alarmingly, the cumulative effects of social contamination, which could launch a nation into a downward spiral into barbarity and chaos. The latter focused on a human liability to atavism or reversion, used to explain the predilection of certain individuals for criminal behaviors. I discuss these as "gothic" versions of evolutionism – discourses that emphasized the potential indifferentiation and changeability of the human species – as well as considering them in relation to the literature.

Part III discusses the Gothic's participation in the ongoing debates over the nature of human sexuality. Despite attempts to stabilize the shifting meanings of human identity by a rigidification of gender roles, the late-Victorian period was one verging on "sexual anarchy," to use Elaine Showalter's evocative phrase.[13] Not only was Victorian gender ideology a site of internal contradiction (for example, identifying women as dangerously defined by their bodies on the one hand and ethereal, essentially disembodied creatures on the other), it was also a site of contestation on a number of social and discursive fronts. The Gothic seemed at times to reinforce normative sexuality by representing such behaviors as aggressive femininity and homosexuality as monstrous and abhorrent. But even within this register (a fundamentally anxious one), the Gothic served to multiply, and thus destabilize, the meanings of sexuality. Here it can be seen as analogous to the emergent discipline of sexology, which could only identify a normative sexuality by itemizing the numerous instances of "perversion" against which it was defined. Gothic plotting, working to invert and more radically admix gender and sexual attributes within a variety of abhuman bodies, unfixed the binarism of sexual difference, exploding the construct of "the human" from within.

My readings of the *fin-de-siècle* Gothic are necessarily filtered through the lens of the twentieth-century theorists who have shaped my own thinking. It is indeed unlikely that the genre's preoccupation with abhumanness would have been thrown so sharply into relief for me without benefit of a variety of recent insights – structuralist, deconstructionist, psychoanalytical, postmodernist – into human symbolic orders and the liminal entities which trouble them. This preoccupation *did* exist nonetheless: the end-of-century Gothic explored the parameters of abhuman, or even "posthuman," identities in terms surprisingly compatible with those of many theorists closer to our own *fin de siècle* than the last.[14]

Thus in considering late-Victorian representations of the abhuman I have drawn freely from such models as Mary Douglas' account of abomination, or Kristeva's of abjection, which among other things work to account for the seemingly excessive affect which liminal entities can elicit. This is not to imply that twentieth-century theorists are in any way supra-historical authorities on the historically specific materials under consideration here. But they do provide useful and provocative lines of departure. Kristeva's *Powers of Horror: An Essay on Abjection*, for instance, describes a human subject who struggles both to engage with, and disengage itself from, the inescapable fact of its own materiality. Within the Kristevan scenario this sometimes anguished ambivalence about the prospect of human embodiedness is set forth as universal, the inevitable product of infantile experience. But one may historicize the *Essay on Abjection* itself by placing it on a continuum with other anguished responses to the particular brand of materialism that arose in the nineteenth century. Or to put it in somewhat different terms, Kristeva's revisionist psychoanalytical model of the subject (liminally human, fragmented, Thing-like, convulsed with symptoms) could not have been conceived without benefit of *fin-de-siècle* models of the abhuman subject drawn from both pre- or proto-Freudian psychology and a constellation of evolutionist discourses. Or to put it in different terms still, a juxtaposition of Kristeva and Hodgson, of the abject and the abhuman, is of benefit to both.

METAPHYSICAL ESTRANGEMENT

Though horror and revolting nausea rose up within me, and an odour of corruption choked my breath, I remained firm. I was then privileged or accursed, I dare not say which, to see that which was on the bed, lying there black like ink, transformed before my eyes. The skin, and the flesh, and the muscles, and the bones, and the firm structure of the human body that I had thought to be unchangeable, and permanent as adamant, began to melt and dissolve . . . Here too was all the work by which man had been made repeated before my eyes. I saw the form waver from sex to sex, dividing itself from itself, and then again reunited. Then I saw the body descend to the beasts whence it ascended, and that which was on the heights go down to the depths, even to the abyss of all being . . . I watched, and at last I saw nothing but a substance as of jelly. Then the ladder was ascended again . . . [*here the* MS. *is illegible*] . . . for one instant I saw a Form, shaped in dimness before me, which I will not further describe. But the symbol of this form may be seen in ancient sculptures, and in paintings which survived beneath the lava, too foul to be spoken of . . . as a horrible and unspeakable shape, neither man nor beast, was changed into human form, there came finally death. (Arthur Machen, *The Great God Pan*)[15]

At the center of Arthur Machen's 1890 novel *The Great God Pan* is a woman of many aliases, named most consistently as Helen Vaughan. She is, despite her surpassing beauty, a woman of blackest infamy, though the text refuses to do more than vaguely characterize the nature of her crimes. Helen Vaughan's genealogy is striking enough: she is the product of experimental neurology and of certain obscure primitive forces, as these are brought to play across the body of a seventeen-year-old virgin named Mary. Dr. Raymond, a neurologist and devotee of "transcendental medicine," surgically alters Mary's brain, the point of the operation being to "level utterly the solid wall of sense." "With a touch [of the knife]," says Dr. Raymond, "I can complete the communication between this world of sense and – we shall be able to finish the sentence later on" (p. 173). The ancients, he explains, called such a communication "seeing the great god Pan" (p. 170).

  The operation is successful – Mary "sees the Great God Pan" – but she is reduced to irremediable idiocy, and nine months later, presumably having been impregnated by Pan himself, she gives birth to Helen Vaughan and dies. Helen grows into a terrible maturity, leaving behind her a string of victims: she begins with Rachel, a pubescent girl, and later devotes herself to the ruin of adult men. None of these are victims, directly, of murder: they succumb suddenly to heart failure, commit suicide, or die more slowly of "nervous prostration" as a result of what they have seen in Helen's presence, or seen occur across the metamorphic body of Helen herself.

As to what exactly this might be, the text remains coy, though it is clearly sexual in nature. Herbert, Helen's erstwhile husband, relates how "that woman, if I can call her woman, corrupted my soul," and his corruption began on their wedding night: "sitting up in bed . . . she spoke in her beautiful voice, spoke of things which even now I would not dare whisper in blackest night" (p. 192). As "acute suicidal mania" spreads through the bachelor population of aristocratic London, various gentlemen are seen, immediately before their self-inflicted deaths, emerging from Helen's doorway at unseemly hours of the morning with an "infernal medley of passions" etched on their faces: "furious lust, and hate that was like fire . . . and the utter blackness of despair" (p. 225).

The text hints at a correspondence between Helen's perverse activities and primitive, orgiastic rites said to have been practiced by certain of the ancient Romans, cultists of Pan, who once inhabited Britain. The great god Pan, the text indicates, is a "presence" impinging upon human realities, but not explicable within human symbolic systems. Though embodied, this "god" exists at the juncture of various bodily identities, and is "neither man nor beast, neither the living nor the dead, but all things mingled, the form of all things but devoid of all form" (pp. 176–7). Helen Vaughan's body at the moment of her death is similarly undifferentiated, "changing and melting" from "woman to man, from man to beast, and from beast to worse than beast" (pp. 242–3).

When introducing some of the thematic, rhetorical, and narrative strategies characteristic of the *fin-de-siècle* Gothic, one could do worse than begin with a summary of *The Great God Pan*. Readily identifiable as sensationalist, excessive, its plot is typical within the genre in figuring sexuality as horrific, identity as multiple, the boundary between science and supernaturalism as permeable, and the "normal" human subject as liable to contamination, affective, moral, and physical, by the gothicized subject. Central to it all is the spectacle of the human body that one "had thought to be unchangeable, and permanent as adamant, beg[inning] to melt and dissolve": the spectacle of Helen's body losing sexual specificity, species specificity, and the specificity that distinguishes form from matter (as she becomes "a substance as jelly"), and finally metamorphosing into a thing so terrible as to resist or exceed language.

The inadequacy of language, as the novella struggles to depict and contain the abhuman realities with which it is obsessed, is prominently foregrounded in *The Great God Pan*. The text consistently sheers off into a gothic rhetoric of the ineffable: Pan is a "horror which we can but hint at, which we can only name under a figure" (p. 238); Helen commits "nameless infamies," and her "human flesh [has] become the veil of a horror one dare not express" (p. 242). Even in the fairly graphic scene of Helen's deathbed metamorphosis, the text can only suggest the nature of the final, most horrible transformation "from beast to *worse than beast*." Rhetorical obfuscation, this refusal to name, finds its parallel in a variety of narrative strategies which serve to disrupt the smooth transmission of the story. For the basic plot of *The Great God Pan* as I've described it is extraordinarily difficult to reconstruct. Events are offered in no chronological sequence; instead, the novella takes sporadically the viewpoint of one of three men, Villiers, Clarke, and Austin, as they move randomly into contact with various of Helen Vaughan's victims. The plot further unfolds through a series of interpolated narratives – manuscripts, letters, medical reports, a collection of sketches by an artist-participant in Helen Vaughan's orgies – which help unravel the central mysteries of the text to Villiers, Clarke, and Austin, but are interrupted at the climactic moment, as they're being read aloud, or are even withheld entirely from the reader.[16]

Remarkable in its own way, *The Great God Pan* nonetheless bears striking similarities to a broad range of texts written at the turn of the century. The strategies it practices may be seen as conventions of the *fin-de-siècle* Gothic, which I will summarize as follows. The plot which the genre reiterates is of the becoming-abhuman of the human subject, with abhumanness theorized in the registers of bodily, subjective, and sexual identity. But the genre is profoundly ambivalent towards its own object of obsession. As a result, it works to develop narrative strategies which enable a simultaneous engagement with and revulsion from its topic – strategies whereby to multiply and aggravate instances of abhumanness, but also to occlude them. And finally, human mutability is figured in terms both supernaturalist and scientific; the *fin-de-siècle* Gothic in fact deliberately confuses the two modes, as I will discuss in the pages below.

The fantastic

When *Dracula*'s Jonathan Harker recovers from his terrible experiences in Transylvania, he doubts his own sanity. "I have had a great shock . . .

and I do not know if it was all real or the dreaming of a madman. You know I have had brain fever, and that is to be mad" (p. 138). The Captain of the *Demeter*, the ship that transports Dracula to England, at first refuses to believe there is a vampire on board. He blames the disappearance of his crew on his officer, who babbles about apparitions: "He is mad, stark, raving mad . . . It was this madman who had got rid of the men one by one" (p. 113). Even after the third blood transfusion to the vampirized Lucy, Seward cannot accept the explanation of her "illness" that is staring him in the face. "What does it all mean? I am beginning to wonder if my long habit of life amongst the insane is beginning to tell upon my own brain" (p. 176).

The unnerving possibility of one's own madness is preferable to the still more unnerving one of supernatural agency disrupting known, familiar realities. These moments of refusal identify *Dracula* as an instance of Todorov's transhistorical genre "the fantastic."[7] What distinguishes this genre, according to Todorov, is the prolonged period of "hesitation" undergone by the character (and by extension, the reader) who witnesses the incursion of supernaturalism into a natural world.

> In a world which is indeed our world, the one we know, a world without devils, sylphides, or vampires, there occurs an event which cannot be explained by the laws of this same familiar world. The person who experiences the event must opt for one of two possible solutions: either he is the victim of an illusion of the senses, of a product of the imagination – and laws of the world then remain what they are; or else the event has indeed taken place, it is an integral part of reality – but then this reality is controlled by laws unknown to us . . .
>
> The fantastic occupies the duration of this uncertainty . . . The fantastic is that hesitation experienced by a person who knows only the laws of nature, confronting an apparently supernatural event. (p. 25)

The fantastic presents what Andrzej Zgorzelski calls "a textual confrontation of two models of reality,"[18] and signals in various ways – through a massing of rhetoric around the supernatural event, through descriptions of the disbelief or terror experienced by the character who witnesses the event – that the confrontation is a distressing one. This sense of metaphysical estrangement instantiated by the fantastic enables one to distinguish it from such related genres as the fairy tale and allegory, in which supernatural or magical events are accepted by character and reader alike with a certain nonchalance.

In theory at least, one should be able to distinguish the fantastic from science fiction along the same lines. Darko Suvin defines science fiction as a genre "distinguished by the narrative dominance of a fictional novelty (novum, innovation) validated both by being continuous with a body of already existing cognitions and by being a 'mental experiment' based on cognitive logic" (*Victorian Science Fiction in the UK: The Discourses of Knowledge and Power*, p. 86). Though the science-fiction text depicts fantastic events, in other words, these do not violate the precepts of reality, however defined within its host culture. Rather, the science-fiction text represents extraordinary possibilities that are consistent with, and may be logically derived from, the knowledge systems of the culture in which it was written. In Zgorzelski's terms, there is no confrontation of models of reality in the science-fiction text, for the text commences in and develops an "alternate" reality.[19]

Gothic science

However, the distinction between science fiction and the fantastic is difficult to maintain in the case of the *fin-de-siècle* Gothic, which could readily be subsumed within either category. Ed Block, Jr. suggests that the Victorian Gothic may be characterized by its modification of earlier Gothic themes – "madness, bloodlust, and evil genius" – in terms of evolution theory, particularly *fin-de-siècle* evolutionist psychology (pp. 445, 463). Donald Lawler proposes a new genre, the "hybrid form of gothic SF." This hybrid genre is a "vehicle of expression for humanizing, however erratically and grotesquely, the unrepresented in nature, as implied in the scientific concepts of devolution, randomness, indeterminacy, and the rest of the new ideas that enthralled the nineteenth-century mind to powerful metaphors of despair" (pp. 249, 257). Judith Wilt's claim is that "in or around December, 1897," with the publication of H. G. Wells' *The War of the Worlds*, "Victorian gothic changed – into Victorian science fiction" (p. 618).[20]

Suvin argues that "an S-F narration is a fiction in which the S-F element [the novum] is hegemonic – that is, so central and significant that it determines the whole narrative logic" (p. 89). Few of the texts I will discuss fit this criterion, yet all of them thematize or otherwise incorporate scientific discourses, featuring scientist-protagonists (doctors, psychologists, chemists, anthropologists, natural historians), describing scientific experiments, quoting scientific jargon. The *fin-de-siècle* Gothic consistently blurs the boundary between natural and supernatural phenomena, hesitating between scientific and occultist accountings of inexplicable events. The realm the genre explores is the grey area at the borderline between known and unknown, or extra-rational phenomena, with the supernatural defined not as the occult per se, but as the product of mysterious natural forces the scientist has not yet been able to explain. In Hugh Conway's *Carriston's Gift* (1886), a doctor-psychologist who observes Carriston's powers of second sight asks, "Could it be possible – could there be in certain organizations powers not yet known – not yet properly investigated?" (p. 57). Or as a "professor of mesmerism and clairvoyance" complains in Joseph Hocking's *The Weapons of Mystery* (1890): "Our science, which is really the queen of sciences, is disregarded ... Never mind, our day will come. One day all the sciences shall bow the knee to us, for we are the real interpreters of the mysteries of nature" (pp. 164, 163).

Occasionally these works simply debunk the supernatural, in the Gothic tradition of Ann Radcliffe. In Sheridan Le Fanu's 1886 "Green Tea," for example, the German physician Martin Hesselius explains how a patient's eerie "visitations" were caused by psychological stress and too much caffeine. But more often they feature a scientist or physician who regards the so-called occult with a certain proprietary interest. In Richard Marsh's *The Beetle* (1897), after witnessing the Oriental villainess' metamorphosis from woman to scarab, Sydney Atherton, chemist and general "inventor," writes, "I felt as an investigator might feel who has stumbled, haphazard, on some astounding, some epoch-making discovery" (p. 546). Supernatural phenomena are presented here as forces that might very well be accessible to scientific inquiry, that might be circumscribed within the realm of natural phenomena and controlled by human agency. "The charlatan is always the pioneer," says a character in Conan Doyle's "The Leather Funnel."[21] "From the astrologer came the astronomer, from the alchemist the chemist, from the mesmerist the experimental psychologist ... Even such subtle and elusive things as dreams will in time be reduced to system and order ... [and the topic] will no longer be the amusement of the mystic, but the foundations of a science" (p. 63).[22]

"Scientific" explanations of seemingly occult phenomena offered by the Gothic range from the imprecise to the highly detailed. Jekyll's "Full Statement of the Case" which concludes Robert Louis Stevenson's *Dr. Jekyll and Mr. Hyde* (1886) is vague in the extreme. "Enough, then, that I only recognised my natural body for the mere effulgence of certain of the powers that made up my spirit, but managed to compound a drug by which these powers should be dethroned from their supremacy, and a second form and countenance substituted" (pp. 105–6). Jekyll does not describe the chemical make-up of the compound nor the means by which it wrought his transformation into Hyde, only mentioning that the impurity of a certain "salt" was what "lent efficacy to the draught" (p. 123). Wells' Dr. Moreau, on the other hand, spends several pages elaborating the vivisectionist and other methods by which he transforms animals into "beast men"; Wells was careful to base Moreau's explanation on recognizable experimental procedures.[23] Wells in fact concludes *The Island of Dr. Moreau* with a somber afterword in which he warns that "strange as it may seem to the unscientific reader, there can be no denying that . . . the manufacture of monsters – and perhaps even *quasi*-human monsters – is within the possibilities of vivisection."[24]

Considered in this light, *Moreau* might be classed as science fiction – the scientific "novum" dictates "the whole narrative logic," and is "continuous with a body of already existing cognitions" – and indeed Suvin claims *Moreau* as a "true" example of the genre (p. 66).[25] Nonetheless, *Moreau* might also be classed as Gothic, most notably in its deployment of certain rhetorical and narrative strategies. In emphasizing the horror Moreau's abhuman creations arouse in the narrator Prendick, the text labors to create that sense of metaphysical estrangement Todorov describes as the crucial element of the fantastic. The textual affect that masses itself around the beast people is intensified as much as possible by a series of typically Gothic narrative devices: the prolongation of uncertainty and suspense; descriptive passages marked by their vagueness and obscurity; narrative elisions, evasions, and discontinuities. The science practiced by Moreau is moderately plausible, but the text frames its results as "gothic."

I am finally less interested in the generic classification of a text like *Moreau* than in its reconfiguration of scientific discourse. The *fin-de-siècle* Gothic stands in ambivalent relation to the contemporary sciences, which on the one hand it demonizes, and on the other cites as sources whose prestige and authority lend credence to its own sensational plot structures.[26] In the middle of *Dracula*, the Dutch psychologist Van Helsing launches into a bizarre rant to his former student Dr. Seward. He is preparing his friend for the revelation that vampires do exist, even in the everyday modern world. The ultra-rationalist Seward, however, will have none of it. Van Helsing chides him in his quaint, imperfect English:

You are clever man, friend John; you reason well, and your wit is bold; but you are too prejudiced. You do not let your eyes see nor your ears hear, and that which is outside your daily life is not of account to you. Do you not think that there are things which you cannot understand, and yet which are; that some people see things that others cannot? But there are things old and new which must not be contemplate by men's eyes, because they know – or think they know – some things which other men have told them. Ah, it is the fault of our science that it wants to explain all; and if it explain not, then it says there is nothing to explain. But yet we see around us every day the growth of new beliefs, which think themselves new; and which are yet but the old, which pretend to be young. (p. 246)

Science, in other words, is only now catching up with seemingly supernatural phenomena which have been around for centuries; the scientist dismisses what he cannot explain, but these phenomena persist nonetheless. Seward rejects theories of "corporeal transference," "materialization," "astral bodies," and "the reading of thought," but accepts hypnotism, because "Charcot has proved that pretty well" (pp. 246–7). Van Helsing points out Seward's contradictory reasoning: he cannot "follow the mind of the great Charcot . . . into the soul of the patient that he influence." Yet he is willing to "accept the hypnotism and reject the thought-reading" (p. 247). Once one allows for hypnotism, invoked here as the most plausible of all the "fringe" sciences then in vogue, one opens the door onto all sorts of seeming improbabilities. Van Helsing then describes science itself as occult: "Let me tell you, my friend, that there are things done today in electrical science which would have been deemed unholy by the very men who discovered electricity – who would themselves not so long before have been burned as wizards. There are always mysteries in life" (p. 247).[27] He concludes with a hodgepodge of such mysteries: Methuselah's longevity, life and death in general, human criminality, the great age of a famous Spanish spider and of tortoises, elephants, and parrots, the vampire bat of the Pampas, the awakening from seeming burials alive by Indian fakirs (pp. 247–8).[28] Seward is understandably bewildered, but he acknowledges the point of Van Helsing's lesson: "Then you want me not to let some previous conviction injure the receptivity of my mind with regard to some strange matter" (p. 249).

In this chapter we see Seward's "hesitation" overcome: he is finally prepared to modify his rationalist world-view by accepting the extra-rational possibilities exemplified by Dracula. The reader, however, stands in an odd position to Seward, for the reader has happily acknowledged the existence of vampires as early as chapter 2. Todorov's assertion that the hesitation or uncertainty of textual characters guides the reader's, that the sense of metaphysical estrangement experienced by the one is experienced by the other (pp. 31, 33, 86), clearly does not pertain here. What happens instead is that as Seward is educated out of purist rationalism, the reader is educated into a more "rationalist" accounting of phenomena like vampirism. Both Seward and reader are trained into an understanding of the permeable boundaries between science and occultism, between natural phenomena and monstrous ones. Science is gothicized, and gothicity is rendered scientifically plausible. *Dracula* finally will not choose between the two competing models. The Count is a vampire, but he is also "a criminal and of criminal type. Nordau and Lombroso would so classify him" (p. 439), and by analyzing the "child-brain" of Dracula (p. 437), the psychologist Van Helsing is able to predict and thwart his movements. Hypnotism is both an occult practice, associated with vampiric seduction, and a scientific practice sanctioned by the actual figure of Charcot, under whom the fictional Van Helsing was a student. Psychology is represented simultaneously as an antidote to magic, an alternate form of magic, and finally, a magical new discourse by which to comprehend irrational behavior.[29]

The most important point here is that the topics pursued by nineteenth-century science were often as "gothic" as those found within any novel – criminal hypnosis is a case in point, as is the criminal anthropological theory of the atavist, whose body was a compendium of human and not-human morphic traits. Models of the (ab)human subject generated by psychology in the first case and and revisionary Darwinism in the second conflict with traditional understandings of the unitary and stable human subject, calling to mind Zgorzelski's assertion that the fantastic text stages a "confrontation of two models of reality." Scientific discourses themselves occasion a sense of metaphysical estrangement in their popular readership,[30] as they reconfigure the known world; in the Gothic which emerges in opportunistic relation to these discourses, that moment of convulsion is made visible.

PART I

The Gothic material world

CHAPTER I

The revenge of matter

In William Hope Hodgson's "The Crew of the *Lancing*,"[1] an unnamed ship, sailing somewhere in the tropics, is becalmed after a submarine earthquake. Entrapped within the "wreathing mists" that arise from the boiling sea, and oppressed by a "general feeling of something impending" (p. 259), the men hear strange noises "far out in the night, a muffled screaming, and then a clamour of hoarse braying like an ass's, only deeper, and with a horribly suggestive human note ringing through it" (p. 260). The source of this braying is a hitherto unknown species of deep-water monstrosities, dislodged from their usual habitat by the earthquake, that have boarded another becalmed ship, the *Lancing*, and eaten its crew.

> Crawling about the decks [of the *Lancing*] now visible in the thinning mist, were the most horrible creatures I had ever seen. In spite of their unearthly strangeness I had a feeling that there was something familiar about them. They were like nothing so much as men. They had bodies the shape of seals, but of a dead unhealthy white colour. The lower part ended in a sort of double curved tail on which they had two long, snaky feelers, and at the ends a very human-like hand with talons instead of nails – fearsome parodies of humans.
>
> Their faces, which, like their arm-tentacles, were black, were the most grotesquely human things about them, and save that the upper jaw shut into the lower – much after the manner of the jaw of an octopus – I have seen men amongst certain tribes of natives who had faces uncommonly like theirs; yet no native I have ever seen could have given me the extraordinary feeling of horror and revulsion that I experienced towards those brutal looking creatures. (pp. 265–6)

The horror of the spectacle, as the narrator emphasizes it, lies in the indifferentiation of the monstrous body, an indifferentiation that serves most notably to defamiliarize human identity. He recurs to the human body consistently as his point of reference, only to note its admixture across a fantastic range of morphic possibilities: arms like tentacles,

23

taloned hands, snaky extremities, faces with octopus jaws. These creatures blend human racial characteristics as well, being black like "natives," but white like Europeans; nor can whiteness (here a color "dead" and "unhealthy") be retained as a privileged term within a racial hierarchy that fixes the meaning of human identity from within.

Monstrosity as liminality

Like other monstrosities of the *fin-de-siècle* Gothic, those on the *Lancing* are interstitial creatures: they exist across multiple categories of being and conform cleanly to none of them. Dracula, for example, is *Nosferatu*, or Undead: living and not living, aglow with a horrible ruddy vitality, and yet stinking of the charnel house. The beast people in *The Island of Dr. Moreau* are between species, occupying a border identity midway between animality and humanity. The villainess of *The Beetle* is ambiguous in bodily identity (both human and animal), in sexual identity (both male and female), and in sexual orientation (as a woman, she seduces Paul Lessingham; as a man, he assaults Robert Holt; as a woman, she assaults Marjorie Linden).

Social anthropologist Mary Douglas' *Purity and Danger: An Analysis of the Concepts of Pollution and Taboo* is a text that has proven very useful in the theorizing of such monstrosities as I am discussing here.[2] Douglas argues that phenomena perceived as impure or otherwise dangerous within a culture are those violating the classificatory systems through which the culture is able meaningfully to organize experience. The dietary taboos in *Leviticus*, for example, prohibit the consumption of animal species which lack categorical integrity:

Hybrids and other confusions are abominated . . . Holiness requires that individuals shall conform to the class to which they belong. And holiness requires that different classes of things shall not be confused . . . [I]n general the underlying principle of cleanness in animals is that they shall conform fully to their class. Those species are unclean which are imperfect members of their class, or whose class itself confounds the general scheme of the world. (Douglas, *Purity*, pp. 53, 55)

An "abomination" is a border entity, existing at the interstices of oppositional categories which "impose system on an inherently untidy experience" by "exaggerating the difference between within and without, above and below, male and female, with and against" (p. 4). Within Douglas' paradigm, the monstrosities of the *fin-de-siècle* Gothic are monstrous precisely because of their liminality. To be Undead, to be simultaneously human and animal, to shift from one sexed identity to another, is to explode crucial binarisms that lie at the foundations of human identity.

Douglas emphasizes the positive aspects of pollution behaviors, arguing that it is only by identifying anomalous phenomena that a culture is able to clarify the boundaries of the categories the anomaly confounds, and continue to experience the world as an epistemologically stable site. Dirt, disorder, impurity, anomaly, abomination – these cannot be perceived unless in relation to a highly organized system which they exceed, and serve to delineate more firmly the taxonomies they violate. "Defilement . . . cannot occur except in view of a systematic ordering of ideas . . . For the only way in which pollution ideas make sense is in reference to a total structure of thought whose key-stone, boundaries, margins and internal lines are held in relation by rituals of separation" (p. 41). Pollution behaviors are thus, for Douglas, functional rather than obsessive or hysterical. By this reading the Gothic could be said to function as a conserving genre: in depicting the abhuman it reaffirms, paradoxically, the "fully human" identity to which abhumanness is opposed, so that human identity is reconfigured at the very moment it is undone.[3]

To read a text like "The Crew of the *Lancing*" along such lines, however, seems wilfully perverse. For it is not just human integrity that this story calls into question, but the possibility of any species integrity whatsoever. Hodgson's braying monstrosities are a bizarre amalgam of bodily characteristics drawn indiscriminately from a range of possibilities, the human body only one among them. Octopus blends with seal, ass, and snake as well as human; non-human species are prone to admixture and thus liminality too. The "natural order" emerges as a disorder, exceeding the human ordering systems (such as natural history's classification of organic life by species) designed to contain it. Structure itself – for the creatures are complex, highly structured entities – is revealed as a chaos. An alternate reading of Douglas could emphasize what is implicit in her argument: that classificatory schema are merely functional, artificial rather than natural, and that anomalous phenomena are abominable because they throw into relief the *provisionality* of the categories they confound.

Compare Jacques Derrida's discussion of the "rupture" or "disruption" that occurred in the humanistic and social sciences "when the structurality of structure had to begin to be thought" ("Structure, Sign and Play," p. 280). For Derrida, this entails the recognition that any semiotic system, at any historical moment, is an arbitrary one. The "play" of differentially related elements within a semiotic system is constrained by the supplementary addition of a "center": "a point of presence" or "fixed origin" (p. 278) which is understood as existing paradoxically within and outside of the system, as both governing the system and transcending it. That is, all elements within the system are limited in their play, in their potentiality for meaningfulness and recombination, by virtue of their relation to this "transcendental signified" (God, Providence, Man, Consciousness). The transcendental signified is conceived as "a full presence . . . beyond play" (p. 279) – as an essence which means only itself, and thus transcends the vicissitudes of the recalcitrant material world – and as such it provides the reference point by which all elements in the set can be ranked and fixed. Derrida, however, exposes the transcendental signified as merely a "function," a "sort of nonlocus" (p. 280) within which one culture after another substitutes a different term, and thus arrives at a different mode of organizing human experience. Structures, in other words, are constituted by nothing more than the desire for order.

Derrida situates the "rupture" within the extended moment of later modernity, instantiated by the birth of ethnography, the "Nietzschean critique of metaphysics," the "Freudian critique of self-presence," and the "Heideggerean destruction of metaphysics" (p. 280). It is during the later nineteenth century, in other words, that the "structurality" – the arbitrary, provisional nature – of structure begins to become visible. It is a period of accelerated taxonomical activity, characterized by attempts on all sides to classify and rank the races of man, the natural world, the types and variations of human sexuality, the gradations of insanity and other pathologies. And yet the sum effect of this drive towards organization is disorder: a proliferation of competing paradigms, a multiplication of mental and sexual pathologies behind which the "normal subject" is occluded. As in *Dracula*, the impulse towards classification – Dr. Seward invents a new category for the insane Renfield, the "zoophagous maniac" (p. 95) – may accomplish nothing. Renfield is neither cured by Seward (he continues to erupt into periodic bouts of compulsive fly-, spider-, and bird-eating) nor prevented from assisting Dracula; the variety and unpredictability of material life is not contained by the taxonomies designed to hold it. Any master-terms which could render meaningful the chaotic flow of information they provide are lost. In a secular, Darwinian age, neither God nor Providence remain as agents of design; nor is their logical substitute,

"Man," available any longer as a transcendental signified in relation to which the world takes its meaning.

I do not mean here to downplay the power and appeal of the sciences for the late nineteenth century, nor the pernicious consequences (cliterodectomy, institutionalization, imprisonment) of what were in many ways successful attempts to fix the boundaries between normality and deviance, human and abhuman, through the elaboration of pathological types. As I will argue, a science like criminal anthropology works vigorously to recuperate the category of "human identity" even as it allows for the inevitability of abhuman identities as theorized within Darwinism. My point is rather that the rupture of classificatory systems holding "the human" in place, so visible in the *fin-de-siècle* Gothic, did not originate with the genre. Within the culture in general such systems were subject to massive stress, no longer able to do their proper work of separating anomalous from normative realities.

Here is where Douglas' analysis becomes less relevant for a study such as this one. In the first place Douglas, as a structuralist, focuses on *functional* systems; there is no room in her account for systems under transformation, particularly those in which principles of organization are under stress to the point of dysfunctionality, unable to manage disorder. In the second place, Douglas' arguments are drawn from the study of so-called primitive cultures, by which she means among other things cultures marked by a relatively low rather than high degree of complexity and concomitant taxonomical sophistication. One needs slightly to shift grounds in order to consider a culture in which classificatory activities operate at a pace that could be deemed frenetic. Working from the suggestive but undeveloped point in *Purity and Danger* cited earlier – that the act of separation and demarcation serves "to impose system on an *inherently untidy experience*" (p. 4; my emphasis) – one might read the "pollution behaviors" of the late nineteenth-century sciences, the proliferation of discourses attempting to frame and contain the anomalous human subject, as compulsive or hysterical.

Pollution behaviors are mechanisms whereby the "untidiness" of human experience, of life within an ineluctibly material and chaotic universe, are held at bay. In Douglas' words, they create "a *semblance* of order" (p. 4; my emphasis). They may be said to constitute a form of revulsion against the forces of disorder which underpin them, and are always threatening to exceed and contravene them.[4] An excessive drive towards classification, then, may be seen as an extreme version of this revulsion, one aware of the futility of its endeavor even as it seeks mastery by specifying an "order of things." Late nineteenth-century science, which attempts to but cannot fix the identity of "the human," might be compared to the "mad litany" of the beast people in *The Island of Dr. Moreau*. In this pollution ritual, each articulation of a prohibition ("Not to go on all fours") that serves to separate human from animal concludes with the question "Are we not men?" (p. 59). It is as if the iteration of belief in such a stable construct as a human identity, and in one's own possession of that identity, can make it so. The question is framed as a rhetorical one whose answer is "yes," but the text answers "no": there are no "men" in *Moreau*, only grotesque abhumans whose numbers include the protagonist Prendick and other "fully human" characters.[5] Humanness is revealed as a merely discursive construct, a provisional category under erasure even at the moment its delineations are marked out.

Prendick, witnessing the ritual, reports that "deep down within me laughter and disgust struggled together" (p. 59). The *fin-de-siècle* Gothic, witness to the rupture occasioned by the sciences, like them responds with revulsion to the loss of human specificity, deploying many of the same mechanisms – disavowal, displacement, assertions that abhumanness is the condition of others but never of oneself – visible in the sciences. But it also responds, like Prendick, with "laughter," albeit hysterical laughter. Gothic's is the realm of disorder, wherein cultural ordering systems are revealed as always already having collapsed. But a site of chaos is one from which any configuration, however impossible – Hodgson's braying, cavorting octopus-seal-men, for example – can emerge.[6] As Douglas writes, "Order implies restriction; from all possible materials, a limited selection has been made . . . So disorder by implication is unlimited, no pattern has been realised in it, but its potential for patterning is infinite" (p. 94). In its obsession with abominations, the Gothic may be said to manifest a certain gleefulness at the prospect of a world in which no fixity remains, only an endless series of monstrous becomings.

Thing-ness

[T]he poor woman screamed about things in the air which she could not describe. In her ravings there was not a single specific noun, but only verbs and pronouns. Things moved and changed and fluttered, and ears tingled to impulses which were not wholly sound. Something was taken away – she was being drained of something – something was fastening itself on her that ought not to be – something must make it keep off – nothing was ever still in the night – the walls and windows shifted. (H. P. Lovecraft, "The Colour out of Space"[7])

Early on in Prendick's sojourn on Moreau's island, before he has learned Moreau's secrets, he ventures into the forest by himself. On the bank of a stream he sees "something – at first I could not distinguish what it was," sucking up water. "Then I saw it was a man, going on all fours like a beast!" (p. 38).

This "something" is clad like a human, and utters at least one articulate syllable; yet it behaves like an animal. Prendick agonizes over the question of its identity: "Why should a man go on all fours and drink with his lips? . . . What on earth was he – man or animal?" (pp. 38, 41). Finally, when the anomalous entity begins to stalk him, Prendick abjures the attempt to classify, and "this grotesque half-bestial creature" (p. 38) becomes simply "the Thing" (p. 41). The epithet is repeated eight times as Prendick flees in panic from the "Thing" through the gathering darkness (pp. 43–6).

Here, as in the passage from Lovecraft, the text calls attention to the insufficiency of language to cope with and contain liminal phenomena. Prendick is an amateur natural historian, a student, like Wells, of Huxley (p. 27), and his inability to categorize species life on the island profoundly disturbs him. As he witnesses the collapse of the crucial opposition between animal and human, Prendick's only recourse is to a signifier – Thing-ness – which has no proper signified, unless this be the non-concept of amorphousness. One might also read a certain hysteria into Prendick's compulsive repetition of the word "Thing" over the course of these few paragraphs. For if this "something" Prendick was able initially to identify, at least tentatively, as "a man" is instead a Thing, then what is Prendick? The Thing-ness of the anomalous entity spills over and infects each term of the opposition it confounds, evacuating "the human" of its meaningfulness, and thus stripping Prendick of his own human identity. Prendick, too, becomes a Thing, stalked like an animal, as he runs through the night.

The *fin-de-siècle* Gothic is full of "ravings," to recur to the Lovecraft quote, about indefinite entities for which there are no "specific nouns." Sometimes these entities are not-human anomalies arising from the natural world and impinging on human realities, as in certain of Hodgson's gothic sea stories. "A Tropical Horror," for example, features a giant sea serpent with lobster claws at the end of some tentacles and teeth at the end of others, which cannot be identified except as a "Thing" or "the Horror" (pp. 122–3, 132).[8] In "From the Tideless Sea," a ship stranded in the Sargasso weed is besieged first by a monstrous octopus, then by overgrown anthropophagous crabs, named as "IT," "some dread Thing hidden within the weed," "THAT which was without" (pp. 92, 94, 119).⁹

More commonly, as in *Moreau*, the rhetoric of Thing-ness is deployed to signal the loss of human specificity, the becoming-abhuman of the human body. Barry Pain's "The Undying Thing" (1901) describes an animalized human whose lycanthropy is caused possibly by a wolf-bite to its pregnant mother, possibly by hereditary syphilis.¹⁰ The ape-man of Phil Robinson's "The Hunting of the 'Soko' " (1881) is characterized as a "thing" several times by the narrator, who has travelled to Africa to shoot big game, and is unnerved to find his own simulacrum in the prey he hunts.¹¹ Jekyll's servant Poole refers to Hyde as an "it": he tells Utterson that "him, or it, whatever it is" (p. 83) hiding in Jekyll's laboratory is like a "dwarf" and like a "monkey," but "that thing was not my master . . . God knows what it was" (p. 85). The vampirized Lucy in *Dracula* is an "*it*" and a "foul Thing" (pp. 214, 278), and Dracula himself is a "*something*," an "It," and predictably, a "Thing": in Mina Harker's words, "That is just it: this Thing is not human – not even beast" (pp. 110, 113–4, 293).

When the fungus-man of Hodgson's "The Voice in the Night"¹² tells his story from his rowboat, he is shielded from the narrator's ship, and thus the reader's gaze, by cover of darkness. Initially, one only knows there is a wrongness about him. He hails the narrator's ship with a voice "curiously throaty and inhuman" (p. 153), and the text further hints at his abhumanness with a series of hesitations. "I am only an old – man," he reassures the suspicious narrator (p. 153). When he returns from taking food to his fiancée: "The – lady is grateful now" (p. 158). The word chosen each time is the properly human one; the pause indicates that it is no longer relevant, no longer adequate. His language falters again towards the end of his tale, when he tries to describe the transformation he and his fiancée have undergone. "[A]nd so – and so – we who had been human, became – Well, it matters less each day" (p. 167). The narrator, who catches a glimpse of the fungus-man in the first light of dawn, stumbles in the act of representation as well. "Then the oars were dipped, the boat shot out of the patch of light, and the – the thing went nodding into the mist" (p. 168). The break in the sentence signals a rupture of conceptual systems, a gap wherein identity formations have lost their meaningfulness. Within this rupture, where lies an abhuman identity for which there is as yet no language, is inserted the word "Thing."

This concluding sentence of "The Voice in the Night" illustrates what one might call the syntax of the *fin-de-siècle* Gothic. Within the genre, the demarcations between "the human" and any number of not-human configurations are inexorably erased, so that one must falter at the moment of pronouncing the word "human." The space cleared out by the evacuation of this term is both empty and full: it is a space where the human body, becoming not-itself, becomes a non-signifier, and yet where the possibilities for monstrous embodiments multiply indefinitely. It is the space of Thing-ness, which threatens to burst its bounds and overwhelm the known world.

The Thing-ness of matter

I have told you I was of sceptical habits; but though I understood little or nothing, I began to dread, vainly proposing to myself the iterated dogmas of science that all life is material, and that in the system of things there is no undiscovered land, even beyond the remotest stars, where the supernatural can find a footing. Yet there struck in on this the thought that matter is as really awful and unknown as spirit, that science itself but dallies on the threshold, scarcely gaining more than a glimpse of the wonders of the inner place. (Machen, *The Three Imposters*, pp. 281–2)

To be a Thing is to inhabit a body having no recognizable or definite form, but it is unmistakably to inhabit a *material* body. The term signals indifferentiation, sometimes to the point of amorphousness, while at the same time it calls attention to the inescapable fact of embodied-ness, and to the ineluctibility of matter that resists and exceeds form. For the increasingly secularized late nineteenth century, coming to terms with what T. H. Huxley had called "the physical basis of life" in 1868,[13] the universe is in the process of becoming-Thing. Within a materialist reality there are nothing but Things: matter subjected, provisionally, to the contingency of forms.

Within a materialist reality, in other words, there is a reveral of the hierarchized terms form and matter. Form is no longer the dominant term within the binarism, because matter is intransigent and resists containment within a fixed and unitary form. Moreover, form, as we have seen, is shifting, variable, revealing itself as "structurality" (a *tendency* towards shape and meaningfulness) rather than structure (a stable ordering of things). The possibility of formlessness always looms in the *fin-de-siècle* Gothic. In the passage cited earlier, Helen Vaughan's body "melt[s] and dissolve[s]" into "a substance as of jelly" (*The Great*

God Pan, pp. 236–7); matter is no longer subordinate to form. But the gothicity of matter also threatens to spill over and infect form itself. Villiers speaks of "the terror" occasioned by "that which is without form taking to itself a form" (*The Great God Pan*, p. 232). Here the horrificness of matter, manifested by its absolute formlessness, is redoubled rather than lessened by its organization into a discernible body: Helen Vaughan becomes "a Form . . . too foul to be spoken of . . . a horrible and unspeakable shape" (p. 237).

The state of bodily indifferentiation may be said to represent the contamination of form by matter. The undifferentiated body is a body in process: it has lost its "proper" configurations and is proceeding towards a state of pure disorganization, or perhaps reorganizing into new configurations, unknown and hence terrible. Both narrative possibilities, one of entropy and one of chaotic metamorphosis, pertain in the *fin-de-siècle* Gothic. Each disallows the narrative of human transcendence of the material universe, for in each human identity is enmeshed within the Thing-ness of matter, entrapped within a body always in danger of becoming-Thing.

In "On the Physical Basis of Life," Huxley argues that "all the multifarious and complicated activities of man are comprehensible under three categories. Either they are immediately directed towards the maintenance and development of the body, or they effect transitory changes in the relative positions of parts of the body, or they tend towards the continuance of the species." Human activities, in other words, are explicable within "physiological language," and this includes "[e]ven those manifestations of intellect, of feeling, and of will, which we rightly name the higher faculties" (pp. 130–1). "And if so, it must be true . . . that the thoughts to which I am now giving utterance, and your thoughts regarding them, are the expression of molecular changes in that matter of life which is the source of our other vital phenomena" (p. 140).

Huxley's essay accomplishes a number of things, most notable of which is the circumscribing of "the human" within a relentlessly material reality. Consciousness, will, volition – all of those intangibles that comprise unique and wonderful "human subjectivity" – are theorized as physical phenomena, as intractible in their materiality as is the solid human body. But at the very same time, the seeming solidity of this body is undone by Huxley's discussion of protoplasm, the essential substance of cells. When viewed under the microscope, human and other life appears as grotesquely unfamiliar. As Huxley describes the basic structure of "the common nettle":

The whole hair consists of a very delicate outer case of wood . . . [within] which is a layer of semi-fluid matter, full of innumerable granules of extreme minuteness. This semi-fluid lining is protoplasm, which thus constitutes a kind of bag, full of a limpid liquid . . . When viewed with a sufficiently high magnifying power, the protoplasmic layer of the nettle hair is seen to be in a condition of unceasing activity . . . The spectacle afforded by the wonderful energies prisoned within the compass of the microscopic hair of a plant, which we commonly regard as a merely passive organism, is not easily forgotten . . . [C]ould our ears catch the murmur of these tiny Maelstroms, as they whirl in the innumerable myriads of living cells which constitute each tree, we should be stunned, as with the roar of a great city. (pp. 131–2)

The microscopic analysis of cell structure reveals what we may call the *gothicity of matter*. Matter is not mute and stolid, but rather clamorous and active. In its viscosity, in its oozing mobility, in its unexpected, incessant animation, this "physical basis of life," protoplasm,[14] emerges as a testament to the horrific potentialities of a sheerly physical world. As in the quote from *The Three Imposters* above, matter is "awful and unknown"; the doctrine of materialism, disturbing enough to begin with, cannot even comfort one in its very facticity.

Theorizing slime

By characterizing Huxley's essay as a sort of treatise on the gothicity of matter, I am of course reading it against the grain. Huxley, far from working to hystericize the Victorian audience, took some pains to reassure his readers that materialism was not so terrible a thing as they might have feared. Human consciousness and volition, albeit "physiological" in origin, mattered intensely in the world, he said (p. 145); and as to the "threatened extinction" of "spirit" by materialist science, spirit is but "a name for an unknown and hypothetical cause of states of our own consciousness" (p. 143).

Nonetheless, the gothic implications of Huxley's argument emerge clearly when one reads "On the Physical Basis of Life" alongside the Gothic fiction that followed it, and was, directly or indirectly, influenced by it. The essay serves beautifully to illustrate the sheer uncanniness of organic life in general, and human life in particular. When a drop of human blood is put under the microscope and kept at body temperature, writes Huxley, certain "colourless corpuscles" can be "seen to exhibit a marvelous activity, changing their forms with great rapidity, drawing in and thrusting out prolongations of their substance, and creeping about as if they were independent organisms" (p. 133). Here Huxley is careful to emphasize that like the nettle's, human life is essentially protoplasmic. A "nucleated mass of protoplasm turns out to be what may be termed the structural unit of the human body . . . Beast and fowl, reptile and fish, mollusk, worm, and polype [sic], are all composed of structural units of the same character, namely, masses of protoplasm with a nucleus" (pp. 133–4). Human particularity is thus disallowed in two ways: the most basic human structure is no different from that of any other organism, animal or vegetable; and the human body at this basic level (one imperceptible to the ordinary workings of the senses) is a quasi-differentiated mass, pulsating and viscous.

Nothing illustrates the Thing-ness of matter so admirably as slime. Nor can anything illustrate the Thing-ness of the human body so well as its sliminess, or propensity to become-slime. Slimy substances – excreta, sexual fluids, saliva, mucus – seep from the borders of the body, calling attention to the body's gross materiality. Huxley's description of protoplasm indicates that sliminess is the very essence of the body, and is not just exiled to its borders. Within an evolutionist narrative, human existence has its remote origins in the "primordial slime" from which all life was said to arise. In the minus narrative of devolution, sliminess may be posited as well as the logical terminus of mutable human identity. "The Novel of the White Powder," one of the interpolated tales within Machen's *The Three Imposters*, is the story of a young man who suffers both a fall into evil practices and an increasing loss of bodily specificity. In the last moments before he is put to death, Francis Leicester is revealed as having degenerated into a slime-entity, "unctuous," "writhing," and Thing-like:

There upon the floor was a dark and putrid mass, seething with corruption and hideous rottenness, neither liquid nor solid, but melting and changing before our eyes, and bubbling with unctuous oily bubbles like boiling pitch. And out of the midst of it shone two burning points like eyes, and I saw a writhing and stirring as of limbs, and something moved and lifted up what might have been an arm. The doctor took a step forward, raised the iron bar and struck at the burning points; he drove in the weapon, and struck again and again in a fury of loathing. At last *the thing* was quiet. (*The Three Imposters*, pp. 326–7; my emphasis)

In all of these instances, the body's sliminess signals human entrapment within the realm of matter.[15] Such a predicament, figured as "gothic" within a range of *fin-de-siècle* discourses, would haunt the twentieth century as well. Of particular interest is the response of the existentialist philosopher Jean-Paul Sartre, whose *Being and Nothingness* (1943) confronts the problem of the "sheer thingness" of the human body and "the recalcitrant meaninglessness of the material world," as Martin Jay puts it in his discussion of Sartre in *Downcast Eyes*.[16] Sartre proposes a rough correspondence between the following binarisms: the "In-itself" and the "For-itself," solid and liquid, matter and consciousness, passivity and activity. The latter term is in each case the privileged one: the human subject, enmeshed within the suchness of the material universe, must rise above it; human consciousness must comprehend, mark its absolute difference from, and thus transcend mere matter. The brutish and abject "whatness" of existence is in this way brought to order.

Troubling the dualism of the Sartrean ontology, however, is the problem of slime. Slime is first of all anomalous: "neither liquid nor solid," like Francis' deliquescing body in the *Imposters* quote above, it is a liminal phenomenon. "[T]he slimy reveals itself as essentially ambiguous because its fluidity exists in slow motion; there is a sticky thickness in its liquidity; it represents in itself a dawning triumph of the solid over the liquid – that is, a tendency of the indifferent in-itself, which is represented by the pure solid, to fix the liquidity, to absorb the for-itself which ought to dissolve it" (Sartre, p. 774).

As this passage begins to make clear, slime is disturbing not only in its anomaly; it also constitutes a threat to the integrity of the human subject. If the distinction between liquid and solid can be effaced, then other, more crucial oppositions – between human consciousness and the material body, for instance – threaten to collapse as well.[17] Sartre emphasizes that sliminess is contagious, contaminating the integral "For-itself" with its own glutinous indifferentiation.

The slimy... [seems] *docile*. Only at the moment when I believe that I possess it, behold by a curious reveral, *it* possesses me ... [H]ere is the slimy reversing the terms; the For-itself is suddenly *compromised*. I open my hands, I want to let go of the slimy and it sticks to me, it draws me, it sucks at me ... [T]here exists a poisonous possession; there is a possibility that the In-itself might absorb the For-itself ... and that in this new being the In-itself would draw the For-itself into its contingency, into its indifferent exteriority, into its foundationless existence. (p. 776; emphasis in text)

In other words, matter in all its It-ness adheres to consciousness and impedes transcendence; the infectious quality of matter renders the human subject a Thing, contingent, indifferent, foundationless. (As Huxley puts it, "the best minds of these days" are terrorized by the prospect of materialism: "The advancing tide of matter threatens to drown their souls."[18]) Nor is this matter in its "proper" form, characterized by the "reassuring inertia" of solidity (Sartre, p. 776). It is a *gothic* version of matter, disturbingly animate like Huxley's protoplasm. "The slime is like a liquid seen in a nightmare, where all its properties are animated by a sort of life and turn back against me. Slime is the revenge of the In-itself" (p. 777).

Slime is the revenge of matter. In slime, matter displays itself in all its ineluctibility. As an anomalous phenomenon, slime testifies to the inability of human classificatory systems to contain and master matter; as a tactile experience, sliminess is a reminder of the utter Thing-ness of matter. From here it is a short step to positing matter as somehow malevolent. Sartre imagines a resistless human subject, sucked into the whirlpool of Thing-ness, being drained of will and sentience; in an odd reversal, these become the property of matter, which manifests the hostile intention of absorbing everything into itself and rendering it as amorphous and Thing-like as itself.

Hodgson describes precisely this scenario in "The Derelict,"[19] a story of an encounter with a slime-mold entity. Somewhere north of Madagascar, the crew of the *Bheotpte* boards a derelict ship which seems to be encrusted all over with "smooth great masses . . . of a dirty-white mould," and whose decks "gave under our tread, with a spongy, puddingly feel" (pp. 38–9). Every direction they turn they find this quasi-solid substance "converting the deck-fittings" and the outlines of the ship "into indistinguishable mounds of mould" (p. 39). The mold is "blotched and veined with irregular, dull purplish markings" and exudes a faint sweat (pp. 39, 43); it is covered with sea-lice, parasites that feed on marine animal species; when kicked, it gushes forth a purplish fluid.

Gradually the men come to realize that the ship is not simply covered with mold, it has become mold: "She's ALIVE!" the Captain shouts in terror (p. 54). It is inorganic matter transformed into a living entity with a "reg'lar skin" (p. 39), a heart which the men hear thudding in the hull beneath them, a circulatory system, and a sluggish mobility – a "lower" organism, mold, has attained the morphic organization of a properly higher one. As this entity awakens to their presence, it ripples and undulates, "wobbl[ing] sloppily, like a mound of unhealthy-looking jelly" (p. 44), and sucks at their feet. For the entity is also a voracious one. The hapless seaman Tom Harrison is consumed by the mold:

All about him, the mould was in active movement. His feet had sunk out of sight. The stuff appeared to be *lapping* at his legs; and abruptly his bare flesh showed. The hideous stuff had rent his trouser-legs away, as if they were paper. He gave out a simply sickening scream, and, with a vast effort, wrenched one leg free. It was partly destroyed. The next instant he pitched downward, and the stuff

heaped itself upon him, as if it were actually alive, with a dreadful savage life . . .
The man had gone from sight. Where he had fallen was now a writhing,
elongated mound, in constant and horrible increase, as the mould appeared to
move towards it in strange ripples from all sides. (pp. 47–8; emphasis in text)

The doctor who tells the story to the narrator and his friends
speculates on the conditions (the nature of the cargo, "the juxtaposition
of the various articles of her cargo, plus the heat and time she had
endured"; p. 58) that enabled the derelict's transformation. He argues
that "The *Material* . . . is inevitably the medium of the Life-Force" (p. 29;
emphasis in text). All life is "a Force made manifest through Conditions .
. . and can take for its purpose and Need, the most incredible and
unlikely Matter; for without Matter, it cannot come into existence" (p.
31). "The Derelict" is an attempt fully to realize the horrific potentialities
of an utterly material universe, to theorize such concepts as life, volition,
consciousness in materialist terms. Dismissing the narrator's protest that
life is "spiritual," the doctor says, "[I]n my heart, I believe that it is a
matter of chemistry" (p. 30). This material universe is characterized by
its "Need," its "urgent" and yet "indiscriminate" hunger (p. 29), its
all-encompassing malevolence: the doctor refers to the "Life-Force" as
"the Brute" (30). As this "Brute" manifests itself in inert matter, like the
derelict ship, inert matter, too, becomes hostile and ravenous. Matter in
all its Thing-ness, undifferentiated and viscous, engulfs all those distinctions
which maintain form's ascendency over matter: the specific outlines of
the derelict; the sea around it, which has turned thick and scummy; the
human form, become a "writhing, elongated mound."

In an extraordinary passage from his 1879 Presidential Address to the
British Association for the Advancement of Science, G. J. Allman
describes "behavior in the Petri dish":

Let us observe our Amoeba a little closer. Like all living beings, it must be
nourished. It cannot grow as a crystal would grow by accumulating on its
surface molecule after molecule of matter. It must FEED. It must take into its
substance the necessary nutriment; it must assimilate this nutriment, and
convert it into the material of which it is itself composed . . . A stream of
protoplasm instantly runs away from the body of the Amoeba towards the
destined prey, envelops it in its current, and then flows back with it to the central
protoplasm, where it sinks deeper and deeper into the soft yielding mass, and
becomes dissolved, digested, and assimilated in order that it may increase the
size and restore the energy of its captor.[20]

The perspective of the microbiologist reveals that a Darwinian struggle
for the "survival of the fittest" takes place continually even at a level

invisible to the naked human eye. More notably, as in the case of the Huxley article,[21] the microscope reveals the slimy and mobile Thing-ness of basic organic life. Albeit a known form of animal life, the amoeba appears as a liminal entity: a body which has no proper form but is instead characterized by indeterminacy, as its boundaries are remade again and again by the streaming fluidity of the pseudopods.

Allman's eruption into capital letters underscores the *hunger* of the protoplasmic being. Like the Sartrean "In-itself" which has become-animate by becoming-slime, like Hodgson's rampaging slime-mold entity, this Thing is voracious. Propelled by irresistible want, it envelops the object of hunger into its own viscous body; the object of hunger loses its bodily specificity as it becomes absorbed into that of the predator – which is no specificity at all, only a "soft yielding mass." "She's ALIVE." "It must FEED." Slime is the revenge of matter, which seeks to swallow up the known and bounded world into its own amorphousness.

CHAPTER 2

Symptomatic readings

As the doctor boards the derelict ship early in Hodgson's story, he remarks on the "peculiar smell" it emits: "I felt that in some way, it was vaguely familiar; yet I could give it no name" ("The Derelict," pp. 35–6). His inability to place the smell disturbs him so much that he recurs to it: "there was again a vague odour of something half familiar, that somehow brought to me a sense of half-known fright" (p. 39). It is not the odor itself that frightens him so much, perhaps, as its incomplete familiarity: it stirs in him a memory of something he cannot quite bring to mind.

Similarly, upon Prendick's first meeting with M'Ling, one of Moreau's beast people, he comments on the haunting sense of *déjà vu* with which M'Ling inspires him. "I had never beheld such an extraordinary and repulsive face before, and yet – if the contradiction is credible – I experienced at the same time an odd feeling that in some way I *had* encountered exactly the features and gestures that now amazed me" (*The Island of Dr. Moreau*, p. 11; emphasis in text). The boy Pibby in Hodgson's "The Adventure of the Headland,"[1] hunted by strange dogs somewhere on the African coast, hears the baying of the pack that pursues him, "and for the second time the vague yet frightening familiarity of it stirred the boy's memory oddly" (p. 184).

The uncanny

Sigmund Freud attempts to account for precisely such a sensation in his essay "The 'Uncanny'." The uncanny, he writes, is that which "arouses dread and creeping horror," akin to and yet distinct from that which is "fearful" (p. 122), and thus the sensation of uncanniness is not a response to an object or event that is simply strange and unknown. Instead, "the uncanny is that class of the terrifying which leads us back to something long known to us, once very familiar" (pp. 123–4). The uncanny object is simultaneously *heimlich* and *unheimlich*, familiar and unfamiliar; it violates a crucial binarism by which we organize the world.

In the terms I have outlined above, the sensation of uncanniness is a symptomatic response to liminal phenomena, which confound and exceed the classificatory systems designed to contain matter. The anomaly has no "proper" form; by crossing the borders that separate one category from another, by occupying two categories at once,[2] the anomaly defamiliarizes both. M'Ling presents the spectacle of the animal become-human, or the human become-animal, as do the dogs in "Adventure of the Headland," whose numbers include certain regressed humans who run and bay with the pack and hunt human flesh. The doctor cannot initially recognize that the smell of the derelict has "something animal-like in it" (p. 41) because the familiar smell is inappropriate, defamiliarized by the improper context.

Thus far the sensation of the uncanny bears a strong similarity to that of the "hesitation" described by Todorov, the symptomatic response to an anomalous phenomenon (a supernatural event) situated within an inappropriate context (the natural setting). Freud, however, is careful to distinguish the sensation of the uncanny from that of "intellectual uncertainty" (p. 124), or metaphysical estrangement. The symptom, for Freud, redounds upon the subject who experiences it, denoting resistance or refusal on the part of the subject. The object of uncanniness is "something familiar and old-established in the mind that has been estranged only by the process of repression" (p. 148): it is *heimlich* within the occluded level of the unconscious, *unheimlich* to the conscious mind. Uncanniness constitutes a moment of near-rupture, wherein the repressed contents of the unconscious struggle to come to the surface and are repressed again.

The Freudian uncanny, then, draws into intimate relation the subject who incurs the symptom and the object which inspires it. That the relation is one of *likeness* is clearest in *Moreau*, where the distinction between beast people and "fully human" characters like Prendick is constantly in danger of collapse at a highly visible textual level. Prendick confronts abhumanness, but he cannot quite comprehend it as such; he finds M'Ling uncanny. The symptom compromises him as one who recognizes, but then denies, the possibility of his *own* abhumanness.

The scenario Freud finds most conducive to uncanniness is that which recalls the trauma of Oedipality, whereby desire for the mother was foreclosed by the threat of castration by the father.[3] He does, however, briefly consider the uncanny in relation to pre-Oedipality, "a time when the ego was not yet sharply differentiated from the external world and from other persons" (p. 143).[4] Anything which threatens to dissolve the boundaries the ego has erected to distinguish itself from other people, other things (Freud's example is the figure of the *Doppelgänger*) provokes in the subject a half-recollection of this period of amorphous identity. The doctor's sensation of uncanniness in "The Derelict," then, is multi-valenced: it is a symptomatic response to the anomalous nature of the slime-mold entity, but it also pulls him within the field of indifferentiation, or Thing-ness, that the entity represents.[5] This dynamic is still more evident in Hodgson's "The Thing in the Weeds," which describes yet another sea-going encounter with a slimy-bodied monstrosity. The narrator comments on the Thing's smell, "faint and sickly, yet vaguely suggestive of something I had once smelt before" (p. 60). Later the "indefinable familiarity" of the smell (p. 61) is traced to the stench of rotting human bodies: the First Mate jokes that "I'm thinking it's Davy Jones come up for a breather" (p. 61), and recalls smelling a similar odor when he once boarded a derelict ship full of dead men (p. 62). The uncanniness of the Thing's smell speaks to a fact the narrator would rather not remember: that he, too, is a Thing, circumscribed wholly within the materiality of human embodiedness.

Abjection

Prendick finds M'Ling uncanny, but the emotion is also tinged with disgust. Later on he tells Montgomery that "it gives me a nasty little sensation, a tightening of my muscles, when he comes near me" (p. 35). In "Disgust and Other Forms of Aversion," David Pole argues that in order to disgust, disgusting objects must fulfill two conditions. The first is liminality:[6] "Nothing is more fearfully disturbing than experiences that seem to call in doubt the whole scheme of known distinctions by which we live" (p. 227). This alone, however, cannot account for the intensity of the affect of disgust, nor for the essential ambivalence of an emotion compounded of both aversion and desire, revulsion and fascination. "What is lacking is some element of self-identification . . . that makes the horrifying thing also a part of me" (p. 227). Pole, whose field is the philosophy of aesthetics, does not discuss the mechanisms of resistance which might block the disgusted subject's recognition of its likeness to the disgusting object, and thus aggravate the intensity of the affect. The

Freudian uncanny, however, allows us to identify Prendick's disgust as symptomatic of a particularly violent denial of his doubling relationship with M'Ling, as a particularly intense version of the recognition/repression dynamic of uncanniness.

I will return to the issue of disgust shortly. But I wish for the moment to remain with Freud's hint that a doubling relationship, which on the surface accomplishes a simple bifurcation of the self, gestures towards a more radical fissioning of the self – towards an amorphous version of the self which is a non-self, because it has forfeited all the boundaries that enabled it to distinguish itself from the world of things that surround it. Stevenson makes a similar gesture in *Dr. Jekyll and Mr. Hyde.* Jekyll's researches bring him "steadily nearer to that truth . . . that man is not truly one, but truly two," and his potion allows him to literalize the "truth" of a bifurcated subjectivity through a doubling of bodies. But Jekyll qualifies his assertion. "I say two, because the state of my own knowledge does not pass beyond that point. Others will follow, others will outstrip me on the same lines; and I hazard the guess that man will be ultimately known for a mere polity of multifarious, incongruous and independent denizens" (p. 104).[7] This gesture undoes the most basic and readily accessible interpretation of *Jekyll and Hyde*, that it stages a confrontation between good and evil. The human being embroiled within such a Manichæan drama is split in two, but nonetheless fully situated within the field of meaningfulness, wherein meaning arises through the constant and steady tension between terms fixed in an oppositional relation one to the other. But to be a multiple subject – not simply split, but fractured, dissolved – is to spin out of the field, and thus to be evacuated of a meaningful self-identity. "The Derelict" completes the gesture by representing the human subject who has lost all specificity whatsoever: Tom Harrison becomes a glob of undifferentiated matter indistinguishable from the undifferentiated material world that has engulfed him.

This repulsive yet intriguing possibility of loss of self-identity is the topic of Julia Kristeva's *Powers of Horror: An Essay on Abjection.* Abjection, for Kristeva, is a nauseating affective state: like ambivalence but more wracking; more violent than the sensation of uncanniness; too primordial to be called an emotion, for it refers back to the affective state of the self *before* it has become a self. During pre-Oedipality, Kristeva argues, the not-yet subject experiences itself simply as a body crossed by drives, a body, moreover, which has not yet identified itself as a discrete entity,[8] but rather experiences itself as continuous with all other things in its field.

This proto-subject, then, occupies a space which is a chaos, not yet brought to order by the signifying systems (familial configurations, sexual difference, language) that structure the cultural order and determine one's place in it, not even yet provisionally ordered by the basic distinction me/not-me.

Abjection begins when this proto-subject, very tentatively, begins to clear out a space on which the ego will be constructed and from which an "I" will emerge. The moment is a terrifying one, recalling the trauma of birth, "the immemorial violence with which a body becomes separated from another body in order to be" (p. 10). Nor does the ambivalent proto-subject, though impelled towards self-differentiation, wish to relinquish the state of being purely constituted by the fierce, directionless energies of the id.

Moreover, the attempt to empty out a space upon which to erect a self is an impossible one, for the objects that surround the proto-subject have not yet become distinguished as such – as objects in counterdistinction to an integral subjectivity. "Even before things for him *are* – hence before they are signifiable – he drives them out" (p. 6; emphasis in text). What the proto-subject "drives out," then, is itself. In a moment of anguish, it "throws up everything" (p. 6), and by evacuating a world until this instant utterly continuous with itself, evacuates itself. "I expel *myself*, I spit *myself* out, I abject *myself* within the same motion through which 'I' claim to establish *myself* . . . During that course in which 'I' become, I give birth to myself amid the violence of sobs, of vomit" (p. 3; emphasis in text).

The primordial experience of abjection remains as a trace memory long after the proto-subject has constituted itself as a "full" (discrete and integral) subject – not a repressed memory, because the experience occurred before the creation of the unconscious, but rather a body-memory of nausea and convulsion. This memory can be triggered by confrontation with anomalous phenomena:[9] objects or events which spill over the lines of demarcation meant to contain them, and thus call into question the permanence and efficacy of any boundaries, most notably those erected by the "self" to maintain itself as a distinct entity. "It is thus not lack of cleanliness that causes abjection but what disturbs identity, system, order. What does not respect borders, positions, rules. The in-between, the ambiguous, the composite" (p. 4). Abjection "draws me toward the place where meaning collapses" (p. 2) and where the self, too, dissolves into indifferentiation and meaninglessness.

The crucial point for Kristeva is that the symptom of nausea does not

denote a repression, but something quite different. Abjection, albeit
nauseating, is a fundamentally ambivalent affective state. The abject[10]
is "a vortex of summons and repulsion"; it "simultaneously beseeches
and pulverizes the subject" (pp. 1, 5). The subject confronting the abject
is torn between two ontological possibilities: one which is rigidly
invested in the construct of a stable self-identity, one which is attracted
to the turbulence, chaos, and indifferentiation associated with pre-
Oedipality. In the experience of abjection one can have it both ways:
abjection is a "jouissance in which the subject is swallowed up but in
which the Other [the abject], in return, keeps the subject from
foundering by making it repugnant" (p. 9). The subject is dissolved, but
in the convulsions of nausea its body-boundaries, at least, are re-made.
"One thus understands why so many victims of the abject are its
fascinated victims" (p. 9).

Nausea

What I am moving towards here, slowly, are speculations as to why the
readers of the *fin-de-siècle* Gothic were (and are) its "fascinated victims."
What can account for the phenomenal popularity of what was, with few
exceptions, a thoroughly nauseating genre? For there are two things the
fin-de-siècle Gothic represents again and again. The first is the spectacle of
the human subject undergoing dissolution, a spectacle which provokes
hysterical anxiety in Sartre's analysis, a sense of metaphysical estrangement
in Todorov's, repression and denial in Freud's, abjection in Kristeva's.

The second is the symptom of nausea. From *Dracula*: "As the Count
leaned over me and his hands touched me, I could not repress a
shudder. It may have been that his breath was rank, but a horrible
feeling of nausea came over me, which, do what I would, I could not
conceal" (pp. 28–9). From *Jekyll and Hyde*: "Mr. Hyde was pale and
dwarfish, he gave an impression of deformity without any nameable
malformation . . . [a]ll these were points against him, but not all of these
together could explain the hitherto unknown disgust, loathing, and fear
with which Utterson regarded him" (p. 52). From Conan Doyle's "Lot
249": "The features [of the mummy], though horribly discoloured,
were perfect, and two little nut-like eyes still lurked in the depths of the
black, hollow sockets . . . In its crouching position, with bent joints and
craned head, there was a suggestion of energy about the horrid thing
which made Smith's gorge rise" (p. 84).[11] From *The Three Imposters*: "I
stood shuddering and quaking as with the grip of ague, sick with

unspeakable agonies of fear and loathing" (p. 324). From Guy Boothby's *Pharos the Egyptian* (1899): "Then the other [Pharos] turned his head and looked at me; and, as he did so, a great shudder, accompanied by an indescribable feeling of nausea, passed over me . . . Once more I experienced the same sensation of revulsion that had overwhelmed me twice before. Again I felt sick and giddy; once more a clammy sweat broke out upon my forehead" (pp. 27, 42). From Frank Aubrey's *A Queen of Atlantis: A Romance of the Caribbean Sea* (1899): "Most strange of all, a cold, sickly horror seized upon the two. It was a feeling of nausea such as might be caused by an aroma of intolerable foulness, and with it the sensation of repulsion and disgust that a human being has for a loathsome, unclean thing" (pp. 77–8).

These examples could be multiplied indefinitely.[12] In its generation of an endless procession of abhuman embodiments, the *fin-de-siècle* Gothic dictates, as the "proper" somatic response to abhumanness, the sensation of disgust. Pole writes that "Disgust, being . . . contagious, contaminates its subject as well" (p. 221): that is, the subject is compromised by its confrontation with the disgusting object, drawn into the field of its Thing-ness, an analysis consistent with both Sartre and Kristeva. It is by no means a given that a reader's affective state must correspond to that of the text's characters, but characterly nausea offers at least a strong suggestion as to how the reader should respond. As D. A. Miller writes of a genre in vogue several decades before the Gothic, the Victorian sensation novel:

[It] offers us one of the first instances of modern literature to address itself primarily to the sympathetic nervous system, where it grounds its characteristic adrenalin effects: accelerated heart rate and respiration, increased blood pressure, the pallor resulting from vasoconstriction, and so on . . . [The sensation text] can mobilize [the reader's] sympathetic nervous system only by giving it something to sympathize with. In order to make us nervous, nervousness must first be represented.[13]

In order to make us nauseous, nausea must first be represented. That characterly nausea is always in danger of spilling over the boundaries of the text and infecting the reader is most startlingly apparent in this quote from Hodgson's *The Boats of the "Glen Carrig"*:[14] "Now it is scarcely possible to convey the extraordinary disgust which the sight of these human slugs bred in me, nor, could I, do I think I would; for were I then successful, then would others be like to retch even as I did, the spasm coming on without premonition, and born of very horror" (pp. 69–70).

Hysteria

One evening, however, after Rachel had come home, her mother heard a noise which sounded like suppressed weeping in the girl's room, and on going in found her lying, half undressed, upon the bed, evidently in the greatest distress. As soon as she saw her mother, she exclaimed, "Ah, mother, mother, why did you let me go to the forest with Helen?" Mrs. M. was astonished at so strange a question, and proceeded to make inquiries. Rachel told her a wild story. She said –
Clarke closed the book with a snap . . . (Machen, *The Great God Pan*, p. 187)

In the passage from *The Boats of the "Glen Carrig"* cited on p. 45 above, Hodgson deploys a rhetorical strategy typical of the *fin-de-siècle* Gothic: a simultaneous movement towards, and convulsive retreat from, the representation of horrific bodily realities. Here the strategy is a specious one – the narrator's talk of retching does indeed "convey" his "extraordinary disgust" to the reader – but elsewhere in *"Glen Carrig"* the strategy is used more urgently, as the narrative oscillates between graphic depictions of abhuman and other monstrosities and a refusal to describe them. The text itself, in other words, is rent by the same irresolvable ambivalence as Kristeva's abjected subject, in the throes of both desire and loathing for the prospect of an abhuman becoming.

"They must be men of very cold imagination," writes Ann Radcliffe in her 1826 "On the Supernatural in Poetry," "with whom certainty is more terrible than surmise" (p. 149). Working from Edmund Burke's 1756 *A Philosophical Inquiry into the Origin of Our Ideas of the Sublime and Beautiful*, Radcliffe distinguishes between the dramatic effect of terror, characterized by "uncertainty and obscurity . . . respecting the dreaded evil," and horror, which results from the graphic depiction of the dreaded evil. Horror, for Radcliffe, is the debased emotion, or the cheap literary effect, whereas terror, which exalts and uplifts, is a proper "source of the sublime." "Terror and horror are so far opposite, that the first expands the soul, and awakens the faculties to a high degree of life; and the other contracts, freezes, and nearly annihilates them" (p. 149).

In *The Mysteries of Udolpho* (1794), Radcliffe's sublime and terrible landscapes, described in Burkean terms of majestic obscurity, both correspond to and intensify the powerful but indefinite apprehensions of the mind. As she travels towards Montoni's castle, Emily St. Aubert, oppressed by vague fears of the perils that await her, is aroused by the Alpine scenery into a sense of "dreadful sublimity": the "gloomy grandeur" of the forests, and the "tremendous precipices of the mountains, that came partially to the eye, each assisted to raise the solemnity of Emily's feelings into awe" (pp. 224–5). This passage of sublime "terror" derives its effect, in Burkean fashion, from uncertainty – the uncertain outlines of an immense and overpowering landscape, the uncertainties of a mind in turmoil – and might be contrasted to the "horrid" conclusion of Matthew Lewis' *The Monk* (1796). Nothing is left to the reader's imagination in this scene as Ambrosio's still-living body is shattered upon the rocks and mutilated by insects and birds of prey; here one finds no vague apprehensions or dimly perceived threats, only graphic certainties.

A novel like *The Great God Pan*, seemingly, deploys literary techniques of which Radcliffe would approve, until the very end shrouding its "dreaded evil" (the abhuman Helen Vaughan) from view of the reader by means of obfuscating rhetoric, the multiplication and confusion of narrative layers, and constant interruption of the story being told. Even in the graphic portrayal of Helen's deliquescing body, the text cannot specify the exact nature of her metamorphosis, and hints at worse horrors than those found on the page (". . . *Here the* Ms. *is illegible* . . ."). A scene midway through the text, when Villiers gives Austin a "neat little packet of manuscript" containing "an account of the entertainment Mrs. Beaumont [a.k.a. Helen Vaughan] provided for her choicer guests," is typical. "Austin took the manuscript, but never read it. Opening the neat pages at haphazard his eye was caught by a word and a phrase that followed it; and, sick at heart, with white lips and a cold sweat pouring like water from his temples, he flung the paper down" (p. 231). Villiers, who has read the manuscript through, says, "I can fancy what you saw. Such forces cannot be named, cannot be spoken, cannot be imagined except under a veil and a symbol" (pp. 231–2) – a speech which causes Austin to break out into a cold sweat again. The reader learns no more of what was written.

Despite such strategies of narrative occlusion, practiced consistently throughout *The Great God Pan*, the novel hardly makes an approach towards the sublime. Here the result of textual indefinition is not to "expand the soul," to quote Radcliffe again, but to "contract . . . the faculties," into the visceral response of nausea.[15] Clearly the textual mechanisms which work to produce a nauseating affect are more complicated than those allowed for within Radcliffe. And in fact they bear striking similarities to those described within another *fin-de-siècle* discourse, early psychoanalysis: the mechanisms of hysteria, which work to produce symptoms across the body of the traumatized subject.

At precisely the point where *The Great God Pan* might give specifics rather than the vague effusions about nameless horrors it has offered so far, it interrupts itself, inserting instead the specifics of Austin's nauseated response to the story of Helen Vaughan, his sickness, pallor, and sweat. It then resorts to more obfuscating rhetoric, as Villiers speaks at great length[16] about how what Helen is, what Helen does, is *unspeakable*. The trauma Helen represents is absolutely central to the novel – manuscript after manuscript masses itself around that center – and yet the novel will not, or cannot, say what the trauma is. Instead the novel erupts into symptoms, as one character after another succumbs to nausea, and more and more language is produced (I am reading an excess of language as itself symptomatic) to identify the trauma as one that exceeds language.

To assert that something is too horrible to be spoken of is the privileged utterance of the Gothic, but it is also the privileged utterance of the hysteric. Freud argues that the precondition of hysteria is a "disturbance in the sphere of sexuality" (*Dora*, p. 39) so intolerable that it must be repressed. The memory escapes to the unconscious, and thus is henceforth incapable of expression in conventional discourse; the forces of repression at work ensure its unspeakability. But that which the conscious mind cannot acknowledge, and the subject cannot speak, the body tells instead, resulting in what Freud called "conversion" into any number of hysterical symptoms – including paralysis, enervation, nervous twitchings, dyspnoea, and finally, nausea.[17]

The Great God Pan, like other texts within its genre, responds to the traumatic and intolerable prospect of the loss of human specificity[18] by becoming hysterical. Over and again the novel recurs to its site of disturbance, and over and again it marks its own inability to frame abhumanness within the available language. "Clarke tried to conceive the thing again . . . and again his mind shuddered and shrank back, appalled before the sight of such awful, unspeakable elements enthroned as it were, and triumphant in human flesh" (p. 188). Nor can conventional narrative structures contain abhumanness. The novel is comprised of a confusing mass of interlocking stories, all of which circle around the indescribable phenomenon of Helen Vaughan, all of which interrupt themselves and one another and will not conclude. Narrators suffer aphasia and breakdown; the text and its interpolated texts are ruptured by narrative gaps, elisions, and outright refusals. There's a compulsion to represent, as the almost obsessive proliferation of interpolated manuscripts indicates, but at the same time the novel abjures utterance.

However, *The Great God Pan* deploys quite precise language in detailing the hysterical symptoms of its narrators and readers, particularly, as in the description of Austin's "cold sweat," the symptom of nausea. Symptoms manifest themselves across multiple bodies, as if the Thing-ness of Helen Vaughan were so overwhelming that it could not be expressed through a single displacement, through the hystericization of a single body. A ripple effect of revulsion emanates from without the unspecifiably disgusting body of Helen Vaughan, infecting even the most casual observer: "Everyone who saw her at the police court said she was at once the most beautiful woman and the most repulsive they had ever set eyes on. I have spoken to a man who saw her, and I assure you he positively shuddered as he tried to describe the woman, but he couldn't say why" (pp. 198–9). Helen Vaughan's immediate victims, her husband, her lovers, the girl Rachel, are more fatally hystericized and die of lingering nervous disorders, from sudden heart failure, or from suicide. Hystericization also operates at one remove from Helen's presence: through, for example, the very bodies of Helen's victims, whose hysterical symptoms are catching. Villiers says of Herbert, Helen's husband, "There was something about the man that made one shiver . . . His presence seemed to chill one's blood" (p. 201). Even the London townhouse in which Helen entertained her guest retains an ability to sicken. Villiers, exploring the house, is overcome by dyspnoea, faintness, and nausea; after this incident, he says, "I was in bed for a week, suffering from what my doctor called nervous shock and exhaustion" (p. 203). The contagion of disgust spreads through and overwhelms the text.

Second-remove hysteria, however, is chiefly triggered through reading. *The Great God Pan* especially focuses on the nauseated responses of Clarke, Villiers, and Austin as they read through – or are unable to read – the series of undisclosed interpolated manuscripts. I will not make too much of this point, since such a scenario rarely occurs elsewhere in the *fin-de-siècle* Gothic. Nonetheless, a dynamic which pertains generally across the genre is highly visible in this Machen novel: that the *fin-de-siècle* Gothic is *training* its readership somatically, underscoring that nausea is the proper response to a confrontation with abhumanness. Hystericized itself, the genre seeks to draw its reader into the field of its hysteria.

Pleasure

The question remains as to why the reader would consent to be thus hystericized by the experience of reading. Certainly we enjoy texts that evoke a strong affect, but why *this* affect, the unpleasurable sensation of nausea? When I read *Moreau* as a twelve-year-old, the novel sickened me, and thus I reread it many times more.[19] Perhaps I am the anomaly here. But perhaps not. *Moreau*'s reviewers insisted, in the strongest possible language, that the novel was disgusting. "[T]he author, not content with the horror inevitable in his idea . . . has sought out revolting details with the zeal of a sanitary inspector probing a crowded graveyard" (*The Saturday Review*). "[A]ny ordinarily fastidious reader cannot but be repelled at some of the descriptions of the Beast People" (*The Academy*). "A more gruesomely grotesque and uncanny tale than *The Island of Dr. Moreau* it would be hard to imagine" (*The Critic*). "The horrors described by Mr. Wells in his latest book very pertinently raise the question how far it is legitimate to create feelings of disgust in a work of art" (*Athenaeum*).[20] And yet *Moreau* was a rousing popular success, one of two novels that established Wells' reputation and fortune.[21]

Advertising for Frank Aubrey's *The Devil-Tree of El Dorado* (1896),[22] a particularly densely-plotted novel with many other sensational improbabilities to attract a readership, focused on the anthropophagous tree itself, and emphasized by way of *recommendation* the disgustingness of the tree. "The gruesome devil-tree is about as ghastly a horror as the most jaded appetite could wish." "When once the nightmare of a tree makes its appearance . . . [we are] enthralled by the hideous fascination of a most ghastly tale." "The idea [of the tree] is sufficiently blood-curdling to satisfy the most *blasé* amateur of the gruesome." "For a description of the carnivorous monster we must refer our readers to Mr. Aubrey's own pages, where, if they love to sup on horrors, we can assure them that they will find an ample meal." "[T]o crown all, the awful devil-tree itself [is] a conception sufficiently ghastly and full of horror to satisfy the cravings of the most jaded intellectual appetite." Note how drastically, in the space of seven years (the advertisement appeared in 1903), basic assumptions about the reader and his or her desires have changed: Wells' reviewers feel duty-bound to warn away the "ordinarily fastidious" reader from Wells' nauseating beast people; Aubrey's advertisers worry that the reader, grown "jaded," will not find the devil-tree nauseating enough. It would seem that *fin-de-siècle* readers were not only successfully trained to respond to Gothic texts with disgust, but also to like it.

One critical model identifies horror genres as cathartic, providing a space wherein the reader temporarily may entertain certain illicit or intolerable possibilities represented by monstrosity, only to expel them, along with the text, when the monster is bested at the end.[23] Within this model, nausea – the prelude to vomiting – could be said strikingly to literalize, or somatize, the dynamic of catharsis. However, many *fin-de-siècle* Gothic texts provide only partial closure or none at all: the infection of abhumanness spreads steadily, as it does in *Moreau*, throughout the entire purview of the text; monstrosity is not expelled. Catharsis theory as well assumes a certain predictability on the part of the reader, straightforward mechanisms of identification, straightforward desire for closure and the reconstitution of normality and order. Aubrey's reader, by contrast – at least the ideal reader constructed by the advertisement – is more difficult to characterize, seemingly uninterested in plot or characterization, attracted by the prospect of chaos, craving the sensation of nausea for its own sake. This reader, in fact, emerges as startlingly *hungry* for disgust in the three reviews that speak of readerly "appetite." The advertisement appeals to a reader both sophisticated ("*blasé*") in palate and voracious, in search of an "ample meal" of disgustingness. Aubrey's novel features a tree that eats people, and the reader "eats it up." What mechanisms of identification are at work here?

One must finally, I think, read the symptom of readerly nausea as a multi-valenced one. Within the text, nausea draws the "fully human" character into intimate relation with abhumanness, as occurs with Prendick and M'Ling. The symptom signifies both metaphysical estrangement, as the boundaries that separated humans from Things collapse, and denial, as Prendick fights to maintain the illusion, no longer tenable, of his own "fully human" identity. Across the text, nausea draws the "fully human" reader, as well, into intimate relation with abhumanness. Readerly nausea may be a symptom of denial, like Prendick's: through this emphatic negation, visceral revulsion, the reader may refuse her place within the spectacle of the human becoming other, affirming her identity as a stable and integral human subject.

For Kristeva, nausea allows one to maintain, in the most fragile sense possible, an identity of sorts – not of the specular-ego, unmade by abjection, but of the body-ego, remade in the contractions of disgust. The Gothic, however, disallows even this, most tentative, identity construct, for it is precisely the human body that it reveals as phantasmic and changeful. But it does offer nausea. Nausea throws the subject back into the immediate and unmistakable experience of his own body, affording the subject concrete proof of his own reality, his own undeniable, material Thing-ness, if not of his meaningfulness. As the outlines of the human body dissolve – indeed, as the whole universe around it threatens to dissolve into Thing-ness – the reader is consoled with bodily sensation, however fleeting, however nauseating.

Or perhaps the reader is simply drawn towards the sickening vortex of abhumanness: towards not only the forces of turbulent disorder and indifferentiation, as Kristeva argues, but also the prospect of the terrible and thrilling reconfigurations of identity and meaning that may emerge from the vortex. Whether this is a strategy of identification, or something else entirely, I cannot answer here.

PART II

Gothic bodies

CHAPTER 3

Evolutionism and the loss of human specificity

The philosophical ramifications of Darwin's theories are so immense that they strike at the most fundamental oppositions at the heart of Western culture: the difference between human and animal, male and female, Nature and culture. He reverses a system of signification at least as old as the Greek *polis* with whose emergence the images of hybrid and intermediary forms (centaurs, Amazons, Cyclops) were banished to the realms of monstrosity and otherness. With the disappearance of the Author from Darwin's universe, these oppositions, which had been elevated virtually to the status of logical categories or necessary ways of thinking about the world, collapsed into a kind of Derridean freeplay.

Margot Norris, *Beasts of the Modern Imagination* (p. 37)

In 1884, H. G. Wells came to study at the Normal School of Science in South Kensington, established by T. H. Huxley for the training of science teachers who would staff the new public schools founded after the 1870 Education Act. Though his contact with Huxley was minimal – Wells attended Huxley's lectures for a course on advanced zoology January through June of 1885, and spoke to him only once, in greeting – Wells fell under Huxley's spell. "I believed then he was the greatest man I was ever likely to meet," he wrote in 1901, "and I believe that all the more firmly today."[1] Wells admired Huxley's commitment to his life's project of explaining for the general public, in both his public lectures and his lucid, readable prose, the importance of a scientific education and the significance of new scientific ideas, most notably evolution theory. Wells would model himself along the same lines, as a champion of Darwin who labored to explain evolutionist science to a popular audience and expounded, with some insistence, even the least popular, least palatable implications of evolution theory.

As David C. Smith writes in his biography of Wells, "Darwin's work brought together a body of thought which produced a world explosion of knowledge. H. G. Wells had grown to manhood in the middle of the first burst of creative energy, and his thinking was to a substantial degree forged in the heat of it" (*H. G. Wells*, pp. 50–1). The effect of this "world explosion of knowledge" in Victorian England, even putting aside the tremendous issue of the challenge Darwinian science posed to religious faith, was to demolish the model of human centrality in the universe, and replace it with one of human ephemerality, relativity, and potential "degradation" (to use Wells' term). The new discoveries in the geological and biological sciences required a radical rethinking of humanity's position relative to its environment: its intimate relation to lower species; the role of the mere individual within the far more important history of the human species; human insignificance in a world that, according to geology, had existed far longer than previously had been conceived and that, according to astronomy, occupied a place far more minuscule than previously had been conceived.

Not only did the new sciences demolish a comfortable anthropocentrism, but they also problematized the relation between external appearances and internal reality, most notably in the case of the human body. The human being was not the distinctive creature that it appeared to be on the surface: its lowly origins could be traced by the zoologist, who dissected to find internal structural similarities between human and animal bone, muscle, and tissue; by the embryologist, who posited that ontogeny recapitulated phylogeny – that the human individual passed through its whole history of species evolution during gestation; by the microbiologist, who demonstrated that like all other organisms, humans were, in their most basic components, nothing more than globs of protoplasm.

All of these, like the theory of natural selection, accomplished a radical destabilization of what had formerly been a fixed boundary between man and animal. The narrative of Darwinian evolution could be read as a supernaturalist or Gothic one: evolution theory described a bodily metamorphosis which, even though taking place over aeons and over multiple bodies, rendered the identity of the human body in a most basic sense – its distinctness from "the brute beasts" – unstable. Thus the cultural commonplace of man's bearing "the mark of the beast" became literalized within scientific discourses, and gave rise to two fears. If humans derived from beasts, then they might still be abhuman entities, not yet "fully evolved," not yet "fully human." And worse, the evolutionary process might be reversible: the human race might ultimately retrogress into a sordid animalism rather than progress towards a telos of intellectual and moral perfection.

Various secular popularizers of Darwin (most notably Herbert Spencer) attempted to reformulate evolutionism as a sort of natural progressivism, whereby both living matter and human cultural institutions must inevitably evolve from simple to complex, from barbaric to civilized.[2] Even the Anglican Church managed to come to terms with Darwinism in the latter decades of the century by substituting Darwin's theory of natural selection for the idea of "Divine Purpose," so that the human race could still be seen as God's "supreme achievement," the perfected product of a biological selection engineered by Providence.[3] But figures like Huxley and Wells challenged this glossing of Darwinism, arguing that humanity had come into existence through a random combination of natural processes, and that Nature was ethically neutral and under no compulsion to privilege the human species. The human race could not assure itself of its own stability and continuity, for like any other species it could regress into "lower" forms as well as evolve into "higher" ones, or simply disappear from the face of the earth.

Huxley found some prospect for hope in the fact that Nature had, however accidentally, produced a race with an ethical sense, and he argued that human beings must consciously struggle to perpetuate this ethical sense within their species. Wells rejected even this, quite slender, consolation for the loss of the narrative of divinely ordained human purpose. In the 1890s he produced an impressive corpus of work – newspaper and journal articles, short stories, and novels – exploring the physical and moral implications of the evolutionary process.[4] These implications were often monstrous. For Wells was impatient with what he saw as a facile belief in humanity's inevitable progress, and its status as the point of culmination within a divinely ordained teleology. In both his fiction and his journalism, Wells exposed the fallacies of the belief in human ascendancy, and emphasized the tentativeness of the human species' progress up from savagery.

Using their technical phrases and misquoting their authorities in an invincibly optimistic spirit, the educated public has . . . decided that in the past the great scroll of nature has been steadily unfolding to reveal a constantly richer harmony of forms and successively higher grades of being . . . This belief, as effective, progressive, and pleasing as transformation scenes at a pantomime, receives neither in the geological record nor in the studies of the phylogenetic embryologist any entirely satisfactory confirmation.

On the contrary, there is almost always associated with the suggestion of advance in biological phenomena an opposite idea, which is its essential complement . . . the too sweet harmony of the spheres [sh]ould be enhanced by a discord, this evolutionary antithesis – degradation ("Zoological Retrogression," p. 158).[5]

The purpose of Wells' evolutionary speculations is always the same: to explore the ideas of human impermanence, imperfection, insignificance, and, most especially "degradation," or liability to evolutionary regression. For instance, "The Duration of Life" and its follow-up article, "Death" (*Saturday Review*, 1895), are meditations upon the insignificance of the individual in relation to the species. Wells points out that "the business of the animal seems to be, not to live its own life, but to reproduce its own kind" ("Duration," p. 133), and places the individual human life on the same unenviable scale as that of the lowliest organism. "Mortal man and the immortal protozoa have the same barren immortality; the individuals perish, living on only in their descendants, creatures of their body, separated pieces of their undying protoplasm; the type alone persists" ("Death," p. 139).

The "type," however, even the human type, is no more assured of immortality than the individual. "On Extinction" (*Chamber's Journal*, 1893) compares the human species, now in "the days of [its] triumph," with once-powerful species long extinct, like the "Atlantosaurus," or those teetering on the verge of extinction, like the bison. Though the tone is lyrical – Wells speaks of extinction as a sad but inevitable "tragedy" of scientific law (p. 169) – the message is as plain as that of "A Vision of the Past" (*Science Schools Journal*, 1887), a rather heavy-handed humorous piece. The "author," Sosthenes Smith, awakens into prehistoric times to overhear a monstrous three-eyed amphibian preach to his fellows that their species, "the noblest of all beings who have ever existed or ever will exist," represents "the culminating point of all existence" (pp. 155–6). Smith, unable to contain his contempt for these "absurd claims . . . made by a creature so inferior to [him]self in all respects" (p. 156), leaps up, without perceiving the irony of the situation, to inform the misguided congregation that its race is but a preparation for that true culmination, the human species. He then launches into a discourse on the glories of humanity so displeasing to the monsters that he only awakens just in time to avoid being eaten. "Vision" is a parable about humanity's blindness to its relative inconsequentiality – about human hubris and anthropocentrism – for which Wells, presumably, envisioned an audience as hostile and disbelieving as his man-eating amphibians.

For Wells, the strongest argument for the plausibility of human extinction, developed in "The Rate of Change in Species" (*Saturday*

Review, 1894) and "Human Evolution, an Artificial Process" (*Fortnightly Review*, 1896), involves humans' limited reproductive capacity. Those species which reproduce themselves rapidly, he reasons, are more likely to survive a major cataclysm than those whose young only come to breeding age every twenty years or so: the latter species bear offspring so relatively seldom that they produce few variations from which they could benefit in the event of such a radical environmental change as a global shift in temperature. Man, like that ungainly and unsuccessful species the Atlantosaurus, is at a strong disadvantage here: "His individual adaptability and the subtlety of his contrivance are no doubt great, but his capacity for change as a species is, compared with that of a harvest mouse or a green-fly, infinitesimal" ("Rate of Change," p. 131).

Parallel evolutions

For in that backward glance, he had seen the whole deck of the derelict a-move with living things – giant rats, thousands and thousands of them; and so in a flash had come to an understanding of the disappearance of the crew of the barque ... Whether they were true ship's rats, or a species that is to be found in the weed-haunted plains and islets of the Sargasso Sea, I cannot say. It may be that they are the descendants of rats that lived in ships long centuries lost in the Weed Sea, and which have learned to live among the weed, forming new characteristics, and developing fresh powers and instincts. (William Hope Hodgson, "The Mystery of the Derelict"[6])

Wells emphasizes not only the human species' weaknesses but also the potential strengths of "lesser" species: there is no telling into what fearsome forms these more fertile species might evolve. "The Coming Beast must certainly be reckoned in any anticipatory calculations regarding the Coming Man," he writes in "Zoological Retrogression" (p. 168). Other, "now humble" species may develop into powerful intelligences and supercede humanity; and in Wells' vision, these new species are never benign. This motif occurs again and again in his fiction as well as that of contemporaries like Frank Aubrey, Arthur Conan Doyle, and William Hope Hodgson: the "Beast" may lurk ahead in the future, the monstrous product of some process of evolution no one can now foresee; or it may even now be developing quietly in some dark region of the globe as yet uncharted.[7]

Wells' short story "The Empire of the Ants"[8] offers such a scenario: in the jungles of Brazil, a new species of superintelligent ants, possessing advanced social organization and technological skill, takes over Brazil at its least populated center and begins to colonize, killing (and eating) the human beings who block its way. "What was to prevent the ants evolving also?" asks Holroyd, the protagonist. "Why should things stop at that any more than man had stopped at the barbaric age?" (p. 275). Along similar lines, "The Sea Raiders"[9] depicts a hitherto unclassified species of cephalopod – *Haploteuthis ferox* – that emerges from the depths of the ocean to prey on Cornish bathers and boaters; "The Valley of Spiders,"[10] a species of giant carnivorous spiders that lurk in the southwestern American desert; Conan Doyle's "The Horror of the Heights," a two-hundred foot "glutinous, amoeba-like" creature that seizes pilots who venture above thirty thousand feet.[11]

Gillian Beer writes that "Darwin's theories, with their emphasis on superabundance and extreme fecundity, reached out towards the grotesque. Nature was seen less as husbanding than as spending. Hyperproductivity authenticated the fantastic."[12] In other words, natural selection was a scenario within which any morphic configuration, however implausible, was a plausible one, for Nature rewarded variety and changefulness rather than inflexibility of form. To shift Beer's terms slightly, natural selection authenticated the fantastic. Darwin's narrative proved to be an extraordinarily fertile source for Gothic plotting, which in turn placed its phantasmic entities within an explicitly evolutionist or pseudo-evolutionist framework. In "The Terror of Blue John Gap," for instance, Conan Doyle's narrator concludes his description of an encounter with a subterranean monster as follows:

My view is . . . that in this part of England there is a vast subterranean lake or sea, which is fed by the great number of streams which pass down through the limestone. Where there is a large collection of water there must also be some evaporation, mists or rain, and a possibility of vegetation. This in turn suggests that there may be animal life, arising, as the vegetable life would also do, from those seeds and types which had been introduced at an early period of the world's history, when communication with the outer air was more easy. This place had then developed a fauna and flora of its own, including such monsters as the one I had seen, which may well have been the old cave-bear, enormously enlarged and modified by its new environment. (pp. 85–6)[13]

The protagonist of Phil Robinson's "The Man-Eating Tree" (1881)[14] posits a sort of polymorphous evolutionary potential to all organic life, whereby any organism is capable of drastic readaptation to environmental circumstances. Since "the sensual instincts of beast and vegetable are manifestly analogous," one should not be surprised to discover vegetable species remaking themselves as both "percipient" and "sentient" (p. 3). He notes ominously that "The vegetable world . . . has its revenges" (p. 5).[15]

Gothic stories of parallel evolution represent anomalous phenomena (monsters are properly biological sports) as logical products of natural processes. Monstrosities which disturb the taxonomies of natural history are, paradoxically, legitimated by the Darwinian version of natural history, and in Gothic natural history, the anomalous is reframed as the normal. Inert matter takes on life, vegetable species become mobile, and both these as well as non-human animal species acquire sentience, no longer the exclusive property of humans. As "the human" loses its particularity, it also begins to be evacuated of its meaningfulness. A Darwinian Nature does not privilege, indeed takes no particular notice of, the human species. In "The Empire of the Ants," Holroyd, traveling down the Amazon in a small boat, is oppressed by its inhospitality, wildness, and immensity of the South American jungle: "he had suddenly discovered the insignificance of man . . . He began to perceive that man is indeed a rare animal, having but a precarious hold upon the land" (p. 270).

The consumed human body

One of the great leaves of the flytrap, that had been shut and touchin' the ground as it lay, was slowly rolling back upon its hinges. There, lying like a child in its cradle, was Alabama Joe in the hollow of the leaf. The great thorns had been slowly driven through his heart as it shut upon him . . . [I]t had closed on him as you've seen your little hothouse ones do on a fly; an' there he were as we found him, torn and crushed into pulp by the great jagged teeth of the man-eatin' plant. (Conan Doyle, "The American's Tale"[16])

But "The Empire of the Ants" and other stories that speculate on the possibilities of evolution go a step further and represent an actively hostile Nature, a gothicized Nature, that threatens to draw in and engulf the human observer. The especial terror ascribed to these monstrous nonhuman species lurking within the natural landscape is that they prey on human flesh – and that those beings with super-evolved intelligences, like Holroyd's ants or the Martians in Wells' *The War of the Worlds* (1898), regard humankind as inferior brutes further down the evolutionary scale and thus further down the food chain. The narrator of *War of the Worlds* finds himself "oppressed" by "a sense of dethronement, a persuasion that I was no longer a master, but an animal among the animals, under the Martian heel. With us it would be as with [the animals], to lurk and watch, to run and hide."[7]

Humans, in becoming prey, become Things. Texts like Conan Doyle's "The American's Tale" and Aubrey's *The Devil-Tree of El Dorado* (both feature man-eating plants, like Robinson's story) depict in repulsive detail half-eaten bodies, or the agonies of dying people as they are being preyed upon. In Wells' "The Sea Raiders," a character named Fison sees, from a distance, what he first imagines to be a cluster of birds fighting over "a fragment of food that caught the sun and glistened pinkish-white." As Fison approaches nearer to the object, the story engages the reader in a long tease as the "fragment of food" becomes gradually more distinct, and finally reveals itself to be "the partially devoured body of a human being," covered over with the gleaming bodies and tentacles of half a dozen cephalopods (pp. 652–3). Here the human body is sheerly corporeal, indistinguishable from other raw matter as it is rent and fragmented and absorbed into the viscous body of its predator.

Slimy-bodied anthropophagi like the cephalopod are favored in the Gothic literature of parallel evolution.[18] Human objects of prey are alerted by a track of slime to the presence of their as-yet unseen predators in Weatherby Chesney's "The Crimson Beast" (1898)[19] and Hodgson's *The Boats of the "Glen Carrig"*. Wells' giant spiders travel in floating colonies that are "vast, soft, ragged, filmy thing[s]" resembling an "aerial jelly-fish" (p. 838). Robinson's man-eating tree "glisten[s]" with a "sticky dew" (p. 10). All of the life forms that Conan Doyle's aviator finds in the upper air are "greasy" and protoplasmic in texture, and the thing that chases him looks and moves like an amoeba, a gigantic version of the hungry one described by Allman:

Its method of progression . . . was to throw out a long, glutinous streamer in front of it, which in turn seemed to draw forward the rest of the writhing body. So elastic and glutinous was it that never for two successive minutes was it the same shape . . . [Q]uick as a flash there shot out a long tentacle from this mass of floating blubber . . . A long, gliding, sticky, serpent-like coil came from behind and caught me round the waist . . . ("The Horror of the Heights," p. 25–6)

The viscosity of the predatory natural world may be said to represent the suchness of matter, as it gains sentience and rises up to swallow the bounded human world.

"But it was not properly a man"

And at the sixth fire-hole, I did see that which I did think to be a great man, that did sit to the fire, with monstrous knees drawn upward unto his chin. And the nose was great and bent downward; and the eyes very large, and did shine with the light from the fire-hole, and moved, watching, always this way and that, so that the white parts did show, now this side and now that. *But it was not properly a man.* (Hodgson, *The Night Land*)[20]

But a slimy amorphousness also characterizes the human, who can be "reduced to the slime from which he came, and forced to put on the flesh of the reptile and the snake." When the rash Professor Gregg of *The Three Imposters* speaks the mystic words inscribed upon an ancient Celtic stone, "Something pushed out from the body [of the epileptic boy] there on the floor, and stretched forth, a slimy, wavering tentacle, across my room" (p. 299). The invertebrate or reptile is depicted here as a human ancestor whose loathsome characteristics still lie latent within the human body. As Gregg explains, "human flesh may now and then, once perhaps in ten million cases, be the veil of powers which seem magical to us – powers which, so far from proceeding from the heights and leading men thither, are in reality survivals from the depths of being. The amoeba and the snail have powers which we do not possess; and I thought it possible that the theory of reversion might explain many things which seem wholly inexplicable" (p. 293). The motif of human devolution occurs again and again in the *fin-de-siècle* Gothic, sometimes as a means of literalizing the "beastliness" of which humans are capable, sometimes as a means of demonstrating the cruel randomness of motiveless Nature. In the Machen passage, humans are both imperfectly evolved – always already abhuman, continuous with their beastly ancestors – and liable to reversion to a still worse state of abhumanness, even to utter indifferentiation. Within this scenario, man is not simply threatened by "the Coming Beast." He *is* the Coming Beast, and has been all along.

In "Human Evolution, an Artificial Process," Wells, considering the disadvantages of humanity's limited reproductive capacity on its own terms, argues that the species could have benefitted from such an insignificant amount of modification through natural selection in the last ten thousand years that it can hardly have "undergone anything but an infinitesimal alteration in [its] intrinsic nature since the age of unpolished stone" (p. 214). He scoffs at the notion that any sort of ethical sense could have been bred into the species over a few centuries: the "evolution" of ideas and moral systems must be considered separately, and is distinct from natural evolution undergone through selection of the fittest and subsequent modification. In other words, urgent rage and sexual desire, the love of hunting and killing, are still as strong in "civilized" humanity as they were in Stone Age peoples; the civilized person only keeps these strong emotions in check through the "artificial" devices of social breeding and education.

> In the artificial man, we have all that makes the comforts and securities of civilisation a possibility . . . [W]hat we call morality becomes the padding of suggested emotional habits necessary to keep the round Palæolithic savage in the square hole of the civilised state. And Sin is the conflict of the two factors – as I have tried to convey in my *Island of Dr. Moreau.* (p. 217)

Though Wells rejects the idea of God, he retains a definition of "Sin" as a fall from a state of grace, a lapse from humanity to bestiality that signals, to those who care to discern, humans' imperfect evolution from the state of savagery. Wells rejects as well the belief which comforted Huxley, that the human species has managed biologically to evolve such attributes as a moral sense. He argues on the one hand that significant moral evolution has not actually occurred, and on the other that significant evolutionary change may still take us "backwards," in a direction opposite to that we conceive as progress. Evolution, he reminds his reader in "Zoological Retrogression," has no favorites – its only criterion for success is adaptive capability in response to environment – and no *telos* which involves human values or self-interest. Higher faculties such as intellectual capacity and morality are good for only as long as they last, since regression to a lower form may at some time be a more proper response to environmental change than progression to a higher. And humans are no more exempt from regression than any lower form: "The presumption is that before [humanity] lies a long future of profound modification, but whether that will be, according to present ideals, upward or downward, no one can forecast" (p. 168).

CHAPTER 4

Entropic bodies

The prospect of what Wells called "downward modification" would haunt the European imagination in the last decades of the nineteenth century. Every direction one turned, scientists pointed toward the possibility, even inevitability, of changes within the physical or social environment that would irrevocably reshape the human form and human culture. As nineteenth-century physics, evolutionism, and social medicine generated the highly compatible models of entropy, species "reversion," and human pathology, it became clear that such alterations would be disastrous ones, transforming the human species into something unrecognizable, perhaps even ensuring its extinction. The conflation of these models is best exemplified in degeneration theory, discussed below, prominent throughout Europe at the *fin de siècle*.

Degenerationism is a highly narrative discourse, concerned, as Daniel Pick writes, with "the dynamic patterns which underpinned a chain of changing pathologies across generations."[1] Like that of entropy,[2] degenerationism's is a minus narrative, reversing the direction of ameliorist versions of evolutionism, which proposed natural history as an inevitable progression towards "higher" and more complex forms, and human history as an inevitable progression towards a higher and more rarefied state of civilization. The *telos* of the narrative in the first case was the human form; in the second, European culture. Degeneration theory, however, not only reversed the narrative of progress, proposing a negative *telos* of abhumanness and cultural disarray. It also accelerated the pace of the narrative, emphasizing the mutability and flux of human bodies and societies. Degenerationism, in other words, is a "gothic" discourse, and as such is a crucial imaginative and narrative source for the *fin-de-siècle* Gothic.

4.1 DEGENERATE SUB-SPECIES[3]

When under any kind of noxious influences an organism becomes debilitated, its successors will not resemble the healthy, normal type of the species, with capacities for development, but will form a new sub-species, which, like all others, possesses the capacity of transmitting to its offspring, in a continuously increasing degree, its peculiarities, these being morbid deviations from the normal form – gaps in development, malformations and infirmities. (B. A. Morel, *Traité des dégénérescenses*)

In 1857 Benedictin Augustin Morel published his *Traité des dégénérescenses physiques, intellectuelles et morales de l'espèce humaine (Treatise on the Degeneration of the Human Species)*.[4] Though the idea of human biological degeneration was not original to Morel, he was the first to articulate it into a full-blown theory of heredity, and the *Traité* set the terms of the discussion of degeneration for the rest of the century. Morel posited a gloomy sequence of causes and effects, a hereditary line that began with a first set of defective parents and ended in madness and extinction. The first generation, infected by such modern poisons as urban pollutants and addictive stimulants, passed its infection through the "seed": to a second generation prone to epilepsy, neurasthenia, and hysteria, a third generation hovering near the brink of insanity, and a fourth and final generation doomed to congenital idiocy and sterility.[5]

Degeneration was evolution reversed and compressed. Like evolution theory, degenerationism concerned itself with the long-term effects of heredity within the life-span of a species, and with biological variations from type that affected not just the individual, but the generations to follow. But for the idea of evolution towards ever-higher forms of life, degenerationism substituted a terrible regression, a downward spiral into madness, chaos, and extinction. Heredity was not the vehicle of progress: it was an invisible source of contamination, with the infection jumping across bodies, across the generations, and manifesting itself in visible physical deformity. While the evolution from animal to human, from savage to modern, had taken place gradually, over an unthinkable span of time, degeneration was rapid and fatal. A family line could suffer extinction in four generations, hardly more than a human lifetime; and a culture, too, could sicken and die almost as quickly.

Gothic heredity

In pathological terms, degeneration is "a morbid change in the structure of parts [of the organism], consisting in a disintegration of tissue, or in a substitution of a lower for a higher form of tissue" (*OED*). The individual organism, in other words, wastes away as the result of some disease, substance abuse, or congenital abnormality that causes irreversible deterioration of the tissue. Morel's theory focused particularly on lesions of the brain, which he argued were both degenerative and transmissible to offspring. A lesion might be caused by certain "poisons" characteristic of modern society – narcotics and stimulants (alcohol, tobacco, opium, hashish, arsenic), industrial wastes, and tainted foods – as well as by poor diet, hazardous occupations, such illnesses as marsh fever, syphilis, tuberculosis, and goitre, and even an accidental blow to the head. However the parent acquired the degenerative lesion, the offspring could not fail to inherit it. According to the Lamarckian evolutionism that informed degeneration theory, characteristics acquired during the lifetime of the parent could be passed on to the next generation.[6] And what was worse, the degenerate offspring inherited the parents' acquired morbidity in some aggravated form.

Jules Bernard Luys wrote in *Maladies Mentales* that "The individual who comes into the world is not an isolated being separated from his kindred ... He is bound [to those who preceded him and] to those who follow him, and to the atavic influences which he possesses; he serves for their temporary resting-place, and he transmits them to his descendants."[7] Degeneration was an appalling version of this continuity within the species, a gothic nightmare of heredity. In the first place, degeneracy was easily transmitted. The child could inherit a morbid taint from either parent, thanks to the "law of double fertilization" (Carlson, p. 122); and the smallest possible lapse on the part of the parents was enough to doom the offspring. Cesare Lombroso, in *The Man of Genius* (1864, English trans. 1891), warned that "even habitually sober parents, who at the moment of conception are in a temporary state of drunkenness, beget children who are epileptic or paralytic, idiotic or insane ... Thus a single embrace, given in a moment of drunkenness, may be fatal to an entire generation" (p. 144).

In the second place, degeneracy was self-perpetuating, once the chain of reproduction had been set in motion. Virtually all of the subjects of Richard von Krafft-Ebing's 237 case studies in *Psychopathia Sexualis* (written and revised 1882–1902) are contaminated by what he calls "hereditary taint": a family history of neurasthenia, or hysteria, or alcoholism, or insanity, or all four. Case 126, describing a "sexual invert" (homosexual), is typical:

Ilma S., aged twenty-nine; single, merchant's daughter; of a family having bad nervous taint. Father was a drinker and died by suicide, as also did the patient's brother and sister. A sister suffered with convulsive hysteria. Mother's father shot himself while insane. Mother was sickly, and paralyzed after apoplexy . . . At fourteen, [the patient suffered] chlorosis and catalepsy from fright. Later, marked hysteria and an attack of hysterical insanity. (p. 317)

Another "invert," similarly tainted by a family history of nervous and mental illnesses, sent an autobiography to Krafft-Ebing in which he described how the taint had been passed on to his own children: "[M]y wife gave birth to our first boy in a difficult labor – a boy still afflicted with a melancholy nature. Then came a second, who is very quiet; a third, full of peculiarities; a fourth, a fifth; and all have the predisposition to neurasthenia" (p. 333).

And finally, degeneracy was progressive in its effects, as the original contamination (be it "ever so slight") intensified itself in the offspring, and was manifested in the increasing mental and physical deformity of each successive generation. Morel was a monogenist – that is, he believed that the various human races had degenerated, in greater and lesser degrees, from the Edenic perfection of the first couple, rather than evolving as separate "species" in different regions of the world[8] – and the idea of the Fall from grace heavily influenced the *Traité* and the writings of even the polygenist authors on degeneracy who followed Morel. Degeneration, like syphilis, with which it was often confused,[9] could be seen as a divine punishment for some "original sin." Degenerationists wrote in highly colored, apocalyptic style of the sins of the parents being visited most heavily on the heads of children who had forfeited their innocence even before birth.[10] The perverted morality of one generation – of the alcoholic mother, the father who had contracted syphilis from prostitutes – found literalization in the deformed bodies and minds of the next. Syphilitic children were born shrunken and wizened like little old men and women, and degenerate children were born with a disposition to vice as great as the most depraved adult's.

Cultural contagion

Morel proposed a basically limited model of degeneration, writing that "fortunately, [the morbid deviation] is soon rendered sterile, and after a few generations often dies out before it reaches the lowest grade of organic degradation."[11] But during the last decades of the nineteenth century, this model of degeneration yielded to one that was ever more contagious, ever more progressive in its effects – that could spread wildly through the ranks of society and destroy an entire culture. Within the larger etiology of degeneration constructed after Morel, the social organism was as vulnerable as the individual organism to degenerative disease – to morbid infection, deterioration, and death. In a vicious circle of causes and effects, a poisonous society (locus of both environmental and moral contaminants) infected the individual, the individual passed the infection to its offspring, and the degenerate offspring reinfected society.[12]

The issue of environment's causal relation to degeneracy did not entirely disappear from this larger social etiology. Gareth Stedman Jones' *Outcast London* describes the whole body of work that sprang up around the problem of hereditary urban degeneration, particularly as it affected that problematic sub-species, the inner-city (working-class) Londoner.[13] According to James Cantlie's *Degeneration Amongst Londoners* (1885), the original cause of urban degeneration was the lack of "ozone" in the London air; and subsequent generations born to city-bred parents starved of sunlight and fresh air were launched upon a downward spiral of degradation that matched Morel's worst nightmares.[14] J. P. Freeman Williams (*The Effect of Town Life on the General Health*, 1890) wrote that the second-generation Londoner was "excitable and painfully precocious in childhood, neurotic, dyspeptic, pale and undersized in its adult state, if it ever reaches it." This "town type" became more and more exaggerated in the third and fourth generations – that is, if the type managed to survive that long. "[I]t has been maintained with considerable show of probability that a pure Londoner of the fourth generation [like Morel's fifth-generation degenerate] is not capable of existing."[15] Cantlie located a third-generation Londoner only after considerable difficulties, and he was but a sorry specimen. "Height 5 feet 3 inches. Age 19. Chest measurement 20 inches. His head measured 20 inches round (2 inches below the average). His face is mottled, pale, and pimpled. He squints rather badly. His jaws are misshapen . . . [and] his teeth spiculated" (p. 22).[16]

J. Milner Fothergill (*The Town Dweller*, 1889) warned that urban degeneration was forming a new subspecies of cockney "mannikins," a "race of dwarfs," as successive generations of East-Enders devolved further and further back to the "lowlier" and more primitive "racial types" (Erse, Celto-Iberians, pre-Aryans) from which their rustic ancestors had sprung (pp. 107, 113–14). But the larger issue at stake here was not so much the physical well-being of the working classes as the overall health of the nation. As Fothergill stated rather baldly, "the deterioration, both physical and mental, of the town bred organisms, is a matter not meant for the philanthropist, but for the social economist" (p. 114). In late-Victorian England, the theory of urban degeneration was used to explain away the nation's economic decline after the boom of mid-century: Britain was faltering because it was forced to draw both its labor force and its recruits for the imperial army[17] from a class of degenerates. The new "subspecies" of degenerate proletariat found in the inner city was born with a stunted and weakened physique, and thus was constitutionally incapable of hard work; and born with a stunted and weakened moral character, and thus constitutionally prone to such evils as idleness, criminality, alcoholism, and political agitation. The degeneracy of the inner-city working classes might be temporarily checked by the migration of healthy rural laborers, but these newcomers, too, would become infected by the miasmic London air and miasmic London morals, and breed more defective offspring. As Stedman Jones writes, "If the theory of urban degeneration was correct, then the long-run consequences of the migration into the towns would be a progressive deterioration of the race" (p. 286) – and a progressive deterioration of a British economy whose industries relied so heavily on urban labor pools.

Similarly, any decline in national military power – France's defeat at the hands of the Prussians, Britain's losses during the first half of the Boer War – could be accounted for by the theory of degeneration. Degeneration was linked to the rise of democracy, class mobility, and racial miscegenation,[18] and thus could explain the social instability that seemed to be sweeping across *fin-de-siècle* Europe and postbellum America. Degeneration, which caused a population to drift into "unwise extremes of eating and drinking, religion or revelry, lavishness or effeminacy" (Cantlie, p. 21), could also be seen as the source of all social problems – alcoholism, prostitution, unemployment, crime, a low national birthrate, divorce, suicide, deviant sexual practices. All these were blamed on the deteriorating bodies, deteriorating minds, and deteriorating moral character of the people.[19] Krafft-Ebing wrote that the fall of great nations in the past had always been connected with widespread degeneracy and moral decay. "The material and moral ruin of the community is readily brought about by debauchery, adultery, and luxury, [which] . . . can always be traced to psychopathological or neuropathological conditions of the nations involved" (pp. 34–5).

Morel had opened the door to this type of analysis, in which immorality was both causal and symptomatic, with his emphasis on alcoholism as a primary cause of degeneration. Both the weak-willed alcoholic parents and their miserable descendants (born with a predisposition to alcoholism and too weak to resist addiction) were characterized not only by "dementia," but also by "stupidity, the absence of all intellectual initiative, and the abolition of the moral sentiments . . . [They] have sacrificed to their frenzied desires all which they ought to have held most dear" (p. 109). Though the alcoholic might be "poisoned" by liquor or heredity, alcoholism was also an immoral behavior that went hand-in-hand with other immoral behaviors: riotousness, domestic irresponsibility, idleness, and sexual excess, not to mention theft, violence, prostitution, and labor agitation.

Sexual contagion

In other words, while degeneration was technically a medical term, and denoted a particular sub-category of organic disease, this disease wrought moral effects by inducing in the human organism a "morbid deviation from an original type" whose offspring were congenitally prone (or so the theory went) to sinful behaviors. Symptoms became increasingly confused with causes as degeneration theory became a tool for measuring the moral health of society as well as the health of the individual.[20] A predisposition to vice could be either inherited or acquired during an individual's lifetime; in either case, the contamination could be passed on through either heredity or simple association, through sexual intercourse or social intercourse. Degeneration came to stand in for a sort of general turpitude with which modern society was infecting itself, and against which modern society had to police itself.

Sexual turpitude in particular became synonymous with degeneration in the later decades of the nineteenth century. Deviant sexuality could be classed as "degenerate" in four senses: its recapitulation of the less evolved sexuality of so-called primitives, its hereditability, its deteriorative effect on mind and body, and its general corrupting influence on public morals. In works like Eduard Reich's *History, Natural Laws, Laws of Hygiene in Maturity* (1864), Edward Westermarck's *History of Human Marriage* (1891), and Krafft-Ebing's "Fragments of a System of Psychology of Sexual Life" (the introductory chapter to *Psychopathia Sexualis*), deviant sexuality was synonymous with sociocultural devolution. According to these texts, cultural evolution could be defined as a progression from the

promiscuous or perverse sexuality characteristic of "primitive" societies
to the institutionalization of monogamy, and the elevation of "modesty,
chastity, and sexual fidelity," characteristic in modern Christian nations
(Krafft-Ebing, p. 31).[21] Deviant sexual behaviors – masturbation,
homosexuality, any sexual activity, in fact, besides "normal" intercourse
within Christian matrimony[22] – constituted a sort of behavioral
recapitulation of some ancestral state, and a betrayal of the socioevolutionary process that distinguished the modern Caucasian from the present-day
non-European "primitive."

Though the sexual deviant did not actually devolve before one's eyes,
he or she did deteriorate physically. Masturbation, for example, was said
to debilitate the sexual organs and nervous system: various of Krafft-Ebing's
masturbating patients complain of weakened potency from loss of
sperm, premature ejaculation, "general neurasthenia," even "spinal
irritation" (pp. 321, 287, 383). Masturbation also weakened the moral
fiber and ruined the health of the libido.

Nothing is so prone to contaminate – under certain circumstances, even to
exhaust – the source of all noble and ideal sentiments . . . as the practice of
masturbation in early years. It despoils the unfolding bud of perfume and
beauty, and leaves behind only the coarse, animal desire for sexual satisfaction.
If an individual thus depraved, reaches the age of maturity, there is wanting in
him that aesthetic, ideal, pure and free impulse which draws the opposite sexes
together. The glow of sensual sensibility wanes, and the inclination toward the
opposite sex is weakened . . . [P]remature and perverse sexual satisfaction
injures not merely the mind, but also the body; inasmuch as it induces neuroses
of the sexual apparatus (irritable weakness of the centers governing erection and
ejaculation; defective pleasurable feeling in coitus, etc.), while, at the same time,
it maintains imagination and libido in continuous excitement. (pp. 310–11)

While Krafft-Ebing considered masturbation a bad habit rather than
a congenital perversion (even though he did marvel at how many of his
youthful deviants picked up the habit "without any teaching"),
masturbation was the means by which other vices became rooted in the
vita sexualis. "At the age of thirteen he developed a weakness for ladies'
boots with high heels. He pressed them between his thighs and thus
produced ejaculation . . . He soon added to this fancy the idea that he lay
at the feet of a pretty girl and allowed her to kick him with her pretty
boots" (pp. 199–200). "He began to masturbate excessively. When he did
this . . . he would imagine that he carried out the sexual act with [a
roomful of women] and then killed them" (p. 130). "Since that time the
picture of old men performing the sexual act enlivened his dreams (with

pollution), and was present in his mind during masturbation" (p. 391). Masturbation exacerbated fetishism, sadism, masochism, necrophilia, and homosexuality; and if these vices were not discouraged, they would inevitably cause sexual pathology in the offspring. Even the mildest case of "abnormality" could be "hereditarily transferred . . . in such a manner that it becomes transformed into a perversion [in the next generation]" (p. 234).

Aberrant sexuality, then, could be inherited, and was symptomatic of degeneration, but aberrant sexual practices could also be learned, and thus become a fresh cause of hereditary degeneration in a hitherto untainted family. When this happened, then even "normal" sexuality for the purpose of procreation became the means by which corruption was transmitted. Krafft-Ebing made some effort to distinguish between disease (congenital abnormal sexual behavior) and vice (acquired bad sexual habits), which he also differentiated as perversion and perversity. The congenital "invert," for example, was born with a "neuropathic predisposition" to homosexuality (p. 308), while the sometime homosexual had been corrupted by depraved companions, or weakened his mental health through excessive masturbation. But even acquired perversities, if they continued to be indulged, would rapidly debilitate the mind and body, so that even an individual with an untainted lineage could soon be in as lamentable a condition as the born sexual deviant. And either type was contagious: both would transmit their pathology to their offspring; and both were capable of seducing and corrupting "normal," sexually healthy individuals.

The implosion of modernity

The city still played a primary role in initiating the chain of degeneracy, but this was not the city as site of environmental hazards so much as the city as a modern Sodom and Gomorrah, the "breeding ground of perverse and unnatural sexuality" (Gilman, "Sexology," p. 214). Though degeneration caused a culture to slide back into more primitive behaviors – and even caused the individual, in the case of the "invert," to revert back to a primitive bisexuality "such as still exists in the lowest classes of animal life and also during the first months of fetal existence in man"[23] – degeneration was, unfortunately, the particular plague of modernity, of those European nations that prided themselves on their high state of evolution. Krafft-Ebing wrote that "anomalies of the sexual functions are met with especially in civilized races," and that degenerates could be found "especially in the centers of culture and refinement" (pp. 77, 99).

The reason for all of this, according to Max Nordau's *Degeneration* (1893; English trans. 1895), was that an increasingly evolved society was an increasingly debilitated society: modern European peoples were being enervated by the frenetic pace of modern civilization. Civilized nations, Nordau believed, had grown inordinately exhausted in the last fifty years. Fatigue "changes healthy men into hysterical," and "the whole of civilized humanity has been exposed [to fatigue] for half a century" (p. 39).

Degeneration's analysis of this new phenomenon, *fin-de-siècle* exhaustion, was greatly influenced by George Beard's *American Nervousness: Its Causes and Consequences* (1881). Beard described a new disease he called neurasthenia (lack of "nerve force"), whose symptoms, like the symptoms of degeneration, were legion, and whose cause could be found, quite simply, in modernity.[24] "The chief and primary cause of this development and very rapid increase of nervousness is *modern civilization*, which is distinguished from the ancient by these five characteristics: steam-power, the periodical press, the telegraph, the sciences, and the mental activity of women" (p. vi; emphasis in text). Nordau, however, defined neurasthenia as a secondary manifestation of a much greater problem, modern hysteria. The first generation subjected to such new and stressful phenomena as crowded urban living, railway travel, and daily newspapers had grown hysterical, and the next generation had inherited that hysteria.

All these activities . . . even the simplest, involve an effort of the nervous system and a wearing of tissue. Every line we read or write, every human face we see, every conversation we carry on, every scene we perceive through the window of the flying express, sets in activity our sensory nerves and our brain centres . . . Our stomachs cannot keep pace with the brain and nervous system. And so there follows what always happens if great expenses are met by small incomes; first the savings are consumed, then comes bankruptcy. (pp. 39–40)

Nordau made a distinction between this fatigue-hysteria and organic degeneration caused by a brain lesion or heredity; however, each "disease" was heritable, each caused further susceptibility to the other, and both fed into the greater problem of national or cultural degeneration. The first exhausted generation had turned to stimulants (alcohol and tobacco) for relief, and this began a "disastrous, vicious circle of reciprocal effects. The drinker (and apparently the smoker also) begets enfeebled children, hereditarily fatigued or degenerated, and these drink and smoke in their turn, because they are fatigued" (p. 41). And like the addiction to alcohol and tobacco, the addiction to thrills was hereditary, self-perpetuating, and progressive. The modern man and woman inherited the enfeebled constitution of parents enervated by too much and too-rapid change, and that enfeebled constitution left the modern man and woman hungry for more change, for any innovation – however depraved – that might cause the exhausted nerve synapses to fire again.

The exhausted, hysterical state of the modern public accounted, in Nordau's view, for the widespread social immorality earlier degenerationists had described. But more importantly, it accounted for the growing immorality – the sickness and degeneration – of modern culture. The primary target of *Degeneration* is such *fin-de-siècle* aesthetic movements as impressionism, naturalism, mysticism, and symbolism, "effete" movements which emphasized form over substance, and which Nordau believed to be unhealthy and dangerous. According to him, these movements were the morbid invention of degenerates – masturbators, lunatics, homosexuals, and alcoholics – who knew well how to shock and titillate a jaded public looking for a thrill. They glorified obscenity, filth, and social chaos. They rewrote the end-of-century constitutional exhaustion sweeping across Europe into a sort of romantic decadence, encouraging the public to sink back in a pleasant, dreamy langour rather than fighting against its weakness. And their degeneration was infectious, given the nervous susceptibility of the exhausted public. In Nordau's typical scenario, a Wagner or a Verlaine announces the formation of some new "school," the invention of his diseased brain; "other degenerate, hysterical, neurasthenical minds flock around him" to imitate and promote his work; and the hysterical, impressionable public goes wild with admiration (pp. 31–3).

Nordau dedicated *Degeneration* to his "dear and honoured Master" Lombroso, whose *The Man of Genius* posited that genius was the result of a brain lesion, nothing more than another form of degeneration. Lombroso's book is largely an itemization of geniuses throughout the ages who suffered from all the symptoms of degeneration: alcoholism, insanity, egoism, epilepsy, monomania, delusions, melancholy, and a whole host of nervous disorders. Lombroso argued that genius, like degeneration, was a function of tainted heredity, found in "the children of inebriate, imbecile, idiotic, or epileptic parents" (p. 359). And though genius was a one-time biological phenomenon that could not be transferred to the offspring, it, like degeneration, also resulted in the rapid deterioration and extinction of the hereditary line.

[When transmitted, genius] almost always assumes the form of more and more aggravated neurosis, and rapidly disappears, thanks to that beneficent sterility through which nature provides for the elimination of monsters. The fact would be quite sufficiently demonstrated by the pedigrees of Peter the Great, the Caesars, and Charles V, in which epileptics, men of genius, and criminals, alternate with ever greater frequency, till the line ends in idiocy and sterility. (p. 333)

Despite all this, Lombroso's opinion of the man of genius was fairly benign: he believed that the genius contributed, at the expense of his own health and sanity, to the advancement of science, philosophy, and culture. In other words, a morbid biological aberration, the degenerate-as-genius, was paradoxically the most valuable tool of social evolution.

Nordau, however, broke with his "Master" on this issue. "I do not share Lombroso's opinion that highly-gifted degenerates are an active force in the progress of mankind. They corrupt and delude; they do, alas! frequently exercise a deep influence, but this is always a baneful one" (p. 24). Nordau believed that degenerate aesthetic practices were more widespread (and more dangerous) than Lombroso had realized; their numbers included symbolism, decadence and aestheticism, pre-Raphaelitism, Ibsenism, Tolstoism, and the schools of Wagner, Nietzsche, and Zola. These various degenerate schools he classed as examples of either "Mysticism," "Ego-Mania," or "false Realism," three types of aesthetic perception and expression which resulted from "an exhausted central nervous system" and degenerative malfunction of the brain. "In all three tendencies we detect the same ultimate elements, viz., a brain incapable of normal working, thence feebleness of will, inattention, predominance of emotion, lack of knowledge, absence of sympathy or interest in the world and humanity, atrophy of the notion of duty and morality" (p. 536).[25]

Degeneration was *the* book of the 1890s, phenomenally popular throughout Europe.[26] It was perhaps the most successful example of that late-Victorian sub-genre, the sociomedical text, incorporating biology, evolutionism, psychopathology, moral philosophy, and sociocultural analysis into one sweeping critique of modernity. Nonetheless, *Degeneration* is a cranky book, reading like a 600-page Horatian satire of modern culture. It is a bitter Phillipic against every aesthetic movement that, in Nordau's opinion, showed "contempt for traditional views of custom and morality" (p. 5). To Nordau, any break from traditional forms could never denote progress, only mental and cultural devolution. Modern artists might claim to speak to the future, but in reality they spoke from a "forgotten, far-away past," a human evolutionary past of inarticulateness, childishness, and savagery.

Degenerates lisp and stammer, instead of speaking. They utter monosyllabic cries, instead of constructing grammatically and syntactically articulated sentences. They draw and paint like children, who dirty tables and walls with mischievous hands. They confound all the arts, and lead them back to the primitive forms they had before evolution differentiated them. Every one of their qualities is atavistic. (p. 555)

And *Degeneration* is a gloomy, apocalyptic book, playing to all the fears and uncertainties *fin-de-siècle* Europe entertained during what Nordau called "The Twilight of the Nations." Modern Europe had considered itself the supreme product of sociocultural evolution, but now it worried that the process of evolution had peaked, and that Western civilization, contaminated by the very fruits of its own progress, was sliding into a fatal decline, into senility, dementia, and death. "We stand now in the midst of a severe mental epidemic; of a sort of black death of degeneration and hysteria, and it is natural that we should ask anxiously on all sides: 'What is to come next?'" (Nordau, p. 537).

Recuperating humanness

Judging from the past, we may safely infer that not one living species will transmit its unaltered likeness to a distant futurity. And of the species now living very few will transmit progeny of any kind to a far distant futurity; for the manner in which all organic beings are grouped, shows that the greater number of species in each genus, and all the species in many genera, have left no descendants, but have become utterly extinct. (Darwin, *The Origin of Species*, p. 373)

In degeneration theory the prospect of the loss of human specificity is entertained to an almost overwhelming degree. The human body, the human species, human cultures – all are balanced in such tenuous equilibrium that the slightest disturbance will send the whole human enterprise crashing down. Perhaps nothing will be left in the ruins. Within the disparate but interlocking etiologies proposed by degenerationism, even the as-yet healthy body is dangerously permeable and fragile. Contamination passes swiftly between the individual bodies enmeshed within a densely-packed cultural space, and travels fatally across the generations. One drink at the wrong time, one generation without sunlight, one blow to the head, one masturbatory fantasy, and the whole hereditary line is doomed.

Or perhaps what emerges from the ruins will be an abomination. Degenerationists emphasize the ominous mutability of the human body, its liability to abhuman becomings. Even now, they believe, such transformations are upon us, producing what Morel described as "a new subspecies," Cantlie as a "race of dwarfs," and Lombroso as a strange breed of "monsters."

Despite its obsessive rewriting of a narrative of human entropy, however, degenerationism did offer two main strategies for reconstituting a "fully human" identity. The first was to affirm one's own, through a return to such values as perseverance, hard work, and clean thinking. If the European populations struggled hard to resist the effects of degeneration, they would (at least according to the laws of Lamarckian evolution) pass on to the next generation not idleness and dissipation, but firmness, self-denial, and moral strength, and human civilization would be put back on the track. Krafft-Ebing promised that "willpower and a strong character" could cure all but the most depraved or congenitally defective. He urged his patients to abjure such "filthy" practices as masturbation, homosexual activities, and sadomasochism, and "exercis[e their] imagination in the right direction," towards normal heterosexual intercourse (pp. 34, 377).[27] Nordau predicted that the European nations would, within a few generations, adapt to modernity, and produce a new and vitalized species equipped to cope with the rapid pace of modern life. To do this, however, the present generations would have to practice "the expansion of consciousness and the contraction of the unconscious; the strengthening of will and weakening of impulses; the increase of self-responsibility and the repression of reckless egoism" (p. 554).

The second strategy was to fully acknowledge the possibility of abhumanness, but to acknowledge it only as the possibility of others – the masturbator, the East End denizen, the homosexual, the decadent aesthete – against whom the normative subject emerged as unquestionably human. Each healthy individual must resolve to do "strong and resolute combat with the evil" (Nordau, p. 552). Nordau believed that degenerates were ultimately doomed to extinction because they would be weeded out by the process of natural selection. "The feeble, the degenerate will perish. [They] must be abandoned to their inexorable fate. They are past cure or amelioration." However, one could not just sit back and wait for this to happen. The "misguided" masses, who were only "victims to fashion and certain cunning impostures," would be led further astray, and the recovery of "civilized humanity" proceed much more slowly, if degenerates were not actively suppressed (pp. 550–1). He proposed a league of doctors, professors, authors, politicians, and judges – a "Society for Ethical Culture" which would take it upon itself to educate the public and expose the degenerate.

It is the sacred duty of all healthy and moral men to take part in the work of protecting and saving those who are not already too deeply diseased. Only by each individual doing his duty will it be possible to dam up the invading mental malady... [He] must mercilessly crush under his thumb the anti-social vermin ... Such is the treatment of the disease of the age which I hold to be efficacious: Characterization of the leading degenerates as mentally diseased; unmasking and stigmatizing of their imitators as enemies to society; cautioning the public against the lies of these parasites. (pp. 566–7, 560)

Suppression of the degenerate was demanded as a biological imperative, a social imperative, and a national imperative. As an unchecked source of contamination, the degenerate could destroy a family, a race, a nation, or even Western civilization itself. However, the degenerate could also be the source of further socioevolutionary progress if society drew its ranks and mustered its strength to expel the source of contamination – to "crush . . . the anti-social vermin," in Nordau's evocative phrase. As Sander Gilman has argued, degeneration stands in as the negative term in a positive dialectical model of moral and cultural evolution progressing by action and reaction. Degeneracy, within this model, could be described as ultimately "a positive force as it moves humanity to the necessary changes in forms of human interaction. Society thus benefits from its own repression as it dialectically causes changes within itself" ("Sexology," p. 198). To put it another way, by dehumanizing (abhumanizing) the degenerate, the normative subject humanized itself.

4.2 ABJECTING WHITENESS: H. G. WELLS' *THE TIME MACHINE*

[B]etween the most wretched individual of the Hottentot race and the most accomplished European, viewed as the perfection of his type, there is less dissemblance than between this same European and the sickly degenerated being designated by the name of cretin . . . Between the intellectual state of the wildest Bosjesman and that of the most civilised European there is less difference than between the intellectual state of the same European and that of the degenerate being in whom arrest of intellect is due to cerebral atrophy, congenital or acquired. (Morel, *Treatise*, pp. 219, 221)

Despite such recuperative strategies, one result of degeneration theory was to theorize abhumanness, at least the degenerate variety of it, as a uniquely *European* predilection. The very things said to denote a "high" degree of social evolution – industrialization, urbanization, cultural variety – produced chemical, social, and aesthetic contaminants to which only "civilized" bodies were exposed.[28] Non-European bodies and cultures, of course, served as already-abhuman markers against which the extent of European degeneration could be measured, but these, ironically, remained stable points of reference. The European body by contrast was a body in flux, the body upon which the forces of entropy worked most visibly.

While the *fin-de-siècle* Gothic may represent the non-white body as an abomination, indefinite in species-identity and otherwise abhuman,[29] as frequently it is concerned with the liminality and fluctuability of the white body. Texts like Conan Doyle's "The Third Generation," Walter de la Mare's "A: B: O.," and Barry Pain's "The Undying Thing" bring the prospect of white abhumanness directly home with their scenarios of degeneration in Great Britain, as often as not instantiated by the sorts of sexual excesses or perversions writers like Krafft-Ebing warned against.[30] Each story explores the causal relationship between sexual indiscretion, syphilis, and "constitutional and hereditary taint" ("The Third Generation," p. 1016). The sins of the fathers become embodied in the deformities of the children, to the extent of producing abhuman monsters in "A: B: O." and "The Undying Thing."

M. P. Shiel's "Huguenin's Wife" describes the loathsome exploits of the Sphinx-woman Andromeda, who is descended from "a very antique Athenian family, which by constant effort had preserved its purity of blood."[31] Andromeda is a sorceress dedicated to bringing back the ancient worship, and whose magic yields hideous results. Thus Western civilization is revealed as having long since been poisoned at its very font, classical Greece. The title of the same author's "The Pale Ape" emphasizes the liability of the white body to reversion, in this case caused by hereditary insanity in combination with unmanageable male heterosexual desire.[32] In such texts, whiteness is no guarantor of a fully human identity; indeed, whiteness is identified specifically as the color of abjection. The European body, far from being protected by its putative racial superiority, is a body both grossly corporeal and changeful, capable at any moment of becoming the "white Thing" that Wells' protagonist confronts in *The Time Machine* (p. 76).

The Time Machine

And during those few revolutions [of the earth's pole] all the activity, all the traditions, the complex organizations, the nations, languages, literatures, aspirations, even the mere memory of Man as I knew him, had been swept out of existence. Instead were these frail creatures who had forgotten their high ancestry, and the white Things of which I went in terror. (*The Time Machine*, p. 76)

The Time Machine sets out a narrative of increasing human indifferentiation in three registers: degeneration, devolution, and entropy. The novel jumps ahead eight hundred thousand years to imagine what a particularly remorseless process of "downward modification" of the human species might yield. The protagonist, known only as "the Time Traveller," invents a machine that carries him far into the future, where he finds humanity transmuted into two distinct species. The Eloi are lovely but degenerate beings of atrophied mental powers, who perform no useful labor and live only for pleasure. The Morlocks are species abominations, half-human and half-ape, living deep underground in industrial communities and maintaining the Eloi as their food source. The novel, by projecting itself into futurity, emphasizes the fluctuability of species, prone to variation and divergence. The human form we know now, and thus conceive as a "proper" form, is only a temporary one. The novel, however, manifests a certain obstinate inflexibility of imagination: the human body is mutable, but there is only one narrative direction – backwards – marked out for its changes. *The Time Machine* is a text in thrall to the compelling vision of human entropy, much like degeneration theory.

On one level *The Time Machine* is legible as a cautionary parable about the "dehumanizations" effected by capitalism.[33] Humanity's divergence into two species, according to the Time Traveller's conjectures, is the "logical conclusion" of class differentiation in "the industrial system of today" (p. 61). Practical labor and those who performed it were increasingly forced underground, a process already underway in the contemporaneity, with its basement sweatshops and restaurants and subterranean railways, of the Time Traveller. "Even now," he asks in a passage reminiscent of Cantlie, "does not an East-End worker live in such artificial conditions as practically to be cut off from the natural surface of the earth?" (p. 60). The capitalist classes, meanwhile, enclosed the upper earth to make it off-limits to the workers, and were free to pursue art and science – and with the eventual perfection of these, leisure. In accordance with biological law, each class adapted to its existing environment: the Morlocks, to become a species of underground tunnelers and workers, the Eloi, a species of drones dependent on their former slaves. Thus the Morlocks can be said to constitute the oppressed classes that have risen up to consume their oppressors, and their cannibalism to have its roots in an industrial capitalism within which system human beings do, most savagely, prey upon and exploit one another. I will leave this reading slightly to one side in order to consider *The Time Machine* as a specifically Gothic work, as much concerned with abhumanity as inhumanity.

Manliness

When the Time Traveller arrives in the year 802,701, he expects to find a civilization which has so progressed in art, science, and philosophy as to be incomprehensible to his nineteenth-century mind, and fears that the human species will have evolved so far morally and physically that he will appear as a man of the Stone Age would in Victorian London, "some old-world savage animal . . . a foul creature to be incontinently slain" (p. 25). What he finds instead, at least initially, is a species not improved, but strikingly diminished in both intellectual and physical stature. The Eloi are a graceful, gentle people, characterized by a "Dresden china type of prettiness" (p. 28) and speaking a "very sweet and liquid tongue" (p. 27). They greet him with laughter and garlands of flowers and, most surprisingly to him, without intellectual curiosity. Like so-called primitives, they assume that he has travelled from the sun and fallen out of the thunderstorm; and like five-year-old children, they interrogate him for only a few minutes before wandering off to find some other "plaything" (p. 29).

"[A]ll had the same form of costume, the same soft hairless visage, and the same girlish rotundity of limb" (p. 35). The loveliness of the male Eloi is reminiscent of that of ideal Victorian femininity: "his flushed face reminded me of the more beautiful kind of consumptive – that hectic beauty of which we used to hear so much" (p. 27). Physically, this variation on the human species has lost all secondary sexual characteristics, so that males cannot be differentiated from females. Cultural change has accommodated physical change, or vice versa, so that masculinity and femininity (signalled by costume and behavior) are indistinguishable.

One might call this androgyny, but the narrator is dismayed, and codes it as effeminacy. The species, he laments, has lost its Manhood as well as its complexity. The Eloi are "indolent," "easily fatigued," and almost mindless in their idle pursuit of pleasure (p. 33). "They spent all their time in playing gently, in making love in a half-playful fashion, in eating fruit and sleeping" (p. 51). They have no notion of written language, and their spoken language, composed almost entirely of noun substantives and simple verbs, has no power to express thought (p. 48). They passively live off the decaying plenty of a once-powerful and technologically proficient civilization, in the "ruinous splendour" of crumbling palaces and unkempt gardens (p. 34).

The Eloi are in many ways an embodiment of the worst fears of the degenerationists.[34] As with degeneration theory, mental decay here finds embodiment in the physical alteration of the human species – the weakened, diminished frame, and loss of the secondary sexual characteristics which, Krafft-Ebing argued, distinguished the adult human from children and the human species from lower species of animal life. One strand of evolutionist thinking identified "savages," women, and children as three types of inferior humanity, evincing in common certain moral and mental inadequacies that signaled their incomplete state of evolution; and the Eloi have simultaneously "fallen," or devolved, into primitiveness, effeminacy, and childishness. The Eloi display all those characteristics said to typify savages, women, and children: egoism, simplicity, a love of self-adornment, indolence, short attention span, lack of intellectual curiosity, imitativeness, and inability to think abstractly or creatively.

The Eloi do not suffer from "brain lesions" or any of the mental and nervous illnesses Morel and his followers describe. However, the Eloi, like Nordau's modern civilized European, have been betrayed by progress itself. At some point in the future, the Time Traveller reasons, technological and moral progress secured humanity against hunger, disease, and war, but this security made the qualities of energy, intelligence, and strength – of "manliness," in short – obsolete. "We are kept keen on the grindstone of pain and necessity," in a struggle of the survival of the fittest; and Utopia, for the active Carlylian type, is a "too perfect triumph of man" (p. 40). "What, unless biological science is a mass of errors, is the cause of human intelligence and vigour?" the Time Traveller asks. "Hardship and freedom: conditions under which the active, strong, and subtle survive and the weaker go to the wall" (p. 39). The ancestors of the Eloi adapted to their new environment, a man-made environment constructed to eliminate all obstacles and challenges, by becoming less vigorous, less intellectual, more idle, vapid, and effete. "The too-perfect security of the Upper-worlders had led them to a slow movement of degeneration, to a general dwindling in size, strength, and intelligence" (p. 62). The "fittest" who survived were not the strongest and boldest, but those weaker-minded, indolent individuals who would not fret under the new monotonous conditions of ease and luxury. The Time Traveller concludes in a sentence worthy of Nordau that "this has ever been the fate of energy in security; it takes to art and to eroticism; and then come languor and decay" (p. 40).

Social evolution, for the degenerationist, seems to carry within itself the germ of its own decay: progress towards an ever more refined, ever more productive state of civilization eventually collapses and folds back upon itself. For Nordau, technological advancement leads to widespread immorality and constitutional exhaustion; and within *The Time Machine*, projecting itself even further into the future of humanity, it leads to complacency and indolence. For both, the result is the same: a degenerate, decadent race that has lost its manly vigor and drive. Wells, however, envisions a still greater disaster of devolution, whereby one branch of the human species has degenerated even further, back to the remote, animal origins of the human race. His portrayal of the Morlocks is a revision of the theory of urban degeneration: the industrial classes have indeed, as Fothergill warned, developed into a new and terrible species, stunted, deformed, and morally depraved.

But rather than dying out in the unwholesome urban environment, as the urban degenerationists predicted would happen, the working-class "race" in Wells' text has adapted to it with a vengeance. The bleached-out Morlocks are stooped and light-blind, as befits a species of underground tunnelers, and quick and agile from generations of incessant labor. In *The Time Machine*, the idea of the "lower" classes has become literalized into a sub-species of apish Lower-worlders, scurrying and chattering in their subterranean industrial inferno.

The Time Traveller tries to convince himself that the enslavement of the Eloi in the year 802,701 is only a just revenge for their generations of domination as a callous aristocracy, but he cannot do it. "However great their intellectual degradation, the Eloi had kept too much of the human form not to claim my sympathy" (p. 78). Although he feels contempt for the Eloi, they are not abhuman. Perhaps *because* they are effeminized, they cannot arouse abjection, for the Time Traveller's own distinctly human (here coded masculine) qualities – strength, forcefulness, courage, energy – appear to advantage beside them. But as to the Morlocks, "it was impossible, somehow, to feel any humanity in the things." Like those species in *Leviticus* that defy classification, the Morlocks are "abominations" (p. 95), and they arouse in the Time Traveller a sense of "quivering horror" he cannot quite justify or explain (p. 94).

White Things

The Morlocks are not actually introduced till the second half of the novel. They first appear as dream-creatures, phantasmic apparitions which, the Time Traveller speculates, may be the products of an overheated imagination. For example, he awakens one night to catch a half-glimpse of the "greyish animal" that pawed at his face while he dreamed "most disagreeably that [he] was drowned, and that sea-anemones were feeling over [his] face with their soft palps" (p. 54); and later, in the "ghastly half-light" of early dawn, he sees, in the distance, "white figures" that he half-jokingly decides to be ghosts. "Twice I fancied I saw a solitary white, ape-like creature running quickly up the hill, and once near the ruins I saw a leash of them carrying some dark body" (p. 55).

But finally he meets one of his "ghosts" face to face, and in a highly specular encounter, while their eyes meet and the Time Traveller becomes convulsed with symptoms, the Morlock changes from a ghost to a Thing, from a specter to an abomination. In the dim half-light again, within the "profound obscurity" of the ruins of some massive structure, the Time Traveller discovers a pair of luminous eyes watching him from out of the darkness, and the "old instinctive dread of wild beasts" comes over him. Gradually he makes out a "queer little apelike figure," "dull white . . . [with] strange large greyish-red eyes . . . [and] flaxen hair on its head and down its back"; and this "Thing," as he calls it, retreats down a deep shaft, regarding him steadily all the way (pp. 56–7).

I do not know how long I sat peering down that well. It was not for some time that I could succeed in persuading myself that the thing I had seen was human. But, gradually, the truth dawned on me . . . that my graceful children of the Upper World were not the sole descendants of our generation, but that this bleached, obscene, nocturnal Thing, which had flashed before me, was also heir to all the ages. (pp. 57–8)

Even though the narrator is able to describe the Morlocks in detail, both here and later in the novel after he explores their underground community and then fights an epic battle with them in the forest, the reader's perception of these ape-humans remains shadowy and indefinite, since the Time Traveller is anxious to convey not so much the Morlocks' physical appearance as his horrified reaction to their presence. His response is instinctive and visceral, and to describe it he must resort continually to a gothic language of indefinition. "I had a feeling of intense fear for which I could perceive no definite reason" (p. 63). "I felt a peculiar shrinking from those pallid bodies. They were just the

half-bleached colour of the worms and things one sees preserved in spirit
in a zoological museum. And they were filthily cold to the touch" (p. 63).
The Morlocks, he says, have a "sickening quality" – a "something
inhuman and malign. Instinctively I loathed them" (p. 71).

The overwhelming disgustingness of the Morlocks may be partially
attributed to their cannibalism. Cannibalism is the great "secret" of the
novella, and the narrative works up to it very slowly, with a series of
unanswered questions. What was the "dark body" the Time Traveller
saw the Morlocks carrying up the hill? Why are there no aged or infirm
among the Eloi? Why do the Eloi fear the dark, and sleep together in
huddled bands? Why does the Morlocks' underground habitat reek of
"freshly-shed blood," and just what is that "red joint" of raw meat the
Time Traveller glimpses in their underworld (p. 67), here in a future
where all domestic animals have become extinct?

The reader may have little trouble answering these questions, but the
text nonetheless shrouds them in an aura of mystery and horror. Here
cannibalism is the great unspeakable, a trauma instantiating hysterical
symptoms (including an excess of textual affect), just as abhuman
sexuality does in *The Great God Pan*. The Time Traveller, like the several
Machen narrators, cannot bear to put a name to the unspeakable thing
he has discovered: as he rather belatedly deduces the source of the
Morlocks' food-supply, he breaks off mid-sentence. "I thought once
more of the meat that I had seen. I felt assured of what it was . . .
[Human] prejudice against human flesh is no deep-seated instinct. And
so these inhuman sons of men – !" (p. 77). Within *The Time Machine*,
cannibalism is the ultimate and most disgusting proof of abhumanness.
The human reveals his bestiality by preying on his fellow, and the
cannibalized victim is animalized as well (the Eloi are described as
"cattle"). Both eater and eaten are Things, one manifesting the
indiscriminate appetite of the material world, the other losing all
specificity whatsoever as it becomes absorbed into the digestive tract and
tissue of its predator.

However, while the Time Traveller is willing to undergo a ten-day
fruit diet among the Eloi, when he returns to his own present the first
thing he does is wolf down a meal of red meat. "Save me some of that
mutton," he demands of his dinner guests. "I'm starving for a bit of
meat" (p. 16). Although he casts his allegiance with the Morlocks'
victims, and renounces all kinship with the cannibalistic descendants of
the human race, the novel always emphasizes his greater similarity to the
abhuman ape-men. The Eloi may be more recognizably "human," but

the narrator bears far less resemblance to these mild, effeminate creatures than to the Morlocks. For in contrast to their apish appearance, the Morlocks are exemplary Victorians: they are intelligent, shrewd, and industrious; they operate complex machinery; they are actively employed in the production of useful goods. They are energetically masculine, like the Time Traveller himself (the Time Traveller alternates between the pronouns "it" and "he" in describing the Morlocks). And finally, they are *white*: the raciality of the Eloi is not particularly foregrounded, but the Morlocks' most emphatically is. *The Time Machine* stresses the liability of the white man, the Victorian man, to abhumanness.

For if the Morlocks are savage "beasts," they are still not much worse than the Time Traveller, whose story is always bringing his own savagery to the forefront. He fantasizes about and occasionally indulges in brutality towards the annoyingly passive Eloi, and gives in to the passion of blood-lust when he fights the Morlocks, exulting that "I could feel the succulent giving of flesh and bone under my blows" (p. 92). Visiting the Morlock underworld he remarks, "I stood there with only the weapons and the powers that Nature had endowed me with – hands, feet, and teeth" (p. 68): the reader is always reminded of the narrator's own origins in struggling beasthood. For it is not the "old instinctive dread of wild beasts," nor primitive fears of creatures who hunt in the dark, nor even the knowledge of the Morlocks' cannibalism that can account for the disproportionate terror and disgust they arouse in the Time Traveller. This emotion is perhaps instead an awareness of his own abjectness; while at the same time his overcharged hatred of the Morlocks ("I longed very much to kill a Morlock or two"; p. 83) is an assertion of his own separateness from the Thing-ness they represent.

Entropy

But Thing-ness nonetheless overwhelms *The Time Machine*. The novel does not conclude with the Eloi and the Morlocks, with the twin vision of human degeneration and devolution, though this were terrible enough. The Time Traveller takes his machine many millenia into the future, where he finds a cold, desolate planet: the earth, like the moon, has ceased to rotate, and the sun is dying out. "I cannot convey the sense of abominable desolation that hung over the world. The red eastern sky, the northward blackness, the salt Dead Sea ... the uniform poisonous-looking green of the lichenous plants ... all contributed to an appalling effect" (p. 104).

The human race in this apocalyptic future has long been extinct. All that remains of the world, besides very primitive plant life, is its hunger. The Time Traveller, having just fled from the cannibalistic Morlocks, narrowly escapes being eaten by a "monstrous crab-like creature." "Its evil eyes were wriggling on their stalks, its mouth was all alive with appetite, and its vast ungainly claws, smeared with algal slime, were descending upon me" (p. 103). The crab's voracious mouth – "I could see the many palps of its complicated mouth flickering and feeling as it moved" (p. 103) – is the last vestige of morphic complexity he finds in the near-dead world. Even this disappears. He flees further on into time, where the earth has become still chillier and more desolate, and where the last surviving animal creature has no recognizable form whatsoever. "It was a round thing, the size of a football perhaps, or, it may be, bigger, and tentacles trailed down from it; it seemed black against the weltering blood-red water, and it was hopping fitfully about" (p. 106). Overcome with a "deadly nausea" (p. 106), the Time Traveller returns to the present. The future, he has discovered, holds nothing but indifferentiation and its concomitant, disgust.

CHAPTER 5

Chaotic bodies

In fact, the path of [evolution], so frequently compared to some steadily-rising mountain slope, is far more like a footway worn by leisurely wanderers in an undulating country. Excelsior biology is a popular and poetic creation – the *real* form of a phylum, or line of descent, is far more like the course of a busy man moving about a great city. Sometimes it goes underground, sometimes it doubles and twists in tortuous streets, now it rises far overhead along some viaduct . . . Upward and downward these threads of pedigree interweave, slowly working out a pattern of accomplished things that is difficult to interpret, but in which scientific observers certainly fail to discover that inevitable tendency to higher and better things with which the word "evolution" is popularly associated.
Wells, "Zoological Retrogression"
Early Writings in Science and Science Fiction (p. 159)

Entropic narratives are in their own way highly *directive*: they accomplish a straightforward reversal of narratives of "progress." That is, while entropic plotting is productive, capable of generating an intriguing variety of abhuman possibilities,[1] gothic entropy can be seen as a traditional narrative structure: it moves steadily, without detour or interruption, towards a *telos*, albeit the negative *telos* of loss of specificity. What Wells describes by contrast in the quote above is a narrative model more consistent with Darwin's own: a model of random movement, non-directive, non-telic, aimless and errant. Eric White identifies such a narrative movement as "picaresque" (as opposed to the "comic romance" of progressivist history): "The temporal unfolding of reality is . . . open-ended and unpredictable, a suite of contingent circumstances rather than an inexorable march toward some predestined goal." The random processes of evolution, like the picaresque, comprise "a 'degree zero' form of emplotment whose principle of articulation is not teleological but successive: 'and . . . and . . . and . . .'" ("The End of Metanarratives in Evolutionary Biology," p. 63).

Entropic plotting – which bears rough similarities to tragic plotting – evacuates the world of meaningfulness: complex structures (bodies, cultures) lose their complexity; the achievements, or at least the consolidations, of a "forward-moving" evolutionary process are undone. The entropic imagination is held in thrall to an unbroken prospect of barrenness, emptiness, silence, indifferentiation, much like the prospect that greets the Time Traveller at the end of his journeyings. In "picaresque" evolutionist plotting, by contrast, meaningfulness has never even been an option. All the structures it generates are contingent and provisional – they were produced by accident; others would have done as well; nor will they persist unaltered – and thus are without intrinsic meaning. Or rather, they mean nothing more than what they are.

Such a narrative does not lead to barrenness, however, like entropy. It leads nowhere at all, but on the way to nowhere it reveals itself as highly ingenious and productive. Margot Norris argues that for Darwin, the prospect of the randomness of natural processes was by no means a distressing one: "He was able to recognize that madness was not the only alternative to reason and that chaos does not logically follow the abolition of conscious design" (*Beasts of the Modern Imagination*, p. 29).[2] For Darwin, that is, the intricacy and superb functionality of biological forms contrasted markedly with the chaotic randomness of the processes that, accidentally, generate form. The *fin-de-siècle* Gothic, however, envisioned something rather more terrible. In its plots of both parallel evolutions and abhuman becomings, a randomly-working Nature is figured as *too* imaginative, *too* prolific. Any admixture of diverse morphic traits is possible, so that even highly complex bodies, ingeniously specialized for their environment (the new crew of the *Lancing*, for example), are abominable.

5.1 THE BODY AS PALIMPSEST

Mine Own did struggle terribly with a yellow thing which I perceived to be a man with four arms . . . And surely it was a mighty and brutish thing, and so broad and bulkt as an ox, and the lower arms were huge and greatly haired, and the fingers of the hands did have the nails grown into horrid talons, as that they should grip very bitter . . . And the breath of the Man-Beast came at me, and did sicken me; and I held the face off from me; for I had died with horror, if that it had come more anigh; and surely the mouth of the Man was small and shaped so that I knew it did never eat of aught that it did slay; but to drink as a vampire . . . [And] it did make other sounds, and an horrid screeching, so that truly, by the way of it I conceived that it cried out unknown and half-shapen words at me. (Hodgson, *The Night Land*, pp. 497–9)

It is impossible to maintain the idea of an integral human identity within such a scenario, gothic or otherwise. In the first place, the picaresque narrative of evolution does not mark out humanity as its *telos* (it has none), nor can humanity foresee its own direction within such a narrative. The species was an accident like any other, and the only guarantees made by Darwin were that the vast majority of species would become extinct, and that those who remained would not survive unchanged.[3]

More startling, perhaps, was the notion that man never had been "properly a man," to use the Hodgson phrase quoted in chapter 3. In *The Origin of Species*, talking of species in general Darwin presents the body as a compendium, on and within which the whole history of the species is inscribed. "[E]very highly developed organism has passed through many changes; and . . . each modified structure tends to be inherited, so that each modification will not readily be quite lost, but may be again and again further altered. Hence the structure of each part of each species . . . is the sum of many inherited changes, through which the species has passed during its successive adaptations to changed habits and conditions of life" (p. 143). He would bring this point closer to home in *The Descent of Man*: "We have seen in the last two chapters that man bears in his bodily structure clear traces of his descent from some lower form . . ." (p. 445).[4] Norris describes this newly conceived body as a palimpsest, a document on which many records have been made or stories told, one imperfectly erased to make room for the next, none having any meaningful relation to the others. Her argument is worth quoting at length:

The body, Darwin discovered, was as much a palimpsest as the earth, an irregular, haphazard, and incomplete inscription (and erasure) of its own evolutionary history – of changing conditions and their impact on its form, of habits acquired and abandoned, of necessities emergent and vanished, of instincts developed and repressed, and of shifting affinities and departures. In order to read the body in this way, certain metaphysical preconceptions about its unity and integrity had to be scuttled . . . Darwin, like Freud in his approach to dreams, studied the human body *en detail* rather than *en masse*, not in its unity and internal coherence, but in its fragments (organs, structures, functions) and their correlation to those of other creatures. He found that, quite unlike an efficient machine, the human body exhibits many anachronisms . . . Read in this way, as a palimpsest, the human being is no longer the prototype of ideal form in its unity, its originality, its integrity, and its perfection. Hybrid and even teratoid, as it were, in both body and mind, it contains little bits and traces of other animals . . . (pp. 39–40).⁵

Such a body is not just liable to abhuman becomings, but also reveals itself as always already abhuman, a strange compilation of morphic traits, fractured across multiple species-boundaries. Wells, ever obliging about impressing upon his readers the most unsettling of Darwin's arguments, would describe the human body as a modified fish-body. The skull is "a piscine cranium, ossified and altered"; the nose is "a fish's nasal organ"; the ear-drum "is derived from a gill-slit twisted up to supplement the aquatic internal ear." Nor have the modifications been made with particular skill or care. "Everywhere we look we should find the anatomy of a fish twisted and patched to fit a life out of water; nowhere organs built specially for this very special condition" ("Zoological Retrogression," pp. 164–5).

Criminal anthropology

At the sight of that skull, I seemed to see all of a sudden, lighted up as a vast plain under a flaming sky, the problem of the nature of the criminal – an atavistic being who reproduces in his person the ferocious instincts of primitive humanity and the inferior animals. Thus were explained anatomically the enormous jaws, high cheek-bones, prominent superciliary arches, solitary lines in the palms, extreme size of the orbits, handle-shaped or sessile ears found in criminals, savages, and apes, insensibility to pain, extremely acute sight, tattooing, excessive idleness, love of orgies, and the irresistible craving for evil for its own sake, the desire not only to extinguish life in the victim, but to mutilate the corpse, tear its flesh, and drink its blood.⁶

Any layer of text within the palimpsestic body may be seen as an available narrative possibility, which the body may seize upon and develop. This would constitute a *reversion* to some earlier form, whose history still remains, as a trace memory of sorts, in the body of the descendant.⁷ Such a possibility was of course highly compatible with entropic narratives, but this narrative of reversion was an unpredictable one. So many conflicting and mutually irrelevant histories were stored in the body that the most surprising morphic trait could be accessed and realized. Here we have a body both entropic and chaotic.

The *fin-de-siècle* science of criminal anthropology, most commonly associated with the Italian criminologist Cesare Lombroso,⁸ was focused on such an abhuman body as I have described here. Lombroso is most famous for his theory of the "born criminal," whose innate propensity for criminal behaviors could be explained by his atavism, or reversion to now latent characteristics that had been dominant in some earlier moment of the species-history. The atavist was, in short, an evolutionary throwback, but one who could be thrown back along a number of possible trajectories.

The body, for Lombroso, was a transparency of the intellect, emotions, and moral nature of the subject it contained. Innate criminality bespoke itself in certain physical stigmata: physiognomical characteristics shared with lower species or "lower races," but no longer found in the normal Caucasian.[9] The most common of the visible stigmata included an irregular or disproportionate cranium, facial asymmetry, prognathism (a jutting jaw), large or misplaced ears, receding forehead, and apelike disproportion of the limbs; the dissector's knife also revealed lesions and abnormalities of the brain and other structural irregularities. The marks of reversion, in other words, could be found across the entire body – within the skull, face, eyes, ears, nose, mouth, cheeks, palate, teeth, jaw, hair, thorax, pelvis, abdomen, limbs, and brain, which showed abnormal affinities with those of species or races further down the evolutionary scale. Atavistic anomalies were not in themselves causative, but denoted a savage and animalistic nature that prompted criminal acts.

Rodent-lemur-chicken-men

The range of animal species from which atavistic traits could be drawn was truly remarkable. Lombroso does not restrict himself to the most recent human ancestors, the primates: his criminal also shows abnormal physical correspondences with "remote ancestors"[10] like dogs, rodents, lemurs, reptiles, oxen, birds of prey, and domestic fowl, to name a few (pp. 13–22). For instance, the criminal may exhibit the flattened nose and "sugar-loaf" skull of the ape (p. 7), handle-shaped ears like the chimpanzee's (p. 14), a "lemurine apophysis . . . at the angle of the jaw" (p. 15), and rodent-like cheek pouches (p. 16). His "supernumerary teeth" recall the double row of teeth found in snakes, his hooked nose, the beak of the bird of prey (p. 7). Another study documents "additional ribs and vertebrae in 10 [criminals] out of 100, and also too few, in the same proportion; which reminds us of the great variableness of these bones in the lower vertebrates" ("Illustrative Studies in Criminal Anthropology," p. 189).

The multiplication of examples like these produces a certain dizzying incoherence, not least of all because domestic fowl, for one, do not share with humans a common line of descent. Nor does Lombroso explain how the process of atavism could be so indiscriminate, causing one criminal to recapitulate the ape, another the reptile, another the rodent; nor why one criminal with multiple stigmata would simultaneously recapitulate all of these lower species. Some of his criminal-animal correspondences are governed by metaphor, the criminal's double row of teeth recalling the legendary deceitfulness of the snake, his hooked nose, the fierceness of the bird of prey (Lombroso-Ferrero, p. 7). But other correspondences run counter to logic – that the physical characteristics the criminal shares with omnivores should signal his desire to "mutilate the corpse [of the victim], tear its flesh, and drink its blood"; that those he shares with lemurs, apes, and reptiles should signal his innate tendency to vanity, wantonness, vengefulness, and impulsive rage. Lombroso here seems to be playing on the commonplace that certain human behaviors – thieving, viciousness, love of drunken orgies – are "beastly," rather than developing strict animal-human correspondences.

However, rather than faulting the science of Lombroso, still recalled as an exemplary empiricist,[11] I will note instead the *gothic* quality of his atavistic body. This is something rather worse than Wells' fish-human "twisted and patched to fit a life out of water," perhaps worse than Hodgson's braying octopus-seal-men. Atavism reveals that the human body is too compendious, too full of incompatible histories, too full of strange narrative lines waiting to be developed. The human body, at least potentially, is utterly chaotic, unable to maintain its distinctions from a whole world of animal possibilities.

Other abhumans

Despite its intensive theorizing of abhumanness, criminal anthropology was quite deliberately engaged in reconstituting what Darwinism had undone, the stability and integrity of the human species. Abhuman becomings were always possible, according to the Darwinist or pseudo-Darwinist models on which Lombroso based his work, but not for oneself: atavists were defectives, misfits, criminals, riffraff – anomalies against which the "fully human" subject stood out in relief. One will not be surprised to discover that Lombroso's standard of this fully human subject was the (non-criminal) white European adult male. Besides the wide range of animal species, then, the nature and extent of the white man's atavism could be measured against other subjects who were not quite subjects, not quite fully evolved, not quite human: nonwhites, women, and children.

The psychology of the "savage" races – purported to be an altogether thieving, indolent, childish, dishonest, vicious, licentious, and cannibalistic lot – furnished the reader with a perhaps more compelling point of reference for atavism than did lemurine jaw angles. Criminal behaviors denoted "a return to the early brutal egotism natural to the primitive races, which manifests itself in homicide, theft, and other crimes" (Lombroso-Ferrero, pp. 72–3). "As with savages . . . [criminals'] passions are swift but violent, vengeance is considered as a duty, and they have a strong love for gambling, alcohol, and complete idleness." Like New Caledonians, criminals would "[rather] die than work." Like North American Indians, they enjoy savage games (Lombroso, "Criminal Anthropology," pp. 37–8). They are shameless, like the South American Indians, who do not know how to blush. They are inherently dishonest, like those "inveterate thieves," the natives of British New Guinea (Havelock Ellis, *The Criminal*, pp. 138, 181).

The criminal also recapitulates savage behavior in his cultural practices. This explains, for instance, the primitive drawings and inscriptions found in prison cells, the slang, hieroglyphic codes, and elaborate sign language of the European criminal, and his obsession with elaborate tattoos. Lombroso considered this last a particularly potent proof of the atavism of the criminal. According to one of his prison subjects,

"When [our] tattooing is very odd and grotesque, and spreads over the whole body . . . it is for us thieves what the black dress coat and the decorated vest is to society. The more we are tattooed the greater is our esteem for one another; the more an individual is tattooed, the more authority he has over his companions." "Very often," another told me, "when we visited prostitutes, and they saw us covered all over with tattoos, they overwhelmed us with presents, and gave us money instead of demanding it."

"If all that is not atavism," Lombroso concludes triumphantly, "atavism does not exist in science" ("Illustrative Studies in Criminal Anthropology," p. 195).

Within such an argument, the partial humanness, or abhumanness, of the African, American Indian, Polynesian, and other "savage" peoples is simply a given; they represented a point somewhere between the ape and the white man on the evolutionary scale.[12] According to physical anthropologists like George Samuel Morton and Paul Broca, these races evinced marked physical inferiority to the Caucasian: their lesser skull size (and thus intelligence), more prognathous angle of profile, inferior development of the frontal lobes of the brain, et cetera proved that they simply had not evolved far enough to be characterized as completely human.[13] And according to social evolutionists like Herbert Spencer and Benjamin Kidd, the social institutions of nonwhites were similarly undeveloped. Spencer defined social evolution as increasing complexity, the natural "progress towards greater size, coherence, multiformity, and definiteness" that also characterized physical evolution (Spencer, *Principles of Sociology*, p. 597). All existing and extinct races could be ranked according to their status within the chain of evolution from the simple nomadic tribal structure to the "semi-settled" nation-state to modern industrial civilization (pp. 549–55).

"Less-evolved" races were culturally and behaviorally primitive as well. Spencer's Fuegians, for example, a migratory race governed within only a very loose tribal structure, are characterized by promiscuity, cannibalism, greed, thievery, duplicity, and lack of intellectual curiosity (*Descriptive Sociology*, table I) – all of those characteristics Lombroso deplores in his atavistic criminal type. The Fuegians' spoken language "scarcely deserves to be called articulate." They are less human, in short, than the modern European. Kidd, on the other hand, states with some magnanimity that evolutionary superiority is not determined by color, or descent, or even "high intellectual capacity": it belongs to the race "possessing in the highest degree the qualities contributing to social efficiency," such as "strength and energy of character, humanity, probity and integrity, and simple-minded devolution to conceptions of duty" (*Social Evolution*, pp. 348–9).[14] However, these qualities are possessed only by whites. As dictated by the "cosmic order" of evolution, the "coloured races" have stagnated in those temperate regions where "the conditions of life are easiest," while the northern races, under the press of a harsher climate, evolved into the possession of "energy, enterprise, and social efficiency" (p. 340). Thus, "the long, slow process of evolution has produced a profound dividing line between the inhabitants of the tropics and those of the temperate regions" (Kidd, *The Control of the Tropics*, p. 30).

Ernst Haeckel's biogenetic law of recapitulation provided a further justification for the construction of racial hierarchies during Lombroso's time. Haeckel's theory that ontogeny recapitulates phylogeny – that the human individual passes through its whole history of species evolution during gestation – was extended to both human psychology and sociocultural evolutionism.[15] According to psychological recapitulationism, the intellect and moral sense of the child is also in "embryonic" form; en route to adulthood the child must pass through the process of sociocultural evolution undergone by its remote human ancestors. The child is, in other words, a "little savage," but more to the point, the savage may be profitably compared to the white child. This argument fits comfortably into the imperialist policies of nineteenth-century Europe, resulting, at best, in a model of paternalism: Europe would look after its colonies because their native populations, like little children, were not fit to look after themselves. In particular, they were not fit to manage the tremendous natural resources with which they had been blessed; these resources would have to be administered by the more highly evolved Caucasian races, ever mindful of "questions of responsibility to weaker races . . . [who] take us back to the very childhood of the world, and [with whom] the first principle of successful policy is that we are dealing, as it were, with children" (Kidd, *The Control of the Tropics*, pp. 33–4).

The recapitulationist argument is strongly evident in Lombroso's treatment of nonwhites, who are repeatedly compared, in their egoism, their impatience, their petty dishonesties, their love of bright objects and fancy dress, to children. Lombroso saw the child as a primitive human and a "natural" criminal. "The moral sense is certainly wanting in children in the first months or even the first years of life": young children are impatient, deceitful, obstinate, vain, vengeful, cruel, violent-tempered, obscene, even prone to alcoholism ("Criminal Anthropology Applied to Pedagogy," pp. 54–6). In other words, a certain degree of criminality in children is normal, but as the normal child grows up in a proper environment, "all this criminality disappears, just as in the fully developed foetus the traces of the lower animals gradually disappear which are so conspicuous in the first months of the foetal life; we have a genuine ethical evolution corresponding to the physical evolution" (p. 56).

Lombroso used the recapitulationist argument more systematically in his analysis of femininity and the female criminal. All women are in some sense "born criminals," according to him, or at least they are less fully evolved human beings than men. Within Lombroso's work the woman, the child, the "savage," and the animal become interchangeable. "In figure, in size of brain, in strength, in intelligence, woman comes nearer to the animal and the child" ("Atavism and Evolution," p. 48). "In the psychology of the normal woman dress and personal adornment enter as factors of immense importance . . . A similar feeling is visible in children and in savages." Woman's natural vengefulness is proof of "an inferior psychical development, common not only to children, but . . . also to the lower animals." "What terrific criminals would children be if they had strong passions, muscular strength, and sufficient intelligence; and if, moreover, their evil tendencies were exasperated by a morbid psychical activity! And women are big children . . ." (*The Female Offender*, pp. 165, 156, 151).

And like children, women are natural criminals: a "fund of immorality [lies] latent in every female" (*The Female Offender*, p. 216). Whereas the child (at least the white male child) grows out of his primitive state, woman is incapable of higher development. Among her natural shortcomings Lombroso and his son-in-law William Ferrero, co-author of *The Female Offender*, list dishonesty, spitefulness, greed, vanity, disrespect for property rights, selfishness, and vengefulness. Fortunately, in the normal woman these latent criminal tendencies are held in check by her biological and psychical "conservatism" (p. 109). This conservatism is due on the one hand to "the immobility of the ovule compared with the zoosperm" (p. 109), and on the other to the underdevelopment of "the graphic cerebral centres of women in general" (p. 174). The monotonous female structure, in other words, is less likely than the male to evince an aberration like atavism, and the sluggish female brain less subject to lesions or other abnormalities that might trigger criminal behavior; this explains why the female "born criminal" is less common than the male.[16]

The "natural form of retrogression in women" is prostitution rather than crime (p. 152). "[T]he primitive woman was rarely a murderess; but she was always a prostitute, and such she remained until semi-civilised epochs" (p. 111). The female "born criminal," more rare and less "natural" than the prostitute, loses her claim to femininity because she so closely resembles her male counterpart in her virility of aspect and behavior.[17] She is, however, by dint of her superadded feminine "innate depravity" (p. 264), even more degenerate, more savage, more brutal, than he.

In general the moral physiognomy of the born female criminal approximates strongly to that of the male. The atavistic diminution of the secondary sexual characters which is to be observed in the anthropology of the subject, shows itself once again in the psychology of the female criminal, who is excessively erotic, weak in maternal feeling, inclined to dissipation, astute and audacious, and dominates weaker beings sometimes by suggestion, at others by muscular force; while her love of violent exercise, her vices, and even her dress, increase her resemblance to the sterner sex. Added to these virile characteristics are often the worst qualities of woman: namely, an excessive desire for revenge, cunning, cruelty, love of dress, and untruthfulness, forming a combination of evil tendencies which often results in a type of extraordinary wickedness . . . [T]he female born criminal, when a complete type, is more terrible than the male. (*The Female Offender*, pp. 187–8, 191)

The Female Offender is perhaps less interesting for this portrait of the female offender than for the composite picture of the normal woman one can extrapolate from it. Besides possessing her "latent fund of wickedness" (p. 265), the normal woman is unintelligent, conservative, gossipy, impressionable, without pride, and completely without sexual passion. Thanks to her duller sensibility, she is better equipped than a man to endure both physical and moral suffering (pp. 270–2). The only passion she knows is a stolid maternal sentiment: she loves her husband but "feebly" (p. 277), and is biologically incapable of friendship with other women (p. 286).

Interestingly enough, while some of the authors' characterizations of normal femininity – asexuality, childishness, intellectual vacuity – are certainly consistent with Victorian truisms of sexual difference, many of them run counter to other familiar stereotypes. According to *The Female Offender*, women have no finer sensibilities, no delicate moral scruples, no purity of mind. The authors might admit of a Dora Copperfield, but not an Agnes Wickfield. "[Women's love] is like the affection of children – intense – but incapable of disinterested sacrifices or noble resignation" (p. 161). Their piety is but a dull-minded traditionalism. Even the maternal sentiment is overrated (pp. 254–5).

A question of instinct

Note how abhumanness spreads in Lombroso. It is the condition of the vast majority of peoples across the globe, leaving only two small pockets of "fully human" populations (Europe and North America). Even these are not intact. Abhumanness penetrates the very household, presided over by the imperfectly evolved European woman. The normative subject who remains is himself endangered, menaced from within by the chaos of his own body, upon which the species-history is recorded. And it is in Lombroso's discussion of the "born criminal" himself – that is, the European male atavist – that one sees his most stringent attempts to fix and contain the meanings of the unstable human body.

Lombroso was a self-declared positivist (he described his as the "Positive School" of criminology), and placed great stress on the infallibility of the empiricist practice of science. He began only with facts that could be derived from observation. He developed a system of measurement which relied on scrupulously accurate instrumentation. He painstakingly repeated his measurements so as to include every fact of possible relevance, every aspect of the human body. He performed a detailed quantitative analysis of the data his measurements yielded. He displayed his data in tables showing the relative percentages of physical anomalies in normals and deviants, and then summarized the results of it in prose, outlining its implications clearly for his reader. His conclusions, he believed, were unimpeachable, because each step of the process from which he extrapolated them could be checked and verified. As he admonishes the possible skeptic in "Criminal Anthropology: Its Origin and Application," "The only way to explain the opposition to [my theory] is the reluctance of men to draw a general conclusion from individual observations" (p. 38). Observation, dispassionate "investigation of facts," and logical inference, he argued, were sweeping aside the old system of "idio-emotional judgment . . . characteristic of the primitive periods of science and of periods of scientific degeneracy and decadence" ("Criminal Anthropology," p. 34).

The lay reader was likely to be confused by Lombroso's articles, unable to penetrate the quantitative analyses or to visualize such criminal anomalies as "surcillary arch and frontal sinus enormous; median occipital fossa; suture of the atlas . . . [and] double articular face of the occipital condyle" ("Criminal Anthropology," p. 36). Among the anthropometric instruments Lombroso deployed were the intimidating-sounding spirometer, dynamometer, campimeter, craniometer, Hipp's chronoscope, the *Schlitteninductorium* ("Criminal Anthropology," pp. 50, 53), and finally, the "beautiful discovery" of one Mr. Anfosso, the tachyanthropometer, which Lombroso terms "an anthropometric guillotine; so quickly and with the precision of a machine, does it give the most important measurements of the body" ("Illustrative Studies in Criminal Anthropology," p. 191). And yet Lombroso's instruments, Latinate anatomical terminology, and densely inaccessible figures and percentages give his work the pleasing air of scientific accuracy and credibility. Here one sees "Science" at work, homing in on the abhuman body and chopping it down to a manageable size by means of the anthropometric guillotine.

And Lombroso's overall argument is easy enough, and certainly compelling enough, for the layperson to grasp. Criminal anthropology, like the Lavaterian school of physiognomy which posited that a person's face was a true indication of character,[18] taught the common-sense wisdom of judging human nature by external appearance. Lombroso hoped that his readership would not only comprehend his discipline but also become adept in the practice of criminal anthropology. He emphasizes that the specialized tools of his trade are all "very simple instruments," whose manipulation requires little training. In "Criminal Anthropology Applied to Pedagogy," he instructs school teachers in their use, and even includes instructions for making the home version of Weber's aesthesiometer (p. 53). The tachyanthropometer, however intimidating its name, is designed to make "the practice of anthropometry very easy, even to people who are entire strangers to the science"; it "permits on a grand scale observations which hitherto were only obtainable by the learned" ("Illustrative Studies in Criminal Anthropology," p. 191). The spread of abhumanness, in other words, could be checked by the spread of science as it drew the lay population into its purview. Normative subjects (what few were left), equipped with the tachyanthropometer, could measure their own fully human status against the abhumanness of deviants.

But the most reliable gauges of atavism, startlingly enough, were bodily symptoms, much like the interwoven symptoms of metaphysical estrangement, uncanniness, abjection, and nausea I have described in chapter 2. Traditional folk wisdom documents, among normal subjects, a "universal though involuntary consciousness of the existence of a physiognomy peculiar to criminals" ("Criminal Anthropology," p. 38). The criminal arouses a "shock of horror" in the normal onlooker (Ellis, *The Criminal*, p. 85). The "honest man feels instinctive repugnance at the sight of a miscreant" (Lombroso-Ferrero, p. 51). "[Y]our intuition leads you unconsciously to shrink from a person who has the face of a thief" ("Criminal Anthropology Applied to Pedagogy," p. 57). This intuition is especially strong among women, children, and "the common people" ("Criminal Anthropology," p. 38). Lombroso cites as examples a young lady who labeled two men as malefactors long before the police were aware of their crimes, and a group of schoolgirls who were able to separate "scoundrels" from "honest men" in a set of photographs ("Criminal Anthropology," p. 38).

The criminal is abject; his physiognomy elicits nausea, aversion, revulsion, repugnance at some deep level below consciousness. This dynamic can be explained by heredity: one's sense of revulsion in the presence of the atavist is a survival of the fear one's remote ancestors would have felt confronting man-eating predators or cannibalistic savages, whom the atavist recapitulates.[19] (This would explain the stronger intuition of women, children, and common people, who are less highly evolved and thus more attuned to primitive ancestral fears.)

[I]n the strata of our brain there must exist elements of the sensations experienced by our progenitors, sensations which are reawakened as soon as the causes are re-presented which first awakened them.

And as in ancient times the wicked were the dominating oppressors and the good were the oppressed, though these latter have been emancipated in the course of time, there remain internal instincts which arouse aversion to those who present that totality of exterior signs which anthropological science has at last explained. ("Criminal Anthropology Applied to Pedagogy," p. 58)

Like Gothic nausea, criminal anthropological nausea is multi-valenced. At the most visible level it appears as a symptom of estrangement, provoked by confrontation with an anomalous phenomenon, and denial, whereby abhumanness is the property of others but never oneself. "Anthropological science," having "at last explained" the symptom, serves to naturalize it: anomalies are indeed abominations, and the nauseated body, through its disgust, proves its own integrity.

And yet in manifesting the symptom this body undoes itself. To be wracked with the convulsions of instinct is to be animalized, thrown back into the remote species-memory still inscribed in the body. Here even the normative body is revealed as a palimpsest, bearing within it many "savage" and "animal" histories which are always threatening to reemerge as narratives of abhuman becomings.

5.2 "GENERALIZED ANIMALISM": WELLS' *THE ISLAND OF DR. MOREAU*

The gray creature in the corner leant forward. "Not to run on all Fours; that is the Law. Are we not Men?" He put out a strangely distorted talon, and gripped my fingers. The thing was almost like the hoof of a deer produced into claws . . . His face came forward . . . into the light of the opening of the hut, and I saw with a quivering disgust that it was like the face of neither man nor beast, but a mere shock of gray hair, with three shadowy overarchings to mark the eyes and mouth. (*The Island of Dr. Moreau*, p. 60)

The Island of Dr. Moreau sets out, to a remorseless and almost overwhelming degree, the tenuousness of human identity, and the provisional and mutable nature of species identity in general. The greater part of the novel takes place on an unnamed island[20] inhabited by monstrosities. These are "beast people," the abortive results of vivisectionist experiments by which Dr. Moreau attempts to turn animals into humans. The beast people are liminal entities, like the "gray creature" in the quote above, "neither man nor beast" but something in between which, in resembling both, resembles nothing at all.

One may chart a certain physical likeness between the not-quite-evolved beast people and the atavistic "criminal types" elaborated by Lombroso.[21] Their deformities include some of the stigmata Lombroso identified as prevalent among atavists: "prognathous" face, "malformed" ears and noses, sloping forehead, shifty eyes and "furtive manner," twisted and disproportionate limbs and torso, hunched posture, clumsy, misshapen hands and fingers, and lack of "tactile sensibility" (*Moreau*, pp. 25, 83–4). What interests me more, however, is a broader similarity between Lombroso's and Wells' works: each theorizes a human body both chaotic and entropic, both hybridized and prone to reversion.

Moreau constructs his abhumans[22] from an indiscriminate range of animal materials – the island population includes a Leopard Man, Dog Man, Ape Man, Puma Woman, Sloth Man, Monkey Man, Wolf Woman, and Swine Men and Women. The human body, in other words, reveals its morphic compatibility with, and thus lack of distinction from, the whole world of animal life, including those species occupying different lines of descent. Humanness in general is fractured across many boundaries separating the human from the not-human, and individual beast-people bodies may violate multiple species categories as well. M'Ling, whom Prendick finds so disgusting, is "a complex trophy of Moreau's horrible skill," a human constructed of bear, dog, and ox (p. 85). "Moreau had blended this animal with that" in his experiments, "so that a kind of generalized animalism appeared through the specific dispositions" (p. 129). Like Hodgson's octopus-seal-men, these multiple hybrids – a Hyena-Swine Man, Vixen-Bear Woman, Bear-Bull and Mare-Rhinoceros Person – are chaotic bodies. They are "complex" bodies, as Prendick notes, but complexity here denotes indifferentiation and abomination rather than integrity and perfection.

Moreau's "horrible skill" is insufficient: his creatures approach humanness but inevitably revert, returning to the more compelling animal histories inscribed within their bodies. But "true" humans, as well, are prone to reversion; human identity in *Moreau* is an insubstantial thing, continually in danger of dissolution. Like other entropic narratives, *Moreau* can imagine only one narrative line, which moves inexorably "backwards" into loss of specificity. But the prospect one finds there is not barren and silent. It is teeming with abominations, whose changeful and chaotic forms include the "dwindling shreds" of human identity (p. 129).

Hysterical nausea

Prendick is marooned on the island after a hapless series of accidents, and passes through a prolonged period of uneasy speculation into a longer one of horrified certainty. He knows that Moreau's and Montgomery's odd servants arouse in him, inexplicably, a sense of uncanniness and nausea; he learns that Moreau is a vivisectionist who was forced to leave England after his "shocking" experiments were exposed (p. 32); and he discovers a grotesque community of islanders in the forest and is hunted by one of them, the "Thing" he cannot classify as either man or animal.

In the initial pages, Prendick is haunted by vague impressions. The island is full of anomalies, he senses, but he cannot fathom their nature. At times he cannot see clearly enough to know what is wrong, as when he is hunted after dark by the "Thing," or catches a half-glimpse of some "very grotesque creatures scuttl[ing] into the bushes upon the slope" (p. 26). Other times he sees very clearly, but has no language to describe the objects of his gaze. All he can specify are his own symptomatic responses to the strangeness of the islanders: "I saw only their faces," he writes of Moreau's boatmen, "yet there was something in their faces – I know not what – that gave me a spasm of disgust. I looked steadily at them, and the impression did not pass, though I failed to see what had occasioned it" (p. 25). "I could hardly repress a shuddering recoil as [M'Ling] came, bending amiably, and placed the tray before me on the table" (p. 31).

Prendick's disgust is initially naturalized within the text, identified as an "appropriate" response to M'Ling's anomalousness. The captain of the *Ipecacuanha*[23] (the ship which rescues Prendick and then leaves him with Moreau) says that "My men can't stand him. I can't stand him. None of us can't stand him" (p. 14). These loutish sailors are hardly reliable judges of character, but animals are said to be such, and the dogs on board ship, to whom M'Ling shows no unkindness, savage and worry him at every turn. The animal world itself rises up and identifies M'Ling, the beast man, as an abomination. That Prendick and the crew are also instinctively repelled places them in a continuity with these animals, but nonetheless dogs and men alike are reconstituted through their own revulsion as not-abominable, integral members of a proper type.

M'Ling is, as well, identified as a black man (a "black-faced creature," "the black"; pp. 11, 12), as are other of the islanders (p. 26); Moreau's nauseating boatmen are "brown men" wearing turbans and peculiar wrappings, vaguely resembling East Indians. The text first invites us to characterize Prendick's disgust as the natural response of a white man to odd "natives," who are not quite right to begin with; thus one can account for their *unheimlich* quality, the familiarity that is yet a strangeness. Prendick, in puzzling over the question of the racial identity of the islanders, is distracted from discovering that their uncanniness is a product of the hybridization of the human form. One might say that he hysterically refuses to consider this possibility. When the truth finally overwhelms him, it is notably occasioned by three Swine People, whose "skins were of a dull pinkish drab color, *such as I had seen in no savages before*" (p. 39; my emphasis). Their skin color, that is, approximates his own.

Suddenly, as I watched their grotesque and unaccountable gestures, I perceived clearly for the first time what it was that had offended me, what had given me the two inconsistent and conflicting impressions of utter strangeness and yet of the strangest familiarity. The three creatures engaged in this mysterious rite were human in shape, and yet human beings with the strangest air about them of some familiar animal. Each of these creatures, despite its human form, its rag of clothing, and the rough humanity of its bodily form, had woven into it, into its movements, into the expression of its countenance, into its whole presence, some now irresistible suggestion of a hog, a swinish taint, the unmistakable mark of the beast. (p. 40)

The mark of the beast

At this moment it becomes clear that Prendick's symptoms of nausea and uncanniness, as I argued earlier, draw him into a relation of likeness with the beast people. The beast people are uncanny because they remind Prendick not only of "some familiar animal," but also of himself. Beast people are "grotesque caricatures of humanity" (p. 60), but so, too, are humans; all human beings within the novel are capable of "animalistic" behaviors under extraordinary, and even rather ordinary circumstances. Prendick writes glumly that "A strange persuasion came upon me that, save for the grossness of the line, the grotesqueness of the forms, I had here before me the whole balance of human life in miniature" (p. 97): the novel continually, and with varying degrees of subtlety, makes the point that the beast-community is a mirror of the human community at large.

These grotesque islanders are, as Moreau explains to his terrified guest, animals "carven and wrought into new shapes" by the vivisector's knife (p. 72). Human identity in *The Island of Dr. Moreau* is so unremarkable a thing that it can be duplicated by a few weeks of close labor, wherein Moreau accomplishes what Nature, working through natural selection, accomplished in millenia. By means of tissue grafts, intricate surgery, and blood transfusions he transforms the "lower" species into a higher one capable of speech, reason, erect posture, and the manipulation of tools. "The great difference between man and monkey is in the larynx," Moreau tells Prendick (p. 73); and he considers the "moral" difference between human and animal to be equally negligible. Moreau, like Wells in his article "Human Evolution, an Artificial Process," insists that the human race has progressed very little in terms of moral evolution. "Very much indeed of what we call moral education is . . . an artificial modification and perversion of instinct; pugnacity is trained into courageous self-sacrifice, and suppressed sexuality into religious emotion" (p. 73). Just as human beings are trained to repress their animal instincts through a sort of social brainwashing, so does Moreau train his beast-patients to repress their natural savagery, hypnotizing them and implanting "Fixed Ideas" about acceptable and unacceptable human behaviors in their brains (pp. 81–2). When Prendick visits the beast-community in the heart of the forest, he finds that the inhabitants have codified these "fixed ideas" into oral law. The beast people complete Moreau's training by repeating his hypnotic suggestions in a ceremonial chant called the Saying of the Law; and Prendick, as a "newcomer" to the community, is forced to participate in the ritual.

> Not to go on all-Fours; *that* is the law. Are we not Men?
> Not to suck up drink; *that* is the law. Are we not Men?
> Not to eat Flesh or Fish; *that* is the law. Are we not Men?
> Not to claw Bark of Trees, *that* is the law. Are we not Men?
> Not to chase other Men; *that* is the law. Are we not Men?
>
> (p. 59)

This body of law, a series of injunctions against the natural instincts of the animal, has also become the foundation of a crude religion with Moreau as its God. The beast people, with their "limited mental scope" (p. 81), imagine that Moreau is omniscient and omnipotent, and has created all their known world as well as themselves. "*His* is the deep salt sea . . . *His* are the stars in the sky" (p. 60). They obey Moreau's injunctions because they have been conditioned to do so, because they have developed a pitiful pride in their awkward humanity, and most of all because they fear the wrath of their deity. Any "sinner" who breaks the Law is sent "back to the House of Pain" – back to the hell of the laboratory – for punishment by Moreau. In its ritualism, the beast people's religion parodies Catholicism: the Saying of the Law is described as an "insane ceremony," an "idiotic formula," a "mad litany" (p. 59). And in its emphasis on prohibitions and punishment, and its worship of an angry, vengeful deity, their religion parodies Calvinism.

Though Wells, the contemptuous atheist untroubled by doubt, is certainly not above a gratuitous satire of Christianity, his point here is that religion is only an artificial device by which society attempts to keep savage human nature in check, and that civilization is full of such artifices. Prendick suspects that Moreau was driven to "infect [the beast people's] dwarfed brains with a kind of deification of himself" partially out of megalomania (p. 60); but Moreau's more urgent motive is fear – fear of the fierce instincts that might lead the tamed beasts to turn on their master. Moreau's strictest injunction is against the stalking and eating of other "men." The Sayer of the Law carefully emphasizes this prohibition (albeit with a certain wistful nostalgia), warning Prendick that "Some want to follow things that move, to watch and slink and wait and spring, to kill and bite, bite deep and rich, sucking the blood. It is bad" (p. 61). Moreau loses control of his subjects, and the beast-community begins rapidly to deteriorate, when the beast people once again begin to hunt – killing and devouring the rabbits that Montgomery, incidentally, introduced to the island to satisfy his own craving for fresh meat (p. 28). The taste of blood unleashes all the "deep-seated, ever rebellious cravings of their animal natures" (p. 82), and signals not only general anarchy against the Law and the rule of Moreau, but also the commencement of a rapid process of general devolution.

The beast people, however, are not the only ones to devolve. All of *Moreau*'s human characters, however recognizable their physical humanity, show traces of a savagery no less natural than that of the beast people, and all of them are "law-breakers" of one sort or another. The veneer of civilization, as Wells argued in "Human Evolution, an Artificial Process," is spread most thinly over the "artificial man," who is little more than a dressed-up "Palaeolithic savage" ("Human Evolution," p. 217); centuries of social evolution have done little to alter the basic animal nature of the human species, in whom moral injunctions have taken as superficial a hold as they have in the beast people.

The Island of Dr. Moreau begins immediately with the threat of cannibalism, long before the beast people have been introduced. Prendick and two others are trapped aboard the lifeboat of the shipwrecked *Lady Vain* with little food or water, and after eight days of agony draw lots to see who of the three will be eaten by the others. Wells backs off from the actual depiction of cannibalism[24] – the loser of the draw struggles savagely with his shipmate, and both are flung overboard and drowned – but Prendick's rescue only introduces the reader to a further series of "beastly" men. On board the *Ipecacuanha* all is chaos and brutal cruelty, as the loutish crewmen rough up M'Ling and toss him to the dogs, and the captain throws Prendick off the ship in a fit of drunken rage, roaring, "Law be damned! I'm king here" (p. 22). The two men on the island are not much better. Moreau's assistant Montgomery is a former medical student who had to flee London after indulging in some "shabby vice" (p. 109). Eleven years ago he "lost [his] head for ten minutes on a foggy night" and committed some unnamed "blunder," some violation of the law (pp. 18, 109). The years on the island have further brutalized Montgomery, reducing him into alcoholism and into what Prendick suspects is a "sneaking kindness for some of these metamorphosed brutes, a vicious sympathy with some of their ways" (p. 84).

The novel, partly by refusing to specify the nature of the "shabby vice," hints vaguely at Montgomery's homosexuality and thus degeneracy. Prendick's narrative breaks off in the middle of one of the captain's rants about Montgomery, too discreet to repeat his epithets: "Well, never mind what he called Montgomery" (p. 14). Prendick himself notes primly later on that "I was not curious to learn what might have driven a young medical student out of London. I have an imagination" (p. 18). Montgomery is slightly effeminate, "a youngish man with flaxen hair, a bristly straw-colored moustache, and a dropping nether lip" who speaks "with a slobbering articulation, with the ghost of a lisp" (pp. 6–7). As Regenia Gagnier has noted, *Moreau* was to some extent inspired by Oscar Wilde's trials for homosexuality. Wells wrote in his preface to the book:

There was a scandalous trial about that time, the graceless and pitiless downfall of a man of genius, and this story was a response of an imaginative mind to the reminder that humanity is but animal rough-hewn to a reasonable shape and in perpetual internal conflict between instinct and injunction. This story embodies this ideal, but apart from this embodiment it has no allegorical quality. It is written just to give the utmost possible vividness to that conception of men as hewn and confused and tormented beasts. (cited in Gagnier, *Idylls of the Marketplace*, p. 225)[25]

This quote shows at least that Wells considered homosexual behaviors within the realm of the "beastly." Although Wells denied any "allegorical" significance to his tale, one might posit that the text embodies Wilde's "genius" in the asexual Dr. Moreau, and makes obscure reference to Wilde's homosexuality through the oblique characterization of Montgomery.

Moreau is a "magnificent" specimen of a human being (p. 80), with a high forehead, tranquil features, and piercing, intelligent eyes. He is, however, a cruel, remorseless, even vicious man who feels no emotion save an all-engrossing passion for his research, a "strange colorless delight," he calls it, in "intellectual desires" (p. 75). These "desires" can only be fulfilled by the most prolonged and acute tortures of the victims of the operating table, but Moreau is deaf to their agonized screams. As he tells Prendick, "The study of Nature makes a man at last as remorseless as Nature" (p. 75). While the brilliant Dr. Moreau may represent the apex of human intellectual evolution, he is nonetheless as "inhuman" as, perhaps more inhuman than, any of his grotesque creations – bereft of the civilizing human emotions of compassion and pity, as indifferent to ethical questions and legalities as M'Ling confronted with a freshly-killed rabbit, the three starving men in the lifeboat, or the drunken captain of the *Ipecacuanha*. Prendick even suspects that Moreau's obsession has led him into a secret lust for torture and bloodshed: as he cracks his whip and sentences the Leopard Man to return "back to the House of Pain," Prendick notices the "touch of exultation in his voice" (p. 93).

The namesake of Wells' British doctor is the French neurologist Jacques-Joseph Moreau, whose *Morbid Psychology* (1859) claimed that overexcitation of the part of the brain controlling intellect could cause the malfunction of the rest of the brain, and particularly the atrophy of moral sensibility.[26] J.-J. Moreau places the genius on the same "family tree" as the criminal, the lunatic, and a variety of other pathologues and nervous sufferers: the genius' overexpenditure of cerebral energy results in immorality and criminal behavior as well as monomaniacal insanity.[27] "Just as giants pay a heavy ransom for their stature in sterility and relative muscular and mental weakness," Lombroso wrote in *The Man of Genius*, a work greatly indebted to *Morbid Psychology*, "so the giants of thought expiate their intellectual force in degeneration and psychosis" (p. vi). The inevitable corollary of the "extraordinary imagination" (*Moreau*, p. 32) of the vivisectionist Moreau is the stunted morality he shares with beast people and with Lombroso's "born criminal." He has "fallen under the overmastering spell of research" to the point of monomania (p. 33), and pursues his bloody science with no particular end but the fulfillment of his own curiosity.

"It was the wantonness that stirred me," Prendick writes. "I could have forgiven him a little even had his motive been hate. But he was irresponsible, so utterly careless. His curiosity, his mad, aimless investigations, drove him on" (p. 98). Moreau the "criminal genius" may also be read as a personification of Nature itself, a Nature whose idle experiments on living flesh are as wanton, as aimless, as random, and finally as cruel, as Moreau's. "Each time I dip a living creature into the bath of burning pain," Moreau tells Prendick, "I say, this time I will burn out the animal, this time I will make a rational creature of my own" (pp. 78–9); but what he achieves is only a crude mockery of humanity. "I can see through it all, see into their very souls, and see there nothing but the souls of beasts, beasts that perish – anger, and the lusts to live and gratify themselves . . . There is a kind of upward striving in them, part vanity, part waste sexual emotion, part waste curiosity. It only mocks me" (p. 79). Nature, too, subjects its creatures to pain and suffering through the long process of evolution, refashioning new types of beings, testing their fitness, discarding the failures, only to generate a human species that is itself nothing more than a crude mockery of the idea of humanity, deformed by the "mark of the beast from which [it] came" (p. 75) and thwarted in its "upward striving" by the soul of the beast.

And the work both of Moreau and of Nature is subject to undoing. Prendick's first panicked assumption when he uncovers the secret of the laboratory is that Moreau, like Circe on her island, is laboring to transform humans into animals, and that he is marked out as the next victim of this "hideous degradation" (p. 51): the idea of human devolution is the ultimate horror within the text. The beast people, mutilated into a semblance of humanity, cannot maintain even this pitiful state, but slowly devolve back into animality. "[S]omehow the things drift back again, the stubborn beast flesh grows, day by day, back again," Moreau tells Prendick, musing on his failures (p. 77). After Moreau's death and the end of the Law the beast people revert still more quickly to savagery, degenerating into cannibalism, promiscuity, and other "primitive" human behaviors, and gradually losing speech, manual dexterity, and the ability to walk erect.

That "fully human" bodies are entropic ones as well is made clearest when even Prendick begins to devolve. Prendick is the least "beastly" of the characters in *The Island of Dr. Moreau*. During the struggle on the lifeboat, he intervenes to help the weaker of the two men; he is a teetotaler, in contrast to Montgomery; and his conscience is continually outraged by Moreau's cruel experiments. Early on, however, the text drops a number of hints linking Prendick to the beast people. On board the *Ipecacuanha*, he becomes "excited" by the sight and smell of freshly cooked meat (p. 8); later the novel describes two meat-eating Swine Men, "blood-stained... about the mouth, and intensely excited" (p. 103). The Law states that beast people are "not to go on all-Fours," and Prendick, falling out of his hammock in his bedroom on the island, is "deposited... upon all-fours on the floor" (p. 49). The beast people identify Prendick as one of their own, not a "Master" but one "made," and snicker at him behind his back (p. 88).

Prendick is, furthermore, not a "manly" character. He might be one of Nordau's hysterics, the typically enervated, nervous, and ineffectual modern gentleman. "I waited passively upon fate," he writes when the captain of the *Ipecacuanha* refuses to have him on board and Moreau refuses to take him onto the island, and apologizes for his passivity by explaining that "Hunger and a lack of blood-corpuscles take all the manhood from a man" (p. 22). Throughout the novel he gives way to fits of petulance, hysteria, and morbid indecisiveness. After Moreau's and Montgomery's deaths, Prendick knows that his own life may depend on his ability to instate himself as the new ruler of the beast people, but he breaks down after one feeble attempt at intimidation. "I was still inclined to be nervous and to break down under any great stress... And my heart failed me... My imagination was running away with me into a morass of unsubstantial fears . . . [and I] allowed [my courage] to ebb away in solitary thought" (pp. 119–21). Finally he slinks off to the community and "almost apologetically" asks for food, shelter, and acceptance. "In this way I become one among the Beast People in the Island of Dr. Moreau" (p. 123).

And in this way Prendick gives in to the forces of entropy that overtake the beast people, as the "stubborn beast flesh" grows back upon him as well. As his companions begin to revert to their original behavior and nature, so too does the narrator undergo "strange changes" of a devolutionary kind (p. 129). He picks up animal habits, building himself a "den" and sleeping in it by day to protect himself from nocturnal prowlers. He even takes to "clawing bark," disregarding the fourth injunction of the law.[28] And slowly he comes physically to resemble the beast people: "My clothes hung about me as yellow rags, through whose rents glowed the tanned skin. My hair grew long, and became matted together. I am told that even now my eyes have a strange brightness, a swift alertness of movement" (p. 129).

Though this episode in Prendick's adventures, what he admits is "the longer part of [his] sojourn on this Island of Dr. Moreau" (p. 126), lasts ten months, his narrative gives it the most cursory attention. He excuses this elision by telling his reader that nothing interesting or relevant occurred during the long months he "spent as an intimate of these half-humanized brutes. There is much that sticks in my memory that I could write, things that I would cheerfully give my right hand to forget. But they do not help in the telling of the story" (p. 126). Faced with the ultimate abjection – his own devolution into animality – the narrator finally lapses into silence.

Exemplary abhuman bodies

When Prendick returns home to his native island, England, it is only to be haunted by the nightmare of the inevitable devolution of all of humanity.

I could not persuade myself that the men and women I met were not also another, still passably human, Beast People, animals half-wrought into the outward image of human souls; and that they would presently begin to revert, to show first this bestial mark and then that . . . I look about me at my fellow men. And I go in fear. I see faces keen and bright, others dull or dangerous, others unsteady, insincere; none have that calm authority of a reasonable soul. I feel as though the animal was surging up through them; that presently the degradation of the Islanders will be played over again on a larger scale. (p. 136)

This is one of the exemplary abhuman bodies proposed by *Moreau*: the human body whose humanness is tenuous, incomplete, at all moments liable to regression.

However, this entropic body is a clamorous and energetic one. Back on Moreau's island the night is made "hideous" with "calls and howlings" (p. 131). The beast people are "gripping the quivering flesh" of prey, "gnawing at it and snarling with delight" (p. 131). Moreau's creations devolve not from humans to simple beasts, but into admixed bodies, each recognizable form "tainted" with that of "other creatures" and bearing some faint trace of the human past. This is a second exemplary abhuman body: chaotic, abominable, imbued throughout with a "generalized animalism" (p. 129).

Prendick makes his escape off the island in a lifeboat that drifts on shore, possibly the lifeboat of the *Ipecacuanha*. In the boat he finds two dead men, who "had been dead so long that they fell to pieces when I tilted the boat on its side and dragged them out." Prendick flees in the boat in "repulsion" and "frantic horror" as three beast people, drawn by the smell, come out of the woods to worry at the remains (p. 133).

The reviewer P. Chambers Mitchell was particularly infuriated by this last, to him needless, detail. "Mr. Wells will not even get his hero out of the island decently" (p. 369). But the moment is hardly needless. It is one of many in the *fin-de-siècle* Gothic that accomplishes the utter ruination of the human subject, without apology, without nostalgia, without remorse. The human body in all its gross materiality is fully on display here: the decomposing bodies of the sailors, the hybridized bodies of the hungry beast people, the abjected body of Prendick, which responds to it all with a "spasm of disgust" (p. 133). No human body retains specificity; all have long since become Things.

PART III

Gothic sexualities

CHAPTER 6

Uncanny female interiors

It was the face of a woman, and yet it was not human.
Arthur Machen, "The Inmost Light"[1]

Arthur Machen's "The Inmost Light," much like *The Great God Pan*, details the shocking effects of an experiment in human neurology. A certain Dr. Black labors to reconcile physiological with occult science, his goal being to "bridge over the gulf between the world of consciousness and the world of matter" (p. 182). "[F]rom some human being," he explains, "there must be drawn that essence which men call the soul, and in its place . . . would enter in what the lips can hardly utter, what the mind cannot conceive without a horror more awful than the horror of death itself" (p. 182). Dr. Black here appears to affirm that a human "soul" exists independently from the human body, and thus that human identity cannot be fully explicated within a materialist framework.

Yet the story as a whole will not bear out this conclusion. It dwells obsessively on the horrific prospect of a human being conceived in utterly material terms. The doctor's work establishes that the "soul" is seated within the physiological reality of the brain; once extracted, moreover, it appears as a "splendid jewel" (p. 180) – exquisitely beautiful, but nonetheless most corporeal. The demonic force that then gains entry into the evacuated human body is not malevolent in any spiritual sense: it seems rather a representation of the grossly physical, animalistic potentialities of human beings, like the satyr-deity in *The Great God Pan*. Dr. Black's experimental subject becomes an abomination, the sight of which arouses violent symptoms – nausea, "cold sweat," shortness of breath – in the spectator (p. 160). The text dissolves into hysterical symptoms as it posits that spirit and body alike are circumscribed within the terrible reality of physicality.

The abhuman countenance which the protagonist Dyson glimpses behind a window, and which causes his "heart [to] shudder" and his "bones [to] grind together in an agony" (p. 160), is a female face. Around this face is "a mist of flowing yellow hair, as it was an aureole of glory round the visage of a satyr" (p. 161). Dr. Black, we will learn, had chosen for his experimental subject his own wife, an "uncommonly pretty" woman (p. 159). She is transformed into a monstrosity unrecognizable as either a human being or a "lower animal" (p. 162) – but which retains a definitive identity as female: "a woman, and yet . . . not human." Gothic materiality is a condition which might overtake any human subject, the text implies, but which is particularly compatible with the condition of femininity.

Compare M. P. Shiel's "Huguenin's Wife" (1895), wherein the gothicity of the body is aligned still more insistently with femininity. The story's title character is Andromeda, an Athenian of very pure and ancient descent, who through sorcery transforms herself into this species abomination:

I saw proceeding from the interior a creature whose obscenity and vileness language has no vocabulary to describe. For if I say that it was a cat – of great size – its eyes glaring like a conflagration – its fat frame wrapped in a mass of feathers, grey, vermilion-tipped – with a similitude of miniature wings on it – with a width of tail vast, down-turned, like the tails of birds-of-paradise – how by such words can I express half of all the retching of my nausea, the shame, the hate . . . (p. 208)

This "feathery horror," this "thing" (p. 209), flies from the flaming house onto the landing to bury its fangs and talons in Huguenin's heart; man and wife spiral to the ground in a fiery catherine wheel and die.

This was once a woman who was "more lovely than ever mortal was before," and yet "more loathsome" (p. 196). Huguenin was captivated by her beauty, but repelled by her aggressive and inordinate sexual "fervour": "the extravagance of her passion for him he grew to regard as gruesome" (pp. 200, 201). Andromeda's "unnatural" sexual hunger for her husband is indistinguishable from the savage violence with which she attacks him; for a man to submit to a woman's embrace is to risk the bloodiest and most excruciating of torments.[2] Female sexuality in particular and the female body in general are in this story sites of abjection and danger.

Shiel drives home this point by deploying a series of conventional tropes of female monstrosity. Andromeda is a compelling and deadly "Lamia" (p. 196). She is Medusa, the sight of whose hideous head paralyzes the male spectator: the narrator standing before a self-portrait of Andromeda describes how a "kind of surprise held me fixed as the image slowly took possession of my vision. The Gorgon's head! whose hair was snakes; and as I thought of this I thought, too, of how from the guttering gore of the Gorgon's head monsters rose . . ." (p. 196). And finally, in the climactic moment described above, she is the murderous Sphinx, winged and feline as well as human, a composite entity which nonetheless can be particularized as female.[3]

Dyson's impression of Mrs. Black – a face glimpsed at the window for just one second and then engraven on the memory – comprises a kind of iconographic representation of abhumanness. Though Mrs. Black, we will learn, eventually underwent still more hideous changes, Dyson and the reader retain this snapshot image of a Thing frozen and entrapped between categories. With Andromeda, by contrast, we have a dynamic representation of abhumanness, of a Thing marked by such instability and wild kinetic energy that it is even now, it is perhaps always, in the process of metamorphosis. In the one case we have a body admixed, in the other, a body both admixed and violently changeful.

The Thing-ness of the female body

The Worm's hole was still evident, a round fissure seemingly leading down into the very bowels of the earth . . . At short irregular intervals the hell-broth in the hole seemed as if boiling up. It rose and fell again and turned over, showing in fresh form much of the nauseous detail which had been visible earlier. The worst parts were the great masses of the flesh of the monstrous Worm, in all its red and sickening aspect . . . The whole surface of the fragments, once alive, was covered with insects, worms, and vermin of all kinds. The sight was horrible enough, but, with the awful smell added, was simply unbearable. The Worm's hole appeared to breathe forth death in its most repulsive forms. (Bram Stoker, *The Lair of the White Worm*, pp. 189–90)

And in each case the abomination is a specifically *female* one. One cultural tradition, older than the Victorians but nonetheless prominent within the late nineteenth century, identifies women as entities defined by and entrapped within their bodies, in contrast to the man, who is governed by rationality and capable of transcending the fact of his embodiment.[4] In nineteenth-century social medicine in particular, women were theorized as incomplete human subjects. They are but partially evolved from the state of animalism, as figures like Lombroso had argued, and thus are essentially admixed creatures. They possess the intellectual qualities that distinguish Man from brute only in the most limited and imperfect sense. Woman's consciousness does not transcend physicality; her consciousness rather is enmeshed in and determined by the fact of her overwhelming physicality.[5] As Elaine Showalter argues in her discussion of Victorian medicine in *The Female Malady: Women, Madness, and English Culture, 1830–1980*, the "diseases of periodicity" to which the female body was prone meant that

> women were more vulnerable to insanity than men . . . [T]he instability of their reproductive systems interfered with their sexual, emotional, and rational control. In contrast to the rather vague and uncertain concepts of insanity in general which Victorian psychiatry produced, theories of female insanity were specifically and confidently linked to the biological crises of the female life-cycle – puberty, pregnancy, childbirth, and menopause – during which the mind would be weakened and the symptoms of insanity might emerge. This connection between the female reproductive and nervous systems led to the condition nineteenth-century psysicians called "reflex insanity in women." The "special law" that made women "the victims of periodicity" led to a distinct set of mental illnesses that had "neither homologue nor analogue in man." Doctors argued that the menstrual discharge in itself predisposed women to insanity. (pp. 55–6)[6]

The female body, in other words, was intrinsically pathological, and the subject inhabiting that body was erratic and unstable, its fluctuability and incompleteness a function of the not-quite-human body. As well – this is perhaps the more important point in reference to the *fin-de-siècle* Gothic – the disorders of the female body were inextricably linked to the female reproductive system, so that female sexuality emerged as both causal and symptomatic of female abhumanness. Along similar lines, Michel Foucault describes the "hystericization of women's bodies" that occurred within late nineteenth-century sociomedical discourses as "a process whereby the feminine body was analyzed – qualified and disqualified – as being thoroughly saturated with sexuality; whereby it was integrated into the sphere of medical practices, by reason of a pathology intrinsic to it . . ." (*The History of Sexuality*, vol. I, p. 104). The evacuation of female subjectivity (the woman's lack of rationality, volition, and self-control; her liability to pathological mental states) renders the woman a Thing: a body that is at best imperfectly animated by a "human mind" and a "human spirit." Moreover, the Thing-ness of the all-too-embodied woman is redoubled by both her fluctuability and her thorough sexualization; this changeful female body, "saturated with sexuality," to recur to Foucault's phrase, is inescapably corporeal, bounded within the grossness of the material world.

Angels and devil-women

I tell you, doctor, there is something uncanny about the whole business. The woman is an unnatural woman. She is a she-devil. (Dick Donovan, "The Woman with the 'Oily Eyes'")[7]

This nineteenth-century perception of women as "the sex" – fully constrained within a sexualized identity, and so both corporeal and animalistic – stands in sharp contradistinction to Victorian celebrations of woman as a domestic angel, an essentially disembodied creature. Thus, as any number of cultural critics have noted, Victorian representations of women tend to polar extremes: women are saintly or demonic, spiritual or bodily, asexual or ravenously sexed, guardians of domestic happiness or unnatural monsters. These two incompatible perceptions of femininity (women as angels, women as beasts) are often found side by side within the same text, for instance in *The Lair of the White Worm* (1911), where Stoker juxtaposes the pellucid innocence of Mimi Watford with the lustful cruelty of Arabella the snake-woman.

A wide range of Victorianist scholarship examines the disparity between the seeming rigidity of gender roles and the instability of gender ideologies in the nineteenth century. That is, while the dominant discourses on gendered identity might rely on an understanding of the two sexes in fixed and oppositional relation to one another – masculine activity complementing feminine passivity and so forth – such understandings were in fact broadly contested within the culture, particularly towards the end of the century, when such ambiguously sexed and gendered subjects as the homosexual and the "New Woman" emerged increasingly into public controversy. The New Woman, or 1890s feminist, challenged gender norms in any number of ways, not the least of which was to advocate that women be given access to information about birth control and venereal disease, and, more alarmingly, to claim sexual agency for women, championing their rights to sexual freedom within and outside of marriage.[8]

Such a juxtaposition as that found in *The Lair of the White Worm*, between good and evil women, at one level works to stabilize the meanings of "proper" femininity by identifying the sexually active and aggressive woman as a literal monster, an abhuman, and her chaste and modest counterpart as "fully human" by contrast.[9] The female vampire in *Dracula* is a pathological version of womanhood, seducing men and eating children, "gloating" with "deliberate voluptuousness" and "lick[ing] her lips like an animal" (p. 54), whereas Mina Harker is "one of God's women, fashioned by His own hand to show us men and other women that there is a heaven where we can enter, and that its light can be here on earth" (p. 243).

And yet the novel cannot sustain the opposition between animal-women and "God's women." This is most notable in the case of Lucy, who metamorphoses from angel to beast in just two paragraphs:[10]

[S]he looked her best, with all the soft lines matching the angelic beauty of her eyes . . . For a little bit her breast heaved softly, and her breath came and went like a tired child's.

And then insensibly there came the strange change which I had noticed in the night. Her breathing grew stertorous, the mouth opened, and the pale gums, drawn back, made the teeth look longer and sharper than ever. In a sort of sleep-walking, vague, unconscious way she opened her eyes, which were now dull and hard at once, and said in a soft, voluptuous voice, such as I had never heard from her lips: –

"Arthur! Oh, my love, I am so glad you have come! Kiss me!" (p. 208)

Even Mina, most excellent of woman, is liable to such changes. Van Helsing laments that he "can see the characteristics of the vampire coming in her face . . . Her teeth are some sharper, and at times her eyes are more hard" (p. 415).

Thus the contradiction that fractures the ideology of femininity is made visible across the bodies of *Dracula*'s female characters, which fluctuate and contort as they are made to hold incompatible meanings. Or this contradiction may become startlingly visible all at once. Mrs. Black of "The Inmost Light" is a pure and loving wife, victimized by a science that brings to light the horrific potentialities of the female body. From the street Dyson sees her as both demon and angel, a "satyr" whose face is girded by a halo of gold.

Beast-femininity

This confusion as to the true nature of femininity is made visible as well in *The Island of Dr. Moreau*, during Prendick's brief but suggestive commentaries on the female beast people. The novel's beast-females, pitiful representatives of humanity as they are, appear early on in the text as parodic instances of proper femininity, champions of sexual morality and other civilized values. Prendick notes it as "a curious thing" that they had "an instinctive sense of their own repulsive clumsiness, and displayed, in consequence, a more than human regard for the decencies and decorum of external costume" (p. 86).

But when Prendick chronicles the accelerated process of devolution that overtakes the Beast People after the death of Moreau, he writes: "Some of them – the pioneers, I noticed with some surprise, were all females – began to disregard the injunctions of decency – deliberately for the most part. Others even attempted public outrages upon the institution of monogamy" (p. 128). Here female sexuality both instantiates and aggravates the reversion to animality, such that it can almost be said to stand in metaphoric relation to the animality of the human species. Though he expresses gentlemanly "surprise" at the fact, Prendick aligns female sexuality with the troubling fact of human embodiment and with the forces of disorder and changefulness. The issue disturbs him so much that he abruptly drops it mid-paragraph, saying, "I cannot pursue this disagreeable subject" (p. 128).

Prendick's inability or unwillingness to speak further indicates that a certain hysteria underlies his response to the female beast-human's sexuality. And in fact this is not the first instance of such hysteria. In an earlier passage Prendick remarks on the violent nausea which bodily proximity to a beast-female arouses in him: "in some narrow pathway, glancing with a transitory daring into the eyes of some lithe, white-swathed female figure, I would suddenly see (with a spasmodic revulsion) that they had slitlike pupils, or glancing down, note the curving nail with which she held her shapeless wrap about her" (pp. 85–6). The symptom Prendick experiences in the presence of beast-females and beast-males alike is identical; both inspire "spasmodic revulsion." And his revulsion is of course hysterical in either case, signalling his simultaneous recognition and repression of his own abhuman identity, his own affinity with these admixed and abominable species-bodies. But the two passages above mark Prendick's attempts – albeit fleeting and unsuccessful – to identify abhumanness especially, even exclusively, as the property of the female, whose "lithe" sensuality marks her animal nature. The male, who looks on her and desires her at his peril, then emerges by contrast as the more fully human.

The Island of Dr. Moreau, of course, utterly disallows such a construct as a "fully human" identity, so that one can recognize Prendick's panicked response to beast-femininity as symptomatic in a second sense. These passages map out a widespread cultural hysteria, not just Prendick's – a trajectory of recognition, refusal, and displacement that manifests itself across the *fin de siècle*, and is especially visible within the Gothic. When the male subject is confronted with the fact of his own liminality, his own abhumanness, his own bodily fluctuability, he will attempt to keep this fact at bay by insisting that only the female body is chaotic and abominable, never his own.

If *The Island of Dr. Moreau* diagnoses this cultural pathology, one is tempted to say that *The Lair of the White Worm* enacts it. The "white worm" of the title is a prehistoric survival, the last instance of a now-extinct species that flourished in millenia past, when England was a swamp-land. Lady Arabella was bitten by the "ghastly White Worm" (p. 62) in her youth, and has become its familiar, or perhaps its avatar. The adult Arabella is surpassingly beautiful but snaky: she has a "sinuous figure" (p. 29), sibilant voice, and undulating hands. She is also brutal and sadistic, with a "terrible craving for cruelty" (p. 61).

The Lair of the White Worm, then, marks the abhumanness of femininity in a number of ways. Arabella is an unstable subject, with a transformative, half-animal body. She is linked to the abject prehistory of England, for her estate is built over a morass, and her *Doppelgänger* is a primitive "monster" (p. 40) whose natural habitat is slime and swamp. She confuses gender distinctions: she acts with a forcefulness and aggression befitting a man and a savagery unbecoming a woman. Her monster-double confuses sexual distinctions: the worm inhabits an "enormously deep well-hole," suggesting an exaggerated and phantasmic version of the female genitalia, and yet this gigantic "worm" must also be read as a gigantic phallus, inappropriately bestowed upon (or lurking within) a female body.

And the worm-hole's smell is the disgusting smell of embodiedment and mortality. Sir Nathaniel describes it as the stench of "bilge or a rank swamp. It was distinctly nauseating; when I came out I felt as if I had just been going to be sick" (p. 110). The female subject is Thing-like through and through, but an especially repellent Thing-ness – the Thing-ness of slime and its disgusting smell – characterizes her gothic inner body.

6.1 "THE INNER CHAMBERS OF ALL NAMELESS SIN": RICHARD MARSH'S *THE BEETLE*

In Richard Marsh's 1897 novel *The Beetle*, London is invaded by a supernatural intruder who hails from the mysterious East.[11] Known variously as "The Woman of Songs," "the Beetle," or simply "the Oriental," she is a priestess from the cult of Isis who comes to procure white victims to torment, mutilate, and murder for her Egyptian rituals. While the text refuses to specify the precise nature of the Beetle's atrocities, it clearly points to some gothic version of rape, inflicted upon male and female bodies alike.

The novel shares with other *fin-de-siècle* Gothic fiction the narrative strategy I have identified as hysterical, deploying textual euphemism, elision, or indirection in representing and naming sensational, perverse sexualities, despite the text's nonetheless unmistakably sexual and perverse content. Its hysteria, however, is instantiated by much more than sexual trauma. The Beetle-Woman's unspeakability results as much from her racial difference and her species fluctuability as her metamorphic sexual identity (particularly as this identity violates norms of femininity). The text veers back and forth in attempting to account for the gothicity of the abhuman body, identifying first its raciality, then its femininity, then its variable sexuality, then its morphic fluidity, as the marker of abhumanness. As in *The Great God Pan*, both the gothic body and the hysteria it occasions are overdetermined: constructs of human identity break down on all sides, so that gothic sexuality cannot be examined in isolation within the text.[12]

Displacement of sexual energies occurs consistently within *The Beetle*, at the level of plot and character: while the novel throws into question the sexualities of all the non-supernatural characters in *The Beetle*, these characters are finally exonerated at the expense of the villainess whose monstrous female – and monstrous Oriental – body is the ultimate locus of all perversions. *The Beetle*'s conflation of abject female sexuality with Oriental barbarism enables the text to maintain a certain innocence through a series of slippages. The non-supernatural plot of *The Beetle*, disrupted by the arrival of the Oriental, is comprised of entangled, "comic" configurations of love triangles and misplaced affections. One problematic in particular underlies these configurations: the possibility of aggressive female desire, as both Marjorie Linden and Dora Grayling prove themselves willing to chase after the men they desire. Again at the level of the non-supernatural, a certain process of sublimation softens the edge of this aggression. Both Marjorie and Dora love intensely but not sexually, their desire manifested as admiration of their menfolk's life-work. Marjorie declares that "the first stirring of my pulses was caused by the report of a speech of [Paul Lessingham's] which I read in *The Times*. It was on the Eight Hours' Bill" (p. 580). Dora, the heiress, translates her love for Sydney Atherton into an offer to fund his scientific research.

Marjorie and Dora are socially forward but sexually chaste; however, their girlish aggressiveness serves faintly to mirror the Oriental's sexual ravenousness, and vice versa. The monstrosity of the Gothicized seductress, embodied, in her avatar of the Beetle, as a hungry and emasculating womb equipped with phallic powers of penetration, marks a Victorian horror of female sexual appetite; in other words, the Gothic plot of supernatural female sexuality functions as site of displacement for an active non-Gothic female sexuality the text simultaneously points to and denies. But in a crucial textual slippage, this appetite is revealed to be the ugly secret not so much of (white) women as of the barbaric Oriental. The Beetle's crimes – the sadistic but unspecified perversities to which she subjects her victims – are represented as sexually executed but racially motivated, as if her Egyptian hatred of a white skin only masked a frustrated longing to "possess" a white body herself, in any sense of the word.

The raced and sexed body

You'll find that your filthy Egyptian tricks won't answer in England. (Conan Doyle, "Lot No. 249," p. 102)

In *The Beetle*, conventional methods of criminal investigation prove futile against this foreign intruder whose supernatural, easily metamorphized body is not subject to the usual limitations of time and space. As a supernatural being she defies natural law and eludes scientific definition: she cannot be countered with rational means. Augmenting – or perhaps comprising – her supernatural potency are the dark and primitive natural forces she may call upon both as a woman and as an Oriental. Hers is an aggressive and fearsome femininity that explodes cultural roles, and an Eastern mentality that is utterly foreign: alien, inexplicable, inimical to that of her host nation.

Edward Said has famously described how the Orient, the source of one of the West's "deepest and most recurring images of the Other," has "helped define Europe (or the West) as its contrasting image, idea, personality, experience" (*Orientalism*, pp. 1–2). European values of self-restraint, progress, democracy, scientific precision, and rationality contrast with what is perceived as the sensuality, primitiveness, despotism, superstition, and slovenly mentality of the Orient. According to Said's model, the East, defined by the West in terms of all those qualities the West rejects for or denies in itself, serves as a kind of "surrogate or even underground self" for the West (p. 3). In *The Beetle*, the Oriental represents a barbaric Other (as opposed to the highly civilized Westerner), a sexually perverse Other (as opposed to the chaste and cerebral Westerner), and a magical, supernatural Other (as opposed to the scientific, technologically proficient Westerner). She indulges in primitive religious and social rituals; pursues strange and illicit sexual desires; and has access to an occult realm of magic so ancient that the West has forgotten it, or so unfamiliar that the West cannot fit it into its taxonomies of natural occurrences.

In *The Beetle*, the Orient itself, described secondhand by horrified or disgusted British tourists, is a site of backwardness and primitive chaos. Texts like Stoker's 1903 *The Jewel of Seven Stars* (another novel of gothicized Egyptian femininity) evince at least a certain admiration for ancient Egypt's extraordinary scientific proficiency, tempered of course by disapproval of the brutishness and quarrelsome childishness of modern Egypt's degenerate peoples. But *The Beetle* does not grant any sort of recognition even to Egypt's former grandeur. While Marsh indulges his fascination with Oriental occultism, he depicts a consistently savage Egypt whose ancient history is an inchoate and abject "prehistory." In their practice of magic, in their superstition, in their primitive and animalistic religious rituals, Orientals, both ancient and modern, are abhuman. The Beetle originates from an "idolatrous sect" in the very heart of Egypt

which was stated to still practise, and to always have practised, in unbroken historical continuity, the debased, unclean, mystic, and bloody rites, of a form of idolatry which had had its birth in a period of the world's story which was so remote, that to all intents and purposes it might be described as prehistoric (pp. 689–90)

Present-day Egypt, in other words, is a living reminder of the West's prehistory, of that animalistic or abhuman state from which the Westerner has managed to evolve.

On one level, these textual stereotypes that construct the Oriental as "Other" serve a unifying function for the culture that produces them, a culture which, in the service of a coherent and idealized self-definition, denies those qualities that threaten or undermine its own self-image and projects them onto extra-cultural groups (or onto marginal groups, like women, within the culture). On a level of more material and more insidious effects, a paranoiac text like *The Beetle* serves to reflect and feed into British suspicion of and contempt for Egyptians during a period of heightened British military activity in Egypt:[13] the perceived inhumanity of the Orient becomes a rationale for subjecting it to the humanizing, civilizing process of British colonization. While the novel's primary setting in London means that it cannot be classed strictly as "colonialist literature," it is precisely that setting which masks the British imperialist project informing and underlying the text. *The Beetle* inverts the issue of colonization by presenting the East/West conflict in terms of Oriental aggression – an Oriental incursion, with white slavery and genocide as its end, into the very heart of London;[14] and distorts the issue further by presenting Egypt as a site not of relatively stable English rule during Lord Cromer's occupation, but of Oriental misrule, under which innocent white tourists are kidnapped, tortured, and murdered with impunity. Reversing the territorial actualities, the text transposes the colonized subject into a savage aggressor whose duplicity and desire for mastery swell across the boundaries of the Orient into the homeland of civilized England.

As primitiveness inheres in the "debased, unclean, mystic, and bloody" site of the Orient, so too does it inhere in the debased, unclean, mystic, and bloody body of Woman. *The Beetle* presents the Orient as a feminized space, for a female body embodies the Orient. "The sex" was said to occupy the same space of uncontrolled nature (a space hostile to culture) as the Orient. The East, in fact, was often characterized within the Orientalist discourse as feminine, with its "penetrability" and "supine malleability" (Said, p. 206). Located in the so-called matrix of civilization, the Orient is a highly sexualized site, seeming to suggest "not only fecundity but sexual promise (and threat), untiring sensuality, unlimited desire, deep generative energies" (Said, p. 188). For the West, with its more rigid ethos of sexual behavior, "the Orient was a place where one could look for sexual experience unobtainable in Europe" (Said, p. 190), the sort of experience *The Beetle*'s Paul Lessingham is pursuing when he wanders into the backstreet Egyptian brothel presided over by the Woman of Songs. Not only is the Orient a space in which the Victorian male may pursue the luxury of the body, it is also a space he associates with the body itself, with the body's physicality and fertility, with bodily pleasure. The Orient is synonymous with sexuality in the same way that "Woman" is synonymous with sexuality: to each is attributed the sort of gross corporeality, both in terms of generative power and a sexualized identity, that masculinized Western culture disclaims in itself.

This raw physicality inspires simultaneous fascination, disgust, and terror in the novel's male characters. The Beetle-woman's overwhelming embodiedment is presented as a devouring and engulfing force, constituting a threat to subjective integrity as much as a promise of pleasure. In the novel, the Oriental female, or the feminized Orient, is far from being characterized by any womanly "penetrability" or "malleability." The Orient seduces, certainly, with the lovely body of the Woman of Songs, but she is no cipher or lazily passive object of desire. She is a powerful, aggressive – most "unfeminine" – creature, who seduces only to emasculate and consume her male object of desire. While her unfeminine behavior may partially be attributed to her Orientalness (that is, while one may attribute her savagery to her barbaric racial heritage), one must also read her in terms of a Victorian mistrust of femininity and feminine "nature." As inherently more "natural," less civilized (or civilizable) creatures, women share with Orientals their irrationality, lack of logic, superstition, emotionalism, and so forth; they are the natural opponents of Western cultural values. And just as the supernaturally exaggerated representations of the barbaric, primitive Oriental found in *The Beetle* offer a rationale for xenophobia and for a continued British colonial presence within Egypt, so does its fearsome depictions of unleashed feminine potency offer a rationale for the continued constriction of female roles, particularly in the context of the strong feminist movements at the turn of the century.

Abhuman sexuality

And once again I was conscious of that awful sense of the presence of an evil thing. How much of it was fact, and how much of it was the product of imagination I cannot say; but, looking back, it seems to me that it was as if I had been taken out of the corporeal body to be plunged into the inner chambers of all nameless sin. There was the sound of something flopping off the bed on to the ground, and I knew that the thing was coming at me across the floor. My stomach quaked, my heart melted within me – the very anguish of my terror gave me strength to scream – and scream! (*The Beetle*, p. 485)

The opening narrator of *The Beetle* is Robert Holt, a starving ex-clerk long out of work, who tells of the terrible adventures that befell him after he broke into a seemingly deserted house in a seedy London neighborhood, desperate for shelter from the rain. In the darkness inside, he is assaulted by a slimy, foul-smelling creature the size of a small animal, and later held prisoner by an evil-looking Oriental, of indeterminate sex and age, who seems to be the creature's keeper and can call it up at will. Holt is mesmerized and possessed by this foreigner, who forces him to break into the house of Paul Lessingham, prominent Radical politician, and steal a packet of love letters written to Lessingham by his fiancée Marjorie Linden. When Lessingham confronts Holt in the act of burglary, Holt, as ordered by the mesmerist, hisses the words "THE BEETLE!" to send Lessingham into a fit of hysteria.

Part II is narrated by Sydney Atherton, an inventor who is currently hard at work on a new weapon of chemical warfare. Sydney writes of his unsuccessful wooing of his childhood friend Marjorie Linden and his fierce jealousy of his rival Lessingham, and describes visits to his laboratory by both Lessingham and Holt's mysterious Oriental captor. Lessingham, nervously hinting at some shady incident in his own past, comes to seek information from Atherton, amateur Orientalist: he wishes to discover whether there is a "shred of truth" in the Egyptian belief that a "priest of Isis" could "assume after death the form of a scarabaeus" (p. 509). Atherton scoffs at the legend, but later witnesses exactly such a transmogrification when the Oriental comes to enlist his help (unsuccessfully) in her scheme of vengeance against Lessingham.

Marjorie's narrative describes her love affair with Lessingham, the opposition of her father, a conservative politician, to the engagement, and the events leading to her entrapment by the Beetle. Part IV is narrated by Augustus Champnell, a "confidential agent" enlisted by Lessingham to assist in the search for Marjorie. Through him we finally hear the story of what exactly occurred in the Egyptian temple of Isis twenty years ago, when Lessingham was enslaved by the Woman of Songs, broke free of her influence, and strangled her, only to witness the "transmigration" of her corpse into the body of a scarabaeus. Champnell describes the desperate chase after the Oriental and her two prisoners, Holt (who finally expires in a seedy London hotel) and Marjorie. The fugitives are providentially halted by a train wreck which destroys the Beetle. Marjorie is pulled from the debris scarcely alive: "even after her physical powers were completely restored – in itself a tedious task – she was for something like three years under medical supervision as a lunatic. But all that skill and money could do was done, and in course of time . . . the results were entirely satisfactory" (p. 713).

We never get the Oriental's own story directly; her words and emotions are always filtered by the distaste and revulsion of the characters relating them. Her version of the story is inessential to the novel: what matters is her gothic embodiment as the Beetle, the nameless horror it induces in all who encounter her, the terrible effect she has on her victims. As a "foreigner" to the culture – foreign in the sense of both her Egyptian and her supernatural origins – she confronts late Victorian London with a spectre of gross materiality, and evokes a response of denial and dread. The corporeal body in *The Beetle* is both a thing of terror, and a thing of sickness and fear. In her avatar of the Beetle, the Oriental is characterized by that nauseating amorphousness which one encounters so frequently in the monstrous creations of the *fin-de-siècle* Gothic: she is slimy, foul-smelling, and damp, adhering stickily to the body with her numerous legs. Her hypnotized victims, enthralled by the spectacle of Thing-ness she presents, become entrapped in their own agonized bodies. She drives both Holt and Lessingham into an absolute and gibbering hysteria; with her arcane system of tortures, she reduces Marjorie to the wreck of a human being.

The Beetle, in short, is abject, a creature whose unmistakable physicality and morphic fluctuability simultaneously fascinate and repulse. She is a liminal entity, the fact of whose existence violates multiple structures of meaning, including those that organize sexual and species identity. And she arouses in the onlooker a sense of nausea and dread, instinctive, subrational, and immediate. One knows that there is something wrong about her, but cannot put a finger on it. Holt speaks of "that awful sense of the presence of an evil thing" (p. 485); Marjorie recalls "an altogether indescribable feeling, a feeling which amounted to knowledge, that I was in the presence of the supernatural" (p. 562); for Lessingham, there was "about her something so unnatural, so inhuman" as to fill him "with an indescribable repulsion" (pp. 632, 633). Her very smell is nauseating: Marjorie comments on "an uncomfortable odour" in the Beetle's house, "suggestive of some evil-smelling animal" (p. 615).

At times the characters' "instinctive" revulsion from the Oriental seems indistinguishable from commonplace xenophobia, the habitual British mistrust of racial difference. The Oriental's landlady describes her tenant as a "dirty foreigner, who went about in a bed-gown through the public streets" (p. 666). The local policeman has kept an eye on this "queer fish," with his queer habits, ever since "he" appeared in the neighborhood. "He's known amongst us as the Arab," is his simple and self-evident explanation (p. 675). Whether mistrust of "the Arab" is generated by racism or by the abjectness of this particular Oriental individual matters little: abjectness adheres to, is the condition of, the Orient, and though she may be a particularly loathsome example of the Arab, she is by no means an exception to her race.

Like most "unscrupulous Orientals," the Beetle is savage in her pleasures, and heartless in their execution. She is cruel, and takes a wanton delight in her cruelty. She toys with her victims long after their spirit has been crushed, seeming to delight simply in eliciting their screams of terror and pain. She is secretive, unsociable, untrustworthy, filthy, foul-smelling. She has an Oriental envy of the superior white ("What would I not give for a skin as white as that – ah yes!"; p. 456), which translates into a boundless hatred of that unattainable whiteness, a desire to punish and mutilate white skin. And she harbors a "typically" Eastern (and also, perhaps, feminine) vengefulness, nursing an inveterate grudge against Paul Lessingham, the man who spurned her, travelling to England more than twenty years later to destroy him. "Plainly, with this gentleman [sic]," remarks Atherton, "hate meant hate – in the solid Oriental sense" (p. 540).

For the Oriental, malice is a racial condition, not simply an emotional response. So deeply engrained, so basic is her cruel nature that it distorts and makes hideous her very countenance: she is literally evil incarnate. Her dreadful face is an index to her blighting depravity. As Holt describes her,

> there was not a hair upon his [sic] face or head, but, to make up for it, the skin, which was a saffron yellow, was an amazing mass of wrinkles. The cranium, and, indeed, the whole skull, was so small as to be disagreeably suggestive of something animal. The nose, on the other hand, was abnormally large; so extravagant were its dimensions, and so peculiar its shape, it resembled the beak of some bird of prey . . . The mouth, with its blubber lips, came immediately underneath the nose, and chin, to all intents and purposes, there was none. This deformity – for the absence of chin amounted to that – it was which gave to the face the appearance of something not human – that, and the eyes. For so marked a feature of the man were his eyes, that, ere long, it seemed to me that he was nothing but eyes. (p. 454)

The creature is "supernaturally ugly" (p. 454), with the supernatural effect resulting partly from Oriental magicianship, the power of the mesmeric, compelling eyes and voice, and partly from the gross physiognomical traits the Oriental shares with various animal species. (The Beetle's landlady remarks that her tenant is "more like a hideous baboon than anything else, let alone a man"; p. 666.) The abnormally small skull is a clue to the creature's inherently depraved nature, marking the savagery of the atavistic criminal, or the incomplete moral development of the inferior, less-evolved non-Caucasian.

But even her preternatural ugliness, sadism, and mesmeric potency cannot account for the overwhelming affective response the Beetle-Woman inspires. She is uncanny rather because of her bodily indefinition, her violation of multiple categories. When Holt first meets the creature, he cannot ascertain its age, its sex, or its nationality, except that it is "foreign" (p. 453-4): he cannot even vouch for its species. "I saw someone in front of me lying in a bed. I could not at once decide if it was a man or a woman. Indeed at first I doubted if it was anything human"

(p. 453). He is particularly vexed by the issue of the creature's gender. At first, taking into account his captor's hideousness, Holt states firmly, "I knew it be a man – for this reason, if for no other, that it was impossible such a creature could be feminine" (p. 453). But soon he begins to doubt: his "instinct," as he later tells Marjorie (p. 604), leads him to note that there is something "essentially feminine" in the creature's face (p. 462), and he is further bewildered by "his" manifest desire for Lessingham, and by "his" teasing advances to Holt himself. "Is it not sweet to stand close at my side? You, with your white skin, if I were a woman, would you not take me for a wife?" (p. 486). These doubts are then again quelled by the animalistic countenance, the aggressively unfeminine behavior of his captor: "after all, I told myself that it was impossible that I could have been such a simpleton as to have been mistaken on such a question as gender" (p. 462).

Perhaps the reader is meant all along to guess the femininity of the Oriental and label Holt, as invited, a "simpleton"; but it is more likely that the text intended to shock the Victorian reader with what would have been an unexpected depiction of male homoerotic desire, establishing the general idea of sexual perversion which is to pervade the novel and associating sexual perversity specifically with the Oriental. The Oriental, whatever its gender, is certainly blatantly sexual in its interests. "He" forces Holt to strip and gloats over his naked white skin with a "satyr's smile" and "devouring . . . glances" (p. 456); after a night spent in a deep trance, Holt finds himself being uncovered and closely examined and "prodded" in his nakedness by his satyrlike host. "Fingers were pressed into my cheeks, they were thrust into my mouth, they touched my staring eyes . . . and – horror of horrors! – the blubber lips were pressed to mine – the soul of something evil entered me in the guise of a kiss" (p. 458). The reader witnesses this early scene under the impression that it takes place between two men. Later, though the text might seem to foreclose the possibility of male homoerotic desire by firmly establishing the Oriental's femininity, it provides the reader with a further homoerotic situation – the Oriental's sadistic, quasi-sexual attacks on Marjorie.

The Oriental is able to cross the boundary between one sexual or gendered identity and another, she can cross the boundary separating the human and animal species, and even in her avatar of the Beetle she resists enclosure within the boundary of a definite species classification. After the train wreck which Marjorie barely survives and which squashes the Beetle to death, all that remains of the latter are some "huge blotches" on the seat – "stains of some sort," which "were damp, and gave out a most unpleasant smell" (p. 711). Various experts opine that the stains are comprised of human blood, paint, wild cat blood, or finally, "a deposit of some sort of viscid matter, probably the excretion of some variety of lizard" (p. 712). Whatever the Beetle was, resists scientific analysis and classification: it can fit into no taxonomy of natural history. The usually matter-of-fact Champnell has the last word on the subject: "experience has taught me that there are indeed more things in heaven and earth than are dreamed of in our philosophy, and I am quite prepared to believe that the so-called Beetle, which others saw, but I never, was – or is, for it cannot be certainly shown that the Thing is not still existing – a creature born neither of God nor man" (p. 715).

As we are never able to learn what the Beetle "really" is, so we never learn what she really does. We have all the details of the effects she causes – Marjorie's insanity, Paul's hysterical breakdowns, Holt's enslavement and eventual death – but don't know what terrible action she performs to wreak these effects. Words fail to represent the dread the Beetle induces, and the magnitude and type of the agony she is able to inflict, so these are left more profitably to the reader's imagination, enflamed by the vague hyperbole which masses itself round the unnamed and unnameable events connected with the Beetle. The Beetle's female victims, Marjorie in particular, are subjected to "unimaginable agony," "speechless torture," "every variety of outrage of which even the minds of demons could conceive" (pp. 686, 634). We see the effects of such torture in Marjorie's utter physical and mental debilitation by the end of the novel, as well as in the extremities to which the male victims are reduced: the young English boy's "state of indescribable mutilation" after having suffered "nameless agonies and degradations" (p. 689), Lessingham's lapses into crawling, gibbering idiocy at the mere mention of the Beetle. One does not even know with what instruments the Oriental inflicts her tortures. The landlady of the "disorderly house" to which the Beetle carries Marjorie and Holt says she heard no "sounds of struggling, or of blows," only "shriek after shriek" as Marjorie was somehow molested behind a locked door (p. 701). Perhaps the "Arab" hides her instruments of torture in the mysterious "bundle" – the "lurking place of nameless terrors" (p. 686) – she carries on her head about London. Perhaps her instrument of torture is her terrible body itself. As Holt lies dying with "two abrasions of the skin" on either side of his neck (p. 696), he gasps out that "[the Beetle] took me by the throat . . . [and] killed me" (p. 698).

All phenomena associated with the Beetle are, finally, shrouded in mystery. The main events of the story remain unspeakable and unexplained. Champnell laments that since Marjorie recovered with an absolute memory block as to what the Beetle did to her,

what actually transpired will never, in all human possibility, be certainly known and particularly what precisely occurred in the railway carriage during that dreadful moment of sudden passing from life unto death. What became of the creature who all but did her to death; who he was – if it was a "he," which is extremely doubtful; whence he came; whither he went; what was the purpose of his presence here – to this hour these things are puzzles. (p. 713)

Though all the horrible possibilities which the novel raised seem to be neatly dispatched in Champnell's postscript – the Beetle squashed to death, the subterranean temple of Isis, back in Egypt, destroyed by some unexplained explosion, Marjorie recovered in health and happily married to Paul – Champnell prefers to leave his ending open. "The Thing," or something like it, he warns, might very well return. It might return and wreak the same havoc because it was never understood, and was destroyed only by accident. Indefinition – a world in which it is possible that there might exist "creature[s] born neither of God nor of man" – is the final condition of the novel, just as the Beetle is, in the final analysis, indefinable.

And yet this heightened sense of indefinition, from which *The Beetle* gains most of its dramatic effect, may be seen as a certain coyness on the part of the text. The text censors itself from speaking of what the Beetle does as effectively as Marjorie's memory censors itself from remembering what the Beetle did to her. Other characters besides Marjorie suffer from lapses of memory: their narratives are interrupted by insanity, or aphasia, or a fainting fit. Holt's narrative ends with an occurrence so terrible his very consciousness gives way: "[the Beetle] leaped, shrieking, off the bed, and sprang at me, clasping my throat with his horrid hands, bearing me backwards on to the floor; I felt his breath mingle with mine ... and then God, in His mercy, sent oblivion" (p. 488). After his dreadful weeks in the Temple of Isis, Lessingham suffers a long period of "aphasia" and "semi-imbecility" (p. 637); when he recovers he wills himself to forget by trying to bury his memory of the Beetle in hard work.

The characters in the novel cannot bear to recall what the Beetle did to them – or perhaps the text cannot bear to represent it. All one can be certain about is that the Beetle's predations are sexual in nature. The sadistic tortures inflicted on the naked white bodies of English virgins by the priestesses of Isis seem to require, or at least be heightened by, intercourse with a passive and mesmerized English male sex slave:

Lessingham, the unnamed English teenager, and later (one may speculate), Holt. The three stalwart Englishmen in pursuit of Marjorie and her captor writhe with horror at "the notion of a gently-nurtured girl being at the mercy of that fiend incarnate" (p. 688). The repeated trope for what she and the other English virgins have undergone is "that to which death would have been preferred," a common Victorian euphemism for rape. Paul frets that even if they get his fiancée back alive, "she will be but the mere soiled husk of the Marjorie whom I knew and loved" (p. 688), as if the Oriental villainess (perhaps with some phallic substitute hidden in her mysterious bag of tricks, her "paraphernalia of horror and of dread') could deprive Marjorie of even her virginity.

One thing is clear from the beginning: the Oriental, whatever its gender, has a "savage, frantic longing" for the body of Paul Lessingham. "He is straight – straight as the mast of a ship – he is tall – his skin is white; he is strong – how strong! – oh yes! Is there a better thing than to be his wife? his well-beloved?" (p. 465). This strong sexual desire on the part of the Oriental, metamorphosed into vengeance, is what motivates the plot of *The Beetle*. There does exist a certain amount of insistent, posturing sexual desire amongst the non-supernatural characters in *The Beetle*: as in *Dracula*, several suitors (Sydney Atherton, Lessingham, and Percy Woodville) jockey for the hand of one woman, Marjorie Linden, while an otherwise demure Dora Grayling rather shamelessly pursues Sydney. Most of this sexual rivalry and tension is fairly civilized, often even comic, involving the sorts of mix-ups and awkward situations one might find in a novel like *Barchester Towers*. While the two rivals Atherton and Lessingham snarl and snap at one another, both are adamant about the purity of their intentions toward Marjorie. The novel even indulges in the traditional comic ending of a triple marriage (including the rather gratuitous awarding of a Dora Grayling bridesmaid to the minor character Percy Woodville).

However, this civilized and commonplace comedy of mortal romantic desire is displaced – or perhaps one should say, shown up – by the terrible drama of sexuality brought about by the polymorphously perverse and intense desires of the Oriental villainess as she catches the major characters in her snares. Under her hypnotic suggestion, Sydney suddenly finds himself acknowledging a physical longing for Marjorie: "I thought . . . of the delight of holding her in my arms, of feeling the pressure of her lips to mine. As my gaze met his, the lower side of what the conquest of this fair lady would mean, burned in my brain; fierce imaginings blazed before my eyes" (p. 540). However, Sydney manfully shakes off the suggestion and disclaims the desire as his own. ("Rage took hold of me. 'You hound!' I cried.") Sexual desire, figured by the text as monstrous and violent, is displaced from the romantic relationships and projected onto the depraved Oriental. What the novel presents, in her person, is a terrible, rampant sexuality, taken to deviant extremes of sadism, enslavement, homoeroticism, and a general perversion.

Gothic female genitalia

It often happens that male patients declare that they feel there is something uncanny about the female genital organs. (Sigmund Freud, "The 'Uncanny'," p. 152)

And the perversion of the Oriental is explicitly linked to her femininity, as we see in the remarkable introductory sequence from Holt's narrative of "The House with the Open Window." Seeking shelter, Holt enters this seemingly deserted house through the inviting open window, but no sooner does he enter than he wants nothing more than to leave, for he senses a "presence" in the pitch-dark room, "something strange, something evil." "I had a horrible persuasion that, though unseeing, I was seen; that my every movement was being watched"; and this invisible mesmeric gaze holds him and cuts off his retreat by paralyzing him, mind and body (p. 450).

Immobilized and panic-stricken, Holt watches two glowing eyes, six inches above the floor, advance towards him. The creature, emitting an "unpleasant, foetid odour," stalks and climbs him as he stands with unwilling but utter passivity:

On a sudden I felt something on my boot, and, with a sense of shrinking, horror, nausea, rendering me momentarily more helpless, I realized that the creature was beginning to ascend my legs, to climb my body . . . It was as though it were some gigantic spider – a spider of the nightmares; a monstrous conception of some dreadful vision. It pressed lightly against my clothing with what might, for all the world, have been spider's legs. There was an amazing host of them – I felt the pressure of each separate one. They embraced me softly, stickily, as if the creature glued and unglued them, each time it moved. (p. 451)

The creature, proceeding with an infinitely sickening deliberateness, mounts his "loins" and "the pit of [his] stomach," its odor becoming "so intense as to be unbearable," and slowly proceeds up his neck to "envelope [his] face with its huge, slimy, evil-smelling body, and embrace [him] with its myriad legs," at which point Holt is finally maddened into breaking the paralysis and shaking the thing off (p. 452).

Except for the sight of the two glowing eyes and an occasional "squelching" sound, all Holt has to guide him in envisioning the creature are his senses of touch and smell, which feed him only impressions that nauseate him on a visceral level and quickly dismantle his powers of self-control, volition, and especially, rationality – those powers without which Holt feels himself "unmanned." The creature's teasing advance up Holt's body, the darkness of the setting, the intense, intimate physicality of the contact, combined with the idea of stickiness and overpowering smell, point towards a reading of this as some sort of nightmare of sexual encounter, sexuality at its most primitive and terrible. Where Holt entered seeking warmth, shelter and safety, he is paralyzed and assaulted, emasculated by this unseen thing that is a phantasmic version of the female genitalia. This same Beetle that attacks Holt, as we discover later from Sydney Atherton's amateur Orientalist scholarship, is associated with "the legendary transmigrations of Isis," and "the story of the beetle which issues from the woman's womb through all eternity" (p. 546).

Lessingham's "Woman of Songs" metamorphosed into the Beetle – gave birth to this reduction of herself out of her own death – when Paul Lessingham finally broke free of her mesmeric control and strangled her. Always a sexual predator, a "man-eater," she is transfigured into her own hungry, emasculating womb, damp, adhesive, and overwhelmingly nauseating. Holt and the other male victims, then, are not so much "taken out of the corporeal body to be plunged into the inner chambers of all nameless sin," as Holt describes his experience (p. 485), as trapped within their corporeal bodies by the spectre of the externalized "inner chambers" of that repository of "nameless sin," a woman's body.

The female body, saturated with sexuality, is thus a hideous abomination as exemplified by the Beetle-Woman. The novel nonetheless fractures across its ambivalence as to the essential nature of femininity, uncertain as to whether women are beasts, or angels, or somehow both. The Oriental captivates her male victim with her thrilling melodies as the seductive "Woman of Songs," and she dispatches him, with a combination of powers both occult and sadistic, as the cruel, emasculating votary of the goddess Isis. But she is matched by pure-minded Marjorie Linden, "the daintiest damsel in the land" (p. 679). Though the traditional polarity of good versus bad woman is presented untraditionally by *The Beetle* – Marjorie is too adventurous and outspoken to be a conventional heroine, and the "Woman of Songs," by the time she appears in London, too hideously ugly to be exactly a femme fatale – *The Beetle* does juxtapose a pert, lively, but desexualized heroine with a villainess whose fierce and emasculating sexual aggressiveness has made of her a repulsive, yet sexually potent monster: a "ghoulish example of her sex, who had so yielded to her depraved instincts to have become nothing but a ghastly reminiscence of womanhood" (p. 462). As the novel progresses, each woman becomes transformed into a sheer parody of the polarity of femininity she represents: the Oriental is revealed as a literal monster, cruel, sadistic, castrating, and vile; while Marjorie becomes reduced to complete passivity – physical incapacitation, idiocy, and dependence – after she is captured and tortured.[15]

Femininity as represented by Britannia is all of the finest and most civilized. Essential femininity, the text seems to insist, is the femininity of Marjorie Linden: pure, high-minded, appealingly winsome – and metaphorically speaking, disembodied. The embodied female, with her troublesome sexual desires, her fluid gender identity, her terrible avatar of the Beetle is a thing of abjection; but the text denies that she has anything to do with true Victorian femininity. First, she has become "unwomaned," or masculinized, by her behavior. (In Holt's remark quoted earlier, "it was impossible such a creature could be feminine.") Second, after her femininity has been proved by the undeniable fact of her naked body, the reader is still free to attribute her unnaturally masculine sexual aggression to her Oriental savagery.

The vulnerable white body

The Beetle is a text obsessed with naked bodies. Robert Holt, Marjorie Linden, Paul Lessingham, the many victims of the Isis cult, all are "stripped to the skin" (the full phrase is always used) and leeringly examined, or tormented, or sexually molested in "unspeakable" ways we only have leave to conjecture. The Oriental, too, is briefly displayed to Sydney Atherton and the reader in all her nakedness, and only then, as she metamorphoses from human being to scarab and back again and her robes lie about her on the floor, is the tricky question of her gender settled once and for all. "I had been egregiously mistaken on the question of sex," Sydney informs us. "My visitor was not a man, but a woman, and judging from the brief glimpse which I had of her body, by no means old or ill-shaped either" (p. 547).

When stripped, the Beetle's unexpected essence is her decided femininity; but when stripped, the essence (as the text emphasizes it) of her victims, male and female alike, is their decided whiteness. "What a white skin you have – how white! What would I not give for a skin as white as that," gloats Holt's captor after commanding him to undress (p. 456). Champnell, recalling the rumors he has heard of the depraved Isis cult in Egypt whose "practice" is "to offer young women as sacrifices," remarks that the cult members prefer "white Christian women, with a special preference, if they could get them, to young English women" (p. 690); and Lessingham, an eye-witness to the cult sacrifices, proclaims solemnly of the victims, "they were as white as you or I" (p. 634).

In the ramshackle London house that the Beetle has turned into her headquarters, Marjorie Linden finds, on top of the pile of cushions and rugs that serves the Oriental for a bed, a bedspread representing a naked white woman, her writhings and agony depicted with lifelike verisimilitude, in the very act of being burned alive under the pleased scrutiny of Isis. As she watches, the bedspread begins to move, and the Beetle comes out from hiding to seize Marjorie and begin to subject her to some of the same tortures. This is the point to which Marjorie's compulsively rewritten diary leads again and again, and past which it can go no further: her memory balks after the moment when she meets her Oriental captor face to face. This event depicted on the bedspread is both the moment the text is trying to ward off, the narrative gathering momentum as Marjorie's three champions rush to save her from the fate of the woman on the bedspread, and the point to which the text, like Marjorie's diary, compulsively returns again and again: in Champnell's second-hand narration of the ill-fated young Christian women abroad, in Lessingham's hysterical "attacks" or flashbacks in which he recalls what he witnessed in Egypt twenty years ago. There in the temple of Isis, "young and lovely" Englishwomen were stripped naked, "outraged," and "burnt alive," and then their ashes "consumed by the participants" of the Isis cult in a frenzied "orgie" (p. 635). The scene on the bedspread is a sort of icon of the monstrous potential of the Orient, an Orient which, in its insatiable desire for the whiteness of the West, its frenzied envy and hatred of the West, would destroy and engulf it in all its whiteness, consuming its very ashes.

The text dwells obsessively upon the bodies of two naked women: one a victimizer, the other a victim; one, a masculine-appearing and -behaving creature whose nakedness reveals, terrifyingly, her unexpected femininity, the other, a young "Christian" creature whose nakedness reveals, equally terrifyingly, the vulnerability of the white body – a vulnerability the white male victim shares. The feminine pulchritude of the stripped Englishwoman is not emphasized by the text: in her victimization, she is less a sexual object than a representation of whiteness at its "best" – whiteness in its most fragile, most valuable, most cherished state. Her nakedness reveals her as a member of the purest race, subject to the invidious envy and rage of lesser, dark-skinned peoples.

The Beetle inverts its culture's own fascination with "the Oriental experience," its mania for colonization of the desirable Orient, into a belief in British (white) desirability, and a fear of aggressive Oriental "colonization." At the same time that the novel manifests a terror of engulfment by the Orient, it evinces, from a masculine perspective, a terror of an overwhelming female sexuality as embodied in the supernaturally potent Beetle-woman. Even if the sadism of the Oriental vents itself most fully on her female victims, the real object of her visit is Paul Lessingham: her sexuality is directed towards men, and her desire is to consume her object. Aggressive feminine desire is portrayed by the novel as a devouring force which emasculates its male object and literally dehumanizes the sexualized female. For feminine pulchritude (and the lascivious desires that go along with it) does manifest itself in the Oriental. But the beautiful body of the Woman of Songs is a trap. Like Arabella in *The Lair of the White Worm*, the lovely siren hides beneath her fair form, in her "nether parts," the serpent, the worm, or, in this case, the Beetle: an emasculating and abject embodiment of her genitalia.

In *The Beetle*, a Victorian fear of the hidden depravity, the hidden potency, of the female is literalized, in the novel, by a supernatural occurrence: the Oriental's transformation from woman into Beetle, from woman into a reductive, compressed, and monstrous embodiment of her sexuality. And a Victorian fear of the Orient is given focus by the supernatural powers (of mesmerism, transmogrification, control over the natural elements) which the Western mind associated particularly with the Eastern races, and which the Beetle uses to enslave and destroy her white victims. All of the barbarity and primitiveness which the West attributes to the Orient are borne out by the savage behavior of the Beetle; but that barbarity particularly manifests itself as the sadistic sexual practices of a perverse female subject. By casting its villainess as an Oriental, the text manages to avoid suggesting that abject female sexuality could inhere in any sense in white women, but by casting its Oriental as a woman the text manages to suggest that barbaric sexuality is, in some sense, inherently female.

CHAPTER 7

Abjected masculinities

She is the devil! Beautiful – beautiful; but the devil! . . . How am I to
sleep when I see her sitting down yonder at the foot of the bed with
her great eyes watching and watching hour after hour? I tell you it
saps all the strength and manhood out of me.

Arthur Conan Doyle, "John Barrington Cowles"[1]

The Beetle-Woman presents a spectacle of corporeality at its most
fearsome, of a material body which resists classification within categories
of sexual and species identity from which "the human" takes its
meaning. Besides confounding such oppositions as animal/human,
male/female, and masculine/feminine, she is a creature driven purely
by appetite. Her sexual appetite in particular calls attention to the
embodiedness of (ab)human beings, imperfectly evolved and imperfectly
acculturated subjects disrupted by drives and desires that testify to the
tenuousness of a "civilized" human identity.

Though exploring the Thing-ness of the human body at great length,
The Beetle to a certain extent works to delimit Thing-ness by identifying
it as the peculiar liability of women and non-whites, two discredited
groups already associated with the abject suchness of a purely material
reality. A "fully human" identity, in other words, can be recuperated as
the property of the European male.[2] This strategy is only partially
successful, most notably because the novel cannot decide whether a
fully human identity shall be determined on the basis of sex or race, and
is thus ambivalent towards femininity. When their whiteness is
foregrounded, women's full humanity emerges by virtue of contrast
with the abhumanness of the Oriental. However, women are abhuman
non-subjects in relation to men (particularly when their sexual difference
is compounded by racial difference). The novel fractures across this
ambivalence, opening up a fissure from which abhumanness, no longer
containable, seeps out and begins to spread. If the female subject is "by
nature" an abhuman subject, then the raciality of the white woman

cannot ensure for her a status as fully human. The white body in general – including the white male body – is thus revealed as all-too-corporeal, all-too-abhuman.

The dissolution of masculinity

Moreover, as should be clear from the last chapter, masculinity is an unstable construct to begin with in *The Beetle*. While the novel's male characters remain relatively untroubled in their assumption of racial superiority, regarding Oriental-ness with emotions ranging from horror to disgust to dismissive contempt, they are by and large "unmanned" by the Beetle-Woman. Their own sexual identity is dismantled through contact with her, in part because hers is too fluid to constitute a reference point for theirs, in part because insofar as she is female, she inverts traditional sexual roles, her inappropriately aggressive femininity requiring as object an effeminized version of masculinity.[3] Holt laments that "I was no longer a man; my manhood was merged in [the Beetle's]. I was, in the extremest sense, an example of passive obedience" (p. 454).

This prospect of the relinquishment of "manhood" is presented more urgently in the case of Paul Lessingham, since Lessingham, unlike Holt, is actively engaged in heterosexual courtship, and his suitability as a husband and potential father is questioned by both Sydney and Marjorie's father. At first, by focusing on but refusing to reveal the mysterious incident in Lessingham's past around which the plot turns, the novel seems to offer us a reworking of the Jekyll-and-Hyde plot, the Dorian Gray plot: the plot of the double life, the carefully concealed depravity, of Victorian men.[4] Lessingham is as exemplary a public figure as Dr. Jekyll: Sydney calls his rival, in hateful jest, "the Apostle," for Lessingham's is a reputation of spotless integrity and iron self-command. Yet even Lessingham admits that "in all our lives there are episodes which we keep to ourselves" (p. 571) – that the most upright of Victorian gentlemen have enjoyed some furtive little "episode" which, if made public, might destroy their reputation, and that this is the norm rather than the exception. "It was the old tale re-told," says Sydney, sounding a great deal like Utterson, the frame narrator of *Jekyll and Hyde*, "that to the life of every man there is a background – that it is precisely in the unlikeliest cases that the background's darkest" (p. 543).

Lessingham even seems to evince some of the symptoms associated with degeneracy or perhaps syphilis: he suffers from nervousness, delusions, and attacks resembling epileptic fits. "He sank in a heap on the floor; he held up his hands above his head; and he gibbered – like some frenzied animal" (p. 576). Sydney describes Lessingham as "leprous," and worries that his physical and moral contamination might spread to Marjorie. "[W]hat Upas tree of horror was rooted in his very bones? The thought that her sweet purity was likely to be engulfed in a devil's slough in which he was wallowing was not to be endured" (p. 573).

But Lessingham's great secret, as the text gradually reveals it, is not profligacy and its results, degenerate symptoms or venereal disease. His secret is rather an unmanly susceptibility and weakness, shockingly inappropriate to "Paul Lessingham – the politician – the statesman . . . [who] has the reputation, both in the House and out of it, of being a man of iron nerve" (pp. 464, 505). As he describes his sexual enslavement by the "Woman of Songs":

[H]er touch had on me what I can only describe as a magnetic influence. As her fingers closed upon my wrist, I felt as powerless in her grasp as if she held me with bands of steel. What seemed an invitation was virtually a command . . . [Her eyes] had on me a diabolical effect. They robbed me of my consciousness, of my power of volition, of my capacity to think – they made me as wax in her hands. (p. 631)

The Woman of Songs divests Lessingham of "volition" and rationality, qualities which are traditionally the special prerogative of the masculine subject.[5] Lessingham acknowledges this when he says that her hypnotic powers served to "trick [him] of [his] manhood," but here he also gestures towards a dissolution of his sexual as well as his gender identity. He is, the reader can presume, forced to have intercourse with the Woman of Songs numerous times, an experience Lessingham describes without irony as "emasculat[ing]." "The most dreadful part of it was that I was wholly incapable of offering even the faintest resistance to her caresses. I lay there like a log. She did with me as she would, and in dumb agony I endured" (pp. 634–5).

Lessingham's "emasculation," however, is ambiguously figured, entailing both a metaphorical impotence and a seemingly incompatible sexual potency. He behaves as a female subject – passive, resistless, voiceless, and inert – when under the control of this sexually aggressively, strong-willed, and thus ultra-masculine woman. But to identify this scene as one of symbolic castration obscures the crucial point that, speaking literally for the moment, Lessingham is anything but castrated: he is sexually aroused again and again, despite his "horror," his "loathing," his "indescribable repulsion" (pp. 632–3).

While this scene at one level brings to light the fundamental ambivalence, the simultaneous terror and fascination, with which Victorian men regarded the prospect of an active female sexuality, it interests me here as an exemplary moment in which masculinity is more profoundly troubled than by the ambivalence of its desires. Paul Lessingham's masculinity is undone in the first place through a dynamic of inversion: he is feminized, or rendered passive both bodily and mentally, through contact with the inappropriately masculine Woman of Songs. And the result of this feminization is to transform him into an inert non-subject without volition or consciousness, whose essential identity is only bodily, only sexual. The scenario does not exactly contradict Foucault's assertion, discussed in the preceding chapter, that nineteenth-century social medicine identified women but not men as grossly material Things, "saturated with sexuality," for the Beetle-Woman is precisely such a Thing.

And yet, in the scene of his sexual enslavement by the Beetle-Woman, Lessingham, too, becomes precisely such a Thing. He is a corporeal being only, a mere body without self-identity or volition. Furthermore, *his* is the body that is "saturated with sexuality," for the Beetle-Woman's predations render him nothing more than her sexual tool. Chronologically later scenes will spell out the implications of such a transformation, when the young man grows up into an imperfectly masculine (and thus imperfectly human) subject: as erratic and fluctuable as Foucault's hystericized woman, prone to delusions and other mental aberrations and to fits of gibbering and groveling. "I was conscious of his pallid cheeks, the twitched muscles of his mouth, the feverish glitter of his eyes – this Leader of Men, whose predominate characteristic in the House of Commons was immobility, was rapidly approximating to the condition of a hysterical woman" (p. 685).

Phallus or penis?

The sight of Medusa's head makes the spectator stiff with terror, turns him to stone. Observe that we have here once again the same origin from the castration complex and the same transformation of affect! For becoming stiff means an erection. Thus in the original situation it offers consolation to the spectator: he is still in possession of a penis, and the stiffening reassures him of the fact. (Sigmund Freud, "Medusa's Head," p. 212)

In his speculations on the castration complex in "Medusa's Head," Freud implies that male hysteria is a fully appropriate response to female sexual aggressivity. The sight of an unexpectedly "phallic" woman brings into consciousness the repressed memory of the male spectator's discovery of sexual difference: a traumatic moment in which the male subject, observing the seemingly mutilated female genitalia, was forced to come to terms with the possibility of his own castration.[6] Freud's male subject fears a similar mutilation and thus feminization – thus the loss of an integral self-identity – but can avoid hystericization by deriving "consolation" from his own phallic plenitude, which contrasts, in the original traumatic scenario, with the female's lack.

In Freud's analysis, in other words, the spectacle of the phallic woman initially undermines masculinity, but masculinity is reconstituted by the recognition that the female and not the male body is incomplete, pathological, abhuman.[7] Note the odd reversal Freud accomplishes when he gives it as "a technical rule" that "a multiplication of penis symbols" – here the snakes on Medusa's head – "signifies castration" (p. 212). The penis itself, even when it appears out of place, is not and indeed cannot be "gothic" on its own terms, for it is "the absence of [the penis] which is the cause of the horror" (p. 212). Male sexuality, for Freud, is never horrific, but female sexuality is always so; the spectacle of the penis out-of-place serves to remind one of the abjectness not of the male body, but of female sexual difference.

And yet in the scene discussed above, Paul Lessingham responds to the sight of the phallic Beetle-Woman by "stiffening," but is hardly "consoled" by the fact that "he is still in possession of a penis." His erection signals an abjected rather than transcendent masculine identity, a fully *embodied* masculinity that is saturated with sexuality and voided of integral subjectivity. One can begin to account for this disparity between the Gothic and psychoanalytical text by noting the slippage, in Freud, between penis and phallus, between the fluctuable and material male organ itself and the magnificent idea of it – for the phallus, unlike the penis, never tumesces and detumesces; it is always already erect.[8] As Jean-Joseph Goux argues in his history of the symbolics of the phallus within Western myth and psychology, the "materiality of the penis is of little consequence compared to the 'logical' force of the erection . . . [T]he masculine organ is spiritualized, idealized, to the point of becoming a sign of intelligence" ("The Phallus: Masculine Identity and the 'Exchange of Women'," p. 50).

The phallus is a *masculine* principle of generation, of production. In that sense, *it is the very manifestation of intelligence* . . . Thus the inaugural opposition of metaphysics is implied here. Any engendering is the result of the union of two different principles, a male principle which is intelligible reason (ideas, model, father) and a female principle which is matter. This archaic sexuation of the major metaphysical opposition is still quite legible in Plato and in Aristotle. (Goux, p. 46; emphasis in text)

The idea of the phallus, in short, serves to cover over the fluctuable materiality of the penis and the fact of male embodiedment; male subjects transcend the body, while corporeality is figured through oppositional logic as the exclusive property of femininity. The *fin-de-siècle* Gothic, however, frequently undoes this logic, positing absolute corporeality as the ineluctible condition of masculinity and femininity alike.

The Gothic penis

When Jonathan Harker breaks into the crypt at Dracula's Transylvanian castle, he opens the vampire's coffin-lid and sees "something which filled my very soul with horror":

There lay the Count, but looking as if his youth had been half renewed ... [T]he cheeks were fuller ... [and] even the deep, burning eyes seemed set amongst swollen flesh, for the lids and pouches underneath were bloated. It seemed as if the whole awful creature were simply gorged with blood; he lay like a filthy leech, exhausted with his repletion. I shuddered as I bent over to touch him, and every sense in me revolted at the contact. (*Dracula*, p. 71)

The leech-like Count may here be described as "phallic": he is an engorged and bloated symbol of always-erect potency, triumphantly tumescent even when "exhausted with his repletion." Within these terms, he is more vigorous and commanding – more manly – than the British male characters, who are prone to indecisiveness, hysteria, and ineffectuality. Harker suffers anxiety as a "feminized" subject in contrast to Dracula's overwhelming masculinity,[9] and yet his symptoms of disgust also point towards a perhaps more unnerving relation of similarity between himself and the Count. In Dracula, Harker sees the male organ displayed in all its utter materiality. The Count may be perpetually tumescent, but he is hardly transcendently so; instead, his leech-like body-phallus is "filthy," "awful," "revolt[ing]." The Count is a Thing, and he serves as a reminder that the male organ is not a phallus but a penis, a "sign" not "of intelligence" (Goux, p. 46) but of Thing-ness – of the male subject's embodiedment and thus entrapment within the realm of matter.

Compare William Hope Hodgson's "slug-men" in *The Boats of the "Glen Carrig"*:

[T]he valley all beneath us was a-swarm with moving creatures, white and unwholesome in the moonlight, and their movements were somewhat like the movements of monstrous slugs; though the things themselves had no resemblance to such in their contours; but minded me of naked humans, very fleshy and crawling upon their stomachs . . . [T]hese things below us had each two short and stumpy arms; but the ends appeared divided into hateful and wriggling masses of small tentacles . . . and at their hinder ends, where they should have grown feet, there seemed other flickering bunches. (p. 69)

While the viscosity and "fleshiness" of the slug-men might seem to mark them as female, I would argue that they serve instead as markers of a gross, specifically masculine, corporeality. The slug-men's very "slugness" evokes the spectre of the (temporarily) flaccid penis, "rising up on end" (p. 71) and then falling again. Here the gothic penis is characterized as disgustingly magical (erecting and detumescing uncontrollably) and disgustingly adhesive and damp (the slug-men leave a slime-trail, a semen-trail, on the ground beneath them and the bodies of their victims) – as having an "uncanny" quality more typically ascribed, in psychoanalysis, to the female genitalia. The gothic affect of the slug-men/penis-men is intensified through repetition: thousands swarm up the cliff, each with "wriggling masses of small tentacles" at either end of its body. However, in *Glen Carrig* the "multiplication of penis symbols" denotes not castration anxiety, as Freud would have it ("Medusa's Head," p. 212), but the excessive quality of male embodiedment, the abject suchness of male materiality.

Fractured sexualities

The tree was quivering through every branch, muttering for blood, and helpless with rooted feet, yearning with every branch towards me . . . Every part of it was hysterical with excitement. The agitation of its members was awful – sickening yet fascinating. In an ecstasy of eagerness for the food so near them, the leaves turned upon each other. Two meeting would suck together face to face . . . now grappling in a volute like a double shell, writhing like some green worm, and at last faint with the violence of the paroxysm, would slowly separate, falling apart as leeches gorged drop off the limbs. A sticky dew glistened in the dimples, welled over, and trickled down the leaf . . . Here a large leaf, vampire-like, had sucked out the juices of a smaller one. It hung limp and bloodless, like a carcase of which the weasel has tired. (Phil Robinson, "The Man-Eating Tree," pp. 9–10)

It is impossible to avoid reading Robinson's half-comic, half-Gothic account of a British traveler's encounter with a man-eating tree in other than sexual terms, and yet one does not quite know how to proceed. In its voluptuous, writhing stickiness, the tree – hung all over with "glorious golden ovals, great honeydrops, swelling by their own weight into pear-shaped translucencies" (p. 2) – appears to be coded female. And yet the tree could be said to ejaculate: "It strained, shivered, rocked and heaved . . . I felt the vile dew spurting from the tense veins fall on me" (p. 11). The tree again seems female when its trunk is described as a great "soft body," "shudder[ing]" and "quiver[ing]" beneath the manly blows of the protagonist (p. 11). And yet this trunk is unmistakably phallic in appearance as well, rising "upright" from amidst its fallen boughs, "dripping at every joint" and "glistening" (p. 12). The scene is rounded out by not only a violent moment of sexual climax, but also a sort of post-coital lassitude which overtakes both parties: "I made a rush forward over the fallen foliage, and with a last paroxysm of frenzy drove my knife up to the handle into the soft bole, and, slipping on the fast congealing sap, fell, exhausted and unconscious, among the still panting leaves" (p. 12). The story draws wildly and indiscriminately from the available field of sexual conventions, and in doing so serves utterly to confuse that field. The tree is both "male" and "female," but in being both it is neither. The body of the tree is imbued with sexuality – it glistens and drips with it, spurts it – but its sexuality cannot be specified.

Hodgson's "The Voice in the Night" details the transformation of the distinctive human form into a "thing" (p. 166) half-vegetable and half-animal, discernible as both "an extraordinarily shaped mass of fungus" and "the figure of a distorted human creature" (p. 166). As the protagonist concludes his story of the metamorphosis that has overtaken himself and his fiancée, he interrupts himself with the lament, "Only – only we had been man and maid!" (p. 167). Similarly, Wells' "The Sea Raiders" details the dissolution of the distinctive human form into sheer materiality, as it becomes a "fragment of food," a "pinkish object" (pp. 652, 653), a thing so indefinite one cannot tell "whether . . . [it is] a man or woman" (p. 653). In neither of these texts is the question of sexual difference particularly foregrounded, but nonetheless each passage points towards a crucial component of abhumanness: the loss of human sexual specificity. A "fully human" identity requires the subject to be one thing or the other, male or female, the essential qualities of each defined through their relation of contradistinction. To take on the non-identity of a Thing is to be removed from the traditional field of sexual difference, to become an It, rather than a him or her.

In Wells' story the human body is simply evacuated of all meaningfulness, including that supplied by sexual distinctness. More usually within the

fin-de-siècle Gothic, however, the pronoun "it" by no means denotes the
cancellation or neutralization of sexuality. The condition of It-ness
instead signals a proliferation and confusion of sexual identities and
behaviors. These may lie within the still recognizably human field of
sexual perversion as described by nineteenth-century sexology. Sexually
aggressive or phallic women, homosexual or sexually violent men, may
be read as pathological types of the sort elaborated within sexology,
particularly the literature on sexual inversion which detailed the chaos
resulting when attributes "proper" to one sex manifested themselves in
the other.[10] Sexology attempted to stabilize the meanings of sexuality,
carefully classifying the types and degrees of perversion against which a
normative sexual subject would stand out in relief.[11] Nonetheless,
through its very elaboration of perversions, sexology served to multiply
sexual possibilities, demonstrating the alarmingly wide range of sexual
behaviors of which a human (or perhaps not-quite-human) body was
capable.[12] Human sexuality thus emerges as both a chaotic field and a
field of limitless potentiality, wherein gendered behaviors conflict with
sexual identities, and desire is fluctuable and indiscriminate, marking out
a variety of inappropriate object-choices.

As recent criticism of the genre makes clear, the desiring economies
found within the *fin-de-siècle* Gothic are highly unstable ones, throwing
into confusion such essentialist constructs as "normal masculinity" and
"normal femininity." The sense of nausea inspired by Mr. Hyde, for
example, can be traced to a variety of sexual meanings: a horror of
femininity, of which hateful identity Hyde's body bears traces; anxiety
about the potential violence and pathology of heterosexual masculinity,
which Hyde's behavior throws into relief; or ambivalence about "the
love that dare not speak its name," the unspeakable possibility of male
homosexuality raised by the mysterious intimacy between Jekyll and
Hyde.[13] Similarly, vampirism in *Dracula* has been read as a device
whereby to explore, in hysterical fashion, the meanings of female
sexuality, heterosexual relations, and sexual inversion.[14]

Note the capacious nature of the representations that support such
seemingly contradictory interpretations. Abhuman entities must of
necessity confound traditional sexual identities. They are simultaneously
male and female, masculine and feminine, heterosexual and homosexual
– metamorphic as to sexed identity, indiscriminate as to both gendered
behavior and object-choice.

Afterword

CHAPTER 8

Narrative chaos

More than half-way through *The Devil-Tree of El Dorado*, Jack Templemore is finally enlightened as to the terrible secret that haunts the people of Manoa. The corrupt priesthood of this degenerate kingdom has been maintaining its power by sacrificing citizens to the anthropophagous tree. The reader will not be surprised by this outcome – an illustration of a writhing human body encoiled within the tentacles of the tree faces the title-page of the book – but the revelation of the secret is nonetheless played to great dramatic effect. Templemore, "oppressed by a dim unshapen foreshadowing of some new and nameless horror," watches breathlessly as a "*something*" is regurgitated from the maw of the tree and passed about the mobile and twisting branches (p. 249, emphasis in text). The text lingers over the details of Templemore's sickness and pallor as he finally recognizes the obvious – "Great heavens! *It is a human body!*" (p. 250; emphasis in text) – and lingers as well over the death-agonies of the next human victim selected by the tree and consumed "with an awful deliberation and absence of hurry" (p. 252).

All of this should be enough, to quote the review of *Devil-Tree* mentioned in chapter 2, "to satisfy the most *blasé* amateur of the gruesome." Into a single scene, unfolded by means of a heightened gothic rhetoric of indefinition and suspense, are condensed the themes of gothic nature, the Thing-ness of the consumed human body, spectatorial nausea, and white barbarism or degeneracy (signaled by the practice of human sacrifice). And yet Aubrey goes the extra mile, so to speak, for his reader. In between the tree's disgorging of one victim and consumption of the next are intruded new horrors:

Meantime, from out the dark and filthy water and thick slime of the large pool a few hundred yards away, crawled uncouth monsters the like of which Templemore had never looked upon, save, perhaps, in some fanciful representations of creatures said to have existed in pre-historic times. These mis-shapen reptiles were from ten to twelve feet in length. They had heads and tails like crocodiles . . . but in place of the usual scales they were covered with large horny plates several inches in diameter; and in the centre of each plate was a strong spine or spike, thick at the base but sharp at the point . . . These creatures crawled up to the fateful tree; and it was quickly evident that they came to claim their share in the foul repast – the dry husk and bones from which the tree had sucked the rest. (p. 250)

Note the precision with which the reptiles are described – the length of the plate, the shape of the spike; the text goes on to describe with equal precision the interaction of the reptiles with the tree, an interaction discussed as symbiotic and thus fully consistent with the laws of natural selection and species adaptation. Within an already overdetermined scenario, the text opens and expands to include yet another overdetermined instance, and a carefully elaborated instance at that, of horrific natural phenomena: a prehistoric survival marked by species indifferentiation and metonymically associated with the filth and slime that characterize its habitat.

Gratuitousness

These scavenging reptiles serve as an example of what I will call gratuitous gothicity. The awkward transition "Meantime . . ." which introduces the reptiles signals a slight rupture in narrative coherence, a break in an otherwise tightly plotted scene whereby Aubrey pauses to pile on the details of a secondary, or supplemental, instance of gothic embodiment. These reptiles emerge from the novel as *in excess*: an example of disgusting gothicity generated sheerly for its own sake, for the pleasures of bodying forth nature in still another grotesque form.

Compare a throwaway moment towards the conclusion of Hodgson's *The Boats of the "Glen Carrig"*. The castaways have sent out a line from the island to the trapped ship, and are working to pull the *Seabird* from the Sargasso weed. As they haul on the rope, the narrator notices "a commotion amid the weed," and sees that "the rope had freed itself from the weed, and, clutching it, were, maybe, a score of giant crabs" (p. 86). The reader is by this time fairly inured to the spectacle of giant crabs, having earlier witnessed an extended battle between "an enormous crab . . . a prodigy unsurpassed" (p. 51) and several sailors who narrowly escape becoming its prey. Furthermore, the appearance of twenty giant crabs clutching the rope is wholly unnecessary to the advancement of the plot, and the scene is played to little dramatic effect. No one is eaten or even in danger of being eaten; the ship's sailors fire their guns at the crabs, which drop back into the water, and the rescue of the *Seabird* proceeds smoothly on course. It is as if Hodgson, having invented giant Sargasso crabs, cannot resist a last massification of them; they erupt from the pages of the novel and quickly disappear again, another instance of gratuitous – and in its own way, pleasing – gothicity.

Or compare Marsh's short story "A Psychological Experiment" (1900).[1] Here one Andrew Rolt is literally frightened to death by his ex-business partner Douglas Colston, whom he attempted to murder. Disguised as a "stranger" of "monstrous" girth (p. 2), Colston confronts Rolt in a smoking-room. As he reminds Rolt of the details of his crime Colston slowly undoes his outer garments. From his pockets emerge "hideous things . . . efts, newts, lizards, various crawling creatures" (p. 4). From his overcoat falls "another horde of crawling creatures," which drop "like lumps of jelly on to the floor" and lie there in "a wriggling mass" (p. 7). Beneath the overcoat is an oilskin, writhing with obscene life, and from this "gush[es] forth . . . an amazing mass of hissing, struggling, twisting serpents" (p. 9). While the room comes alive with an impossible number of swarming reptiles – far more than the most capacious overclothes could ever hold – Rolt is entangled in the "quivering tentacles" of a squid-like creature that leaps out from a modified jack-in-the-box (p. 17). The revenge plot is clearly a slender pretext that allows Marsh to present the startling image of a man whose body disgorges reptiles, and steadily to develop the effect generated by the multiplication of slimy, writhing monstrosities. As a psychological study (unless, perhaps, the reader is the object of the "psychological experiment"), the story is hardly notable; as a spectacle of absurd excess, it is remarkable.

Earlier I described the *fin-de-siècle* Gothic as a genre marked by both attraction towards and aversion from the object of its obsession, occluding that object through mechanisms of textual hysteria, and yet compelled by the prospect of abhuman becomings. While the genre manifests horror and nausea at every turn, it nonetheless labors, as in the examples given above, to aggravate and multiply instances of gothic embodiment. The seeming gratuitousness of this labor may be likened to Dr. Moreau's. Moreau produces monstrosities simply because he wishes and is able to do so. The technologies at hand allow him to test "the extreme limit of plasticity in a living shape," and the manipulation of bodies gratifies his "intellectual desires" (p. 75). Similarly, the Gothic seizes upon the opportunity at hand – the evacuation of human identity accomplished within the sciences – in order to experiment with the "plasticity" of human and other bodies. The genre hardly manifests the calm detachment of Dr. Moreau, who speaks of his "strange colorless delight" (p. 75) in the spectacle of morphic chaos. The Gothic's very hysteria testifies to its disgust for that spectacle, and its nostalgia for that "fully human" identity whose passing it marks. And yet its hysteria should also be seen as a form of delirium, wherein pleasure predominates as much as nausea, and indeed the two emotions cannot be separated. The genre's "delight" in morphic chaos is not "colorless," but it is nonetheless as speculative and experimental as Moreau's. What the Gothic demonstrates is that there are no limits to the plasticity of form: any morphic trait can be admixed with any other; any body can be shapen or distorted to, and past, its "extreme limit."

Darwinism especially had opened the door to this kind of speculation, with its theorizing of the absolute fluctuability of morphic structures. Darwin's is a scenario wherein functionality is the only criterion for a species' success, so that abominable bodies are no less "fit" than seemingly integral ones. And in fact no body is integral, for a crucial component of species functionality is morphic flexibility; the most successful species are the most variable ones. The Darwinian narrative, moreover, describes an ordering and re- or disordering of bodies that occurs randomly, governed by chance rather than providential or other design. Thus the plastic Thing-ness of organic matter – its tendency towards some organization, any organization[2] – can be molded according to a limitless number of narrative possibilities.

Darwinian natural selection, in other words, is a process both excessive and gratuitous: capable of producing a dense range of bodily forms, more than are needed or can be imagined, and producing these within no meaningful plot structure, but only as accident arranges. Texts like *Moreau*, or the fictions of parallel evolution, incorporate the Darwinian narrative by "thematizing" the randomness and gothic fertility of evolutionary processes: Moreau's "wanton," sheerly experimental manipulation of bodily structures, parallel to Nature's, is a plot device whereby the novel can generate a striking variety of morphic abominations. While the novel as a formal structure does not resist containment within a traditional field of meaningfulness – *Moreau* is readily legible as allegory, Swiftean satire,[3] and so forth – it is nonetheless designed to produce gothicity in excess, to maximize both instances of abhuman embodiment and the nauseating affect which these occasion.

The Gothic picaresque

[T]here we were, standing up against the blank, unknowable night, and out there in the darkness there surely lurked some thing of monstrousness; and we were at its mercy. I seemed to feel it hovering – hovering over us, so that I felt the sickening creep of gooseflesh all over me . . . [M]y imagination began to awaken to horrible discomforts; a thousand dreadful impossibilities of the sea became suddenly possible . . . I remember how the lamps made just two yellow glares in the mist, ineffectual, yet serving somehow to make extraordinarily plain the vastitude of the night and the *possibilities of the dark*. (Hodgson, "The Thing in the Weeds," pp. 65–7; emphasis in text)

Other instances of the genre utilize the Darwinian narrative in a more subtle, but more extensive, way. Novels like *The Boats of the "Glen Carrig"* and *The Three Imposters*, as well as thematizing, like *Moreau*, the randomness of evolutionary processes, incorporate randomness into their narrative structures, elevating contingency into an organizing – or rather, disorganizing – principle of narrative. Their narrative movement is like that of the Darwinian "picaresque" discussed in chapter 5: non-directive, non-telic, governed by happenstance rather than design. The picaresque narrative of natural selection is one without intrinsic meaningfulness. One circumstance follows another, and a rich density of intricate forms is produced (I use the passive construction deliberately) accidentally; the process continues indefinitely. In the Gothic picaresque, one nauseating gothic incident follows another, one morphic abomination follows another. The placement or sequence of events is without significance, and only the need for textual closure[4] checks a narrative movement which proceeds by means of addition ("and . . . and . . . and"). It is difficult to wrest meaning from such a narrative, which seems to accomplish little more than a demonstration of the gothic potentialities of the changeful material world.

The Boats of the "Glen Carrig" is introduced by a preface, identifying the narrator ("John Witherstraw, Gent."), the date of his narration (1757), and its subject: "Being an account of their Adventures in the Strange Places of the Earth, after the foundering of the good ship *Glen Carrig* through striking upon a hidden rock in the unknown seas to the Southward" (p. 3). The novel proper, however, gives no account of the voyage of the Glen Carrig or the shipwreck. It opens quite abruptly: "Now we had been five days in the [life]boats . . ." (p. 4). The novel does not "begin at the beginning," in other words, introducing characters and delineating the sequence of causes that instantiated their "Adventures in the Strange Places of the Earth." Instead it begins in a state of drift, its protagonists already wandering aimlessly through "unknown seas," and proceeds accordingly, as the elements drive the men, in no particular direction and with no particular purpose, from one site to another. *And then* we found the island of man-eating trees, *and then* we were nearly eaten by a giant octopus, *and then* we were nearly eaten by a giant crab, *and then* we were nearly eaten by the slug-men . . .

Nor is the sequence of gothic events of importance. When they visit the "continent" of the man-eating trees, the castaways board a derelict ship and find the fragments of a journal written by one of its dead passengers. This woman had recorded her panicked thoughts on "gray paper wrappers, such as are used, I believe, for carrying samples of corn," and these wrappers are "all oddly numbered, and having but little reference one to the other" (p. 13). George the cabin-boy begins reading them in haphazard order, but is interrupted by a tree-attack: "there had come at the glass of the unbroken window, a reddish mass, which plunged up against it, sucking upon it, as it were . . . I saw that it had the appearance of a many-flapped thing shaped as it might be, out of raw beef – *but it was alive*" (p. 15, emphasis in text).

George escapes with only one random sheet of the journal, which serves as the final installment of the woman passenger's story for lack of a "proper" conclusion. That is, the woman's terrible narrative, as the novel presents it, is out of sequence, disjointed, and incomplete. The audience nonetheless – George's and Hodgson's audience both – knows exactly what it needs to know. An "indescribable Thing" made search through the ship (p. 14). The crew was eaten. The diarist was eaten. The natural world teems with abominations.

The narrative movement of *The Boats of the "Glen Carrig"* is like that Wells described in the quote which begins chapter 5, where he compares the progression of evolution to "the course of a busy man moving about a great city," doubling and twisting about in no discernible "pattern." Or rather, if there is a pattern in *"Glen Carrig"* – if anything unifies its plot strung together of disjointed gothic events – it is the non-pattern of disorder. The mariners drift through a gothicized Nature, filled with Thing-ness and always threatening to draw the human subject into the field of Thing-ness. Moving at random, they encounter one abomination after another, and are racked with horror and nausea. The novel does not seek to infuse these abominations with meaningfulness (the man-eating trees signify suchly; the giant crabs signify suchly): they simply *exist*, the disgusting products of a natural world both chaotic and fertile in expedient. *The Boats of the "Glen Carrig"*, that is, makes no attempt to contain the disorderly natural world it describes; its narrative structure is rather such as can elaborate that disorder with as much variety and detail as possible. All gothicity is gratuitous in *"Glen Carrig"*, in the sense that its gothic incidents, taken separately or as a whole, point towards nothing except the random meaninglessness of the abominable material world – and in the sense that the novel offers its reader no "moral," only the strange pleasures of nausea, intensified through narrative repetition.

8.1 *THE THREE IMPOSTERS*: ARTHUR MACHEN'S URBAN *CHAOSMOS*

In the quotation from "Zoological Retrogression" discussed above, H. G. Wells describes evolution as an aimless and directionless process, serving but to produce an endless array of complex, yet meaningless, forms. The natural world, we may conclude, is a teeming chaos – but one should not expect that a move from the realm of nature to that of human culture would afford any guarantees of orderliness or meaningfulness.[5] For in elaborating the randomness of the narrative of evolution, Wells looks to the city for his primary metaphor. As natural selection produces a rich array of morphic configurations, so does the modern city breed an intricate variety of human activity and interaction. It is a fertile matrix of narratives – but these are not necessarily orderly, telic, or meaningful narratives. The urban space is a dangerous space of flux, wherein social identities may be undone and remade, and wherein seemingly limitless numbers and types of social interchanges are possible amidst a dense and heterogenous population. And while inhabitants of the city may set out on courses fixed by their own design and purpose, their movements shall nonetheless be redirected according to the logic of contingency, their trajectories disturbed by the sorts of accidental, unexpected encounters that are inevitable within the chaos of the city.

Shifting the frame of reference slightly, one may read the city as an *unheimlich* space: familiar and yet alien, labyrinthine, unknowable. To quote Machen's novel *The Three Imposters*, modern London is as darkly mysterious "as Libya and Pamphylia and the parts about Mesopotamia" (p. 335). *The Three Imposters* deploys two strategies for negotiating the urban labyrinth, the first of which corresponds roughly to picaresque narration. Its two protagonists meet "from one of those myriad chances which are every day doing their work in the streets of London" (p. 233), and henceforth the novel unfolds through a series of impossible coincidences: contingency is the organizing, or rather disorganizing, principle of narrative structure. The frame plot is of three "imposters," who change identities to fit the occasion, and their pursuit of a hapless "young man with spectacles," but this plot is extraordinarily difficult to reconstruct. As the two protagonists Dyson and Phillipps, idle *flaneurs*, wander through London and encounter these other principals accidentally, the frame plot is interrupted by a series of intricate interpolated gothic stories, narrated by the imposters ostensibly to further their pursuit of their victim, but in actuality, I will argue, simply for the pleasure of astonishing and nauseating their conversants.

As one moves randomly through the city, in other words, it generates a strange variety of elaborate stories, but these stories lead nowhere, "mean" nothing, produce nothing but sensational affect. *The Three Imposters* at times seems to offer itself as such an instance of a meaningless text, which circumnavigates the chaotic space of London but makes no attempt to organize it (as *The Boats of the "Glen Carrig"* circumnavigates the chaotic space of Nature but makes no attempt to organize it). But this strategy of picaresque narration is at other times counterposed with the paranoiac mode of narration that more usually characterizes the Gothic. Within a paranoiac epistemology, there is no such thing as coincidence: chance encounters are signs that point towards a dark and occluded reality underlying the ordinary one. "Dyson saw at once that by a succession of hazards he had unawares hit upon the scent of some desperate conspiracy, wavering as the track of a loathsome snake in and out of the highways and byways of the London cosmos . . . he divined that all unconscious and unheeding he had been privileged to see the shadows of hidden forms, chasing and hurrying, and grasping and vanishing across the bright curtain of common life" (p. 336). *The Three Imposters* veers between these two possibilities: of an urban *chaosmos* that cannot be brought to order through narrative and other conventional strategies of organization; and of a gothicized city, whose only order or meaningfulness is as an abjected space.

Gothic London

A great chocolate-coloured pall [of fog] lowered over heaven . . . Utterson beheld a marvelous number of degrees and hues of twilight; for here it would be dark like the backend of evening; and there would be a glow of a rich, lurid brown, like the light of some strange conflagration; and here, for a moment . . . a haggard shaft of daylight would glance in between the swirling wreaths. The dismal quarter of Soho seen under these changing glimpses, with its muddy ways, and slatternly passengers, and its lamps, which had never been extinguished or had been kindled afresh to combat this mournful reinvasion of darkness, seemed, in the lawyer's eyes, like a district of some city in a nightmare. (Robert Louis Stevenson, *Dr. Jekyll and Mr. Hyde*, p. 62)

The neighborhood was badly lighted. It was one in which I was a stranger . . . In the darkness and the rain, the locality which I was entering appeared unfinished. I seemed to be leaving civilization behind me. The path was unpaved; the road rough and uneven, as if it had never been properly made. Houses were few and far between. Those which I did encounter, seemed, in the imperfect light, amid the general desolation, to be cottages which were crumbling to decay. (Richard Marsh, *The Beetle*, p. 446)

The metropolis, historian Judith R. Walkowitz argues, was understood as a dangerous and yet attractive space by the Victorian middle class – as a "dark, powerful, and seductive labyrinth."[6] Perhaps no discourse better illustrates this ambivalent response to the fascinating loathsomeness of the city than that produced by the late-Victorian "social explorers." These middle-class reformers – sociologists, urban missionaries, government agents, journalists – founded their discussions of urban poverty upon a central conceit: that the slum neighborhoods of London were as little known, mysterious, and fearsome as the most obscure reaches of the colonies.[7] In *How the Poor Live* (1883), for instance, George R. Sims "record[s] the result of a journey into a region which lies at our own doors – into a dark continent that is within easy walking distance of the General Post Office."[8] The power of the simile, later elaborated at great length by William Booth's *In Darkest England and the Way Out* (1890), lies in its figuring of London as *unheimlich*: the familiar, well-charted city is revealed as absolutely unfamiliar; the civilized capital of the great Empire is a chaotic space of barbarism and darkness. "[S]eething in the very centre of our great cities, concealed by the thinnest crust of civilization and decency, is a vast mass of moral corruption, of heart-breaking misery and absolute godlessness," writes Andrew Mearns in his 1883 *The Bitter Cry of Outcast London, An Enquiry into the Condition of the Abject Poor* (Keating, p. 92).

Many critics have discussed the combination of disgust and fascination with which the Victorian middle-class subject turned its gaze upon the poor, who were regarded as dangerous, yet intriguing, agents of physical and moral contamination.[9] The rhetoric of the social explorers could only heighten disgust and fascination alike by figuring the slum dweller as an exotic "native" – savage, brutish, driven by animalistic passions.[10] What interests me as well, however, is the way in which this rhetoric constructs the urban slum as an undifferentiated space: an "awful slough," as Mearns describes it, a "seething ... mass" without structure or proper form. As such it resists and exceeds language: the social explorer's quite particularized descriptions of the filthy bodies, houses, and streets of the urban poor are punctuated by assertions that words could never convey the extent and nature of the horrors under consideration – a strategy typical of the *fin-de-siècle* Gothic text, like *The Three Imposters*, which veers back and forth between the most graphic scenes of bodily mutilation and transformation and a vague rhetoric of the ineffable. For certain of the social explorers, particularly the urban missionaries like Mearns, this undifferentiated space is not entirely chaotic, for it can be made to yield a definite (albeit negative) meaning, of "misery, squalor, and immorality" (p. 92). But even writers like Mearns, confronted by this inchoate mass which neither language nor statistical analysis can bring to order, may find it easier to produce affect rather than meaningfulness from the "awful slough." All of the social explorers emphasize, in varying degrees, the thrilling pathos, the shocking brutality, of the urban slums and their inhabitants, from which an endless number of sensational stories can be extracted. Like the *fin-de-siècle* Gothic authors who specialize in the gratuitous elaboration of sensational affect, the social explorers, failing to make sense of the labyrinthine city, offer instead the dubious, intense pleasures of the narrative of horror.

In the *fin-de-siècle* Gothic novel, however, it is the entire metropolis itself, not just its relatively delimited slum neighborhoods, that is figured alternately as a labyrinth, a "seething mass," an "awful slough," an uncharted wasteland. The Gothic certainly does not scruple from identifying the urban slums as sites of especial abjection: as with the surreal Soho neighborhood, "like a district of some city in a nightmare," described in the quote from *Jekyll and Hyde* above; the dockside opium dens of *The Picture of Dorian Gray*; the "waste void" of the squalid neighborhood, "one of the foulest slums of Clerkenwell," in which Walters (*The Three Imposters*' "young man with spectacles") is run to ground (pp. 334, 337). However, perfectly respectable neighborhoods may be sites of chaos and abjection as well, like the unfinished Hammersmith building project in which *The Beetle*'s Robert Holt is entrapped and tortured, described in the quotation above, or suburban Purfleet, home to both Count Dracula's decrepit Carfax estate and Dr. Seward's insane asylum. Dyson first encounters the imposters in a "genteel residential neighbourhood of stucco and prosperity," somewhere near Tottenham Court Road (pp. 235–6). As Dyson describes it, "a man is sauntering along a quiet, sober, everyday London street, a street of grey houses and blank walls, and there, for a moment, a veil seems drawn aside, and the very fume of the pit steams up through the flagstones, the ground glows, red-hot, beneath his feet, and he seems to hear the hiss of the infernal cauldron" (p. 238).[11]

Narrativizing the Gothic city

Dr. Lipsius: "I have often heard very young men maintain that style is everything in literature, and I can assure you that the same maxim holds good in our far more delicate profession. With us style is absolutely everything, and that is why we have friends like yourself."

Walters: "I foresaw that if I fell into his [Lipsius'] hands, he would remain true to his doctrine of style, and cause me to die a death of some horrible and ingenious torture . . . I hardly dare to guess how it will at last fall upon me; my imagination, always a vivid one, paints to me appalling pictures of the unspeakable torture which I shall probably endure . . ." (*The Three Imposters*, pp. 342, 348)

All art is quite useless. (Oscar Wilde, "Preface" to *The Picture of Dorian Gray*)

What Dyson finds in this "genteel neighborhood" into which he has accidentally wandered is a story in progress: when he sees one man, chased by another, fling away an object, Dyson procures the object from his hiding place, and later identifies it as an extremely rare gold coin, the only one remaining from "an issue struck by Tiberius to commemorate an infamous excess" (p. 237). Dyson and the reader will discover much later that the pursued man is in fact Walters, the doomed young man with spectacles. Walters is a would-be scholar who meets a certain Dr. Lipsius in the British Library and is seduced by him into following "the science and art of pleasure" (p. 339) – which involves, among other things, the practice of orgiastic pagan rituals in "a house of quiet and respectable aspect in a street lying to the north of Oxford Street" (p. 340). Walters is enlisted, without his knowledge, to help murder the dealer who carries the gold Tiberius; when he discovers the man's corpse embalmed in an Egyptian mummy case, he flees in horror, accidentally grabbing the valuable Tiberius on his way out, and is thenceforth tracked by the three imposters, emissaries of Lipsius.

Note that this particular narrative strand of *The Three Imposters*, the story of Walters (to which approximately one-tenth of the novel is devoted), is already much too densely and sensationally plotted to summarize with any economy, and I have not even finished with it. It is as if one might wander into any London neighborhood at any moment – Dyson is "addicted" to "aimless walks" through the city (p. 350) – and stumble onto fantastic tales in progress, of orgies, murders, corpses in mummy cases, dramatic pursuits. And indeed, this is how the novel is structured (though its "structure" is of the loosest sort). The city yields narrative, wildly sensational narrative, at every turn. Dyson and Phillipps stroll idly about the city, each man following a random trajectory much like that described by the Wells quote which begins chapter 5, and meet in separate encounters the three imposters. The imposters regale them with lurid gothic stories – for instance, of the young law student who imbibes a mysterious potion and gradually deliquesces into slime; of Dr. Gregg's fatal encounter with savage Celtic survivals who possess the power of reversion[12] – and use their stories as an excuse to inquire as to whether their interlocutor has by chance met up with a young man with spectacles. The imposter sometimes weaves this inquiry into the interpolated story with skill, but at other times makes almost no attempt to do so. Since certain textual evidence supports the case that Dyson's and Phillipps' encounters with the imposters are truly coincidental, Machen's reader can only assume that the imposters are circulating through London telling thrilling stories to *everyone* they meet, using as their excuse the quite slender chance that a random passer-by has seen the young man with spectacles.

However, the reader familiar with traditional narrative conventions – that plots unfold logically, or at least reasonably; that elaborate sub-plots will be integrated into the overall plot, or at least will not remain entirely gratuitous; that stories yield morals, or at least a degree of meaningfulness – may not be able to assume this at all. Other textual evidence supports an alternate reading, that Dyson's and Phillipps' encounters with the imposters are the result of some far-reaching design set in motion by Lipsius and his crew, and the reader's very desire for narrative order may render this alternative the more appealing one. Lipsius has control of a terrible "machine," says Walters, a "relentless mechanism" of espionage and surveillance (pp. 342, 347). Walters' language here brings to mind the "infernal machines" that play such a crucial role in Fanny and Robert Louis Stevenson's *The Dynamiter* (1885), whose narrative structure (sensational interpolated tales held loosely in place by an equally sensational frame plot) is said to have served as a model for *The Three Imposters*. Set in London, "the city of encounters, the Bagdad of the

West," *The Dynamiter* is also a picaresque of sorts, unfolding through a series of accidents and coincidences. "Chance, the blind Madonna of the pagan, rules this terrestrial bustle . . . Chance has brought us three together . . . Chance will continually drag before our careless eyes a thousand eloquent clues, not to this mystery only, but to the countless mysteries by which we live surrounded."[13]

But what "Chance" and the three protagonists of *The Dynamiter* uncover is the nefarious plot of a group of terrorists, possibly Fenians, working to place bombs throughout the city. That these dynamiters are essentially comic bumblers should not obviate the fact that the threat of urban terrorism was perceived as a very real one at the *fin de siècle*.[14] The anxious perception of London as a *chaosmos* – a space of meaningless noise, activity, sensation in which narratives indiscriminately crowd one another and no one narrative has any more significance than the next – has its inverse in the paranoid fantasy of a London whose *seeming* indifferentiation masks a network of deeply-laid and infernal designs. The very swarming disorder of the metropolis might seem instrumental to the paranoid, for that disorder can be used to the advantage of terrorist agents like the Stevensons' dynamiters and Machen's imposters, who continually shift identities and interweave schemes under cover of the anonymity of the city. Fictions such as *The Beetle*, *Dracula*, and Guy Boothby's *Pharos the Egyptian* (1899) must be placed within this tradition of paranoid plotting as well, although in these cases it is a supernaturalized foreigner who plots out atrocities while safely hidden within the chaos of London.

One Victorian narrative tradition uses the device of the chance urban encounter to quite different, relatively benign ends. In novels like *Villette* and *Dombey and Son*, there is no such thing as coincidence; accidental meetings serve eventually to reveal that all subjects are interrelated, and that their every action, however secretly performed, will have very visible consequences, punishments, and rewards. One might say that this tradition initially figures the urban space (Brontë's Brussels, Dickens' London) as a gothic one,[15] but then reorganizes that space into a highly ordered and meaningfully human community. But in novels like *The Three Imposters*, the ordering principle underlying the seeming chaos of the city is a horrific one. Coincidences are not coincidences: they represent instead another click of the "relentless mechanism" that invisibly controls the hapless, doomed urban subject.

The Fenians want Irish independence; Dracula hopes to beget a new "race" and form an empire; the Beetle-Woman and Pharos are engaged in schemes of revenge against the West. These are at least recognizable motives, which might seem to justify a paranoiac figuration of the city as a site organized by the intrigues and machinations of the unscrupulous. But what are the goals of Lipsius' far-reaching and all-powerful organization? Its members engage in arcane sexual pleasures, they pursue victims and murder them artistically, they collect rare artifacts. "With us style is absolutely everything," as Lipsius tells Walters (p. 342): the imposters are indeed conspirators if decadents in relentless and organized pursuit of sensation can be said to be conspirators.

What I am arguing here is that neither *The Three Imposters* nor the urban *chaosmos* through which it wanders can finally be brought to order through the paranoiac reading which the novel seems to encourage. The novel stands in slightly parodic relation to both gothicism and aestheticism;[16] the one tradition emphasizes the production of affect, the other, the practice of style. Dyson insists early on that the "literary man . . . has got to do simply this – to invent a wonderful story, and to tell it in a wonderful manner." But Phillipps counters that "in the hands of the true artist in words all stories are marvelous and every circumstance has its peculiar wonder. The matter is of little consequence; the manner is everything" (pp. 233–4). They are hardly in disagreement, though Dyson privileges content and Phillipps form, for Dyson demands a "wonderful" narrative content and Phillipps a "marvelous" narrative style. Each demands sensation, in other words, and each happily receives it from the tales of the imposters.

For the most important thing that the three imposters do is tell stories – lurid and intricate horror stories, detailed, graphic, utterly and yet pleasingly disgusting – which serve to further their ostensible designs not one whit. Their story-telling is a gratuitous act. As Dyson would have it, the imposters' tales are utterly fantastic; as Phillipps would have it, they make no "sense" and turn out to be brilliant formal exercises, produced sheerly for the pleasures of narrativization. This is what one must finally say about the novel as a whole. It stands in opportunistic relation to the urban *chaosmos* it explores, identifying London as a dense and clamorous space from which to extract sensation, incident, narrative. But it cannot and will not organize that space in any meaningful way. The novel begins and ends with Dyson's and Phillipps' discovery of a corpse:

A naked man was lying on the floor, his arms and legs stretched wide apart, and bound to pegs that had been hammered into the boards. The body was torn and mutilated in the most hideous fashion, scarred with the marks of red-hot irons, a shameful ruin of the human shape. But upon the middle of the body a fire of coals was smouldering; the flesh had been burnt through. The man was dead, but the smoke of this torment mounted still, a black vapour.

"The young man with spectacles," said Mr. Dyson. (p. 353)

The intricate plottings of the imposters produce but one tangible object, the artistically mutilated body of the young man with spectacles; Walters' murder is beautifully realized. The intricate plottings of the novel produce but one tangible object, the body of a reader convulsed with both laughter and disgust. *The Three Imposters*, like so many other *fin-de-siècle* Gothic texts, labors mightily to produce affect, and this, too, is beautifully realized – so much so that I myself cannot do better than to emulate *The Three Imposters* and conclude where I began, with this repulsive and yet compelling scenario of the ruination of the human subject.

Notes

INTRODUCTION: THE ABHUMAN

1 Written 1890–4; first published in its entirety 1895.
2 Hodgson uses the term "Ab-Human" in *The Night Land* (1912; see Hodgson, *"The House on the Borderland" and Other Novels*) and *Carnacki the Ghost-Finder* (1913; the individual *Carnacki* stories were published in various magazines 1910–1912). While Hodgson's "Ab-Human" at times denotes a condition of being in pure opposition to that of "the human," the opposition is continually in a state of collapse within his fiction.
3 Kristeva, *Powers of Horror*, especially pp. 1–31.
4 I have deliberately excluded consideration of Gothic literatures outside of Great Britain in order to focus on the relations of Gothic discourse to a specifically British *fin de siècle*. A secondary but significant goal of this study is to demonstrate the extraordinary density and range of British Gothic literature at the turn of the century. In discussing such discourses as criminal anthropology and degenerationism, however, it has been impossible to consider these as other than fundamentally international, albeit differently inflected within different national contexts. Whenever possible, when drawing on the work of Continental scientists, I have worked from articles translated and published by mainstream British journals.
5 For instance, George E. Haggerty argues that what essentially distinguishes the genre is its high degree of formal innovation, as the earlier Gothic, struggling to articulate a cultural sensibility at odds with that allowed within both empiricist philosophy and the more conventional novel, experimented with narrative devices whereby private or subjective experience could be figured as "external and objective reality" (*Gothic Fiction/Gothic Form*, p. 7). Haggerty's analysis credits the Gothic with being slightly in advance of the cultural mainstream, not simply responding to shifts in social realities, but also producing new modes for the perception, interpretation, and experience of social realities. Here the Gothic accomplishes not just an intensification of more mainstream discourses, as Tzvetan Todorov argues (*The Fantastic: A Structural Approach to a Literary Genre*, p. 93), but an alteration of these discourses, by transfiguring the terms of discursivity itself.
6 I use "Darwinism" to refer to the specific theory of species evolution

through natural selection. The label is more convenient than accurate; many historians of science have pointed out the fallacy of identifying natural selection as Charles Darwin's sole invention. My use of "evolutionism" includes Darwinism, and refers more generally to a range of modes of theorizing the transformations of species and human society and culture (Lamarckianism, Spencerian social evolution, degeneration theory, etc.).

7 My argument here is indebted to Margot Norris' chapter on Darwin in *Beasts of the Modern Imagination: Darwin, Nietzsche, Kafka, Ernst, and Lawrence.* What Darwin imagines, according to Norris, is a scenario in which randomness is productive, creative, capable of manufacturing highly specialized and beautifully intricate forms (pp. 26–52, especially p. 29).

8 Hélène Cixous and Catherine Clément, *The Newly Born Woman.* The quote is from Clément's essay "The Guilty One," p. 9. See also the "Exchange" between Cixous and Clément that concludes the book.

9 Armstrong, *Desire and Domestic Fiction: A Political History of the Novel*; Gagnier, *Subjectivities: A History of Self-Representation in Britain, 1832–1920.*

10 "We must make allowance for the complex and unstable process whereby discourse can be both an instrument and an effect of power, but also a hindrance, a stumbling-block, *a point of resistance and a starting point for an opposing strategy.* Discourse transmits and produces power; it reinforces it, but also undermines and exposes it, renders it fragile and makes it possible to thwart it" (*The History of Sexuality: An Introduction*, p. 101; my emphasis).

11 The collection *Third Sex, Third Gender: Beyond Sexual Dimorphism in Culture and History* is very useful on this point, particularly the editor Gilbert Herdt's introduction ("Third Sexes and Third Genders") and Gert Hekma's "'A Female Soul in a Male Body': Sexual Inversion as Gender Inversion in Nineteenth-Century Sexology."

12 *Consuming Desire: Sexual Science and the Emergence of a Culture of Abundance, 1871–1914*, pp. 49, 99. Birkin explains this contradiction within sexology as the result of the discipline's "emerge[nce] during the transition from a production-oriented to a consumer-oriented culture" (p. 14). The irony is that consumer capitalism has no investment in normalizing desire, only in identifying and exploiting the new markets that the multiplication of desiring economies produces.

13 Showalter, *Sexual Anarchy: Gender and Culture at the Fin de Siècle.*

14 Compare the model of the chaotic posthuman subject articulated by Donna J. Haraway in "A Cyborg Manifesto: Science, Technology, and Socialist-Feminism in the Late Twentieth Century." Here Haraway argues that the boundary between human and not-human has already been breached on multiple fronts. As well, Haraway is without nostalgia for the destroyed concept of "the human." A cyborgic or otherwise admixed bodily and subjective identity, she says, is not only more politically practicable, but also more pleasurable, than an integral, "fully human" one.

15 Machen, *The House of Souls*, pp. 236–7. The last three ellipses and the bracketed italic text are Machen's.

16 In its deployment of what might be called proto-modernist narrative strategies, *The Great God Pan* is an extreme, but not atypical, example of its genre. For a somewhat different treatment of *Dracula* as a proto-modernist text, see Jennifer Wicke, "Vampiric Typewriting: *Dracula* and its Media." Wicke describes Bram Stoker's 1897 novel as a "liminal modernist artifact" (p. 469) which deploys both typically nineteenth-century narrative strategies and those associated with mass-media forms of the twentieth. See also Regenia Gagnier, "Evolution and Information, or Eroticism and Everyday Life, in *Dracula* and Late Victorian Aestheticism," on *fin-de-siècle* ambivalence about the encroachments of modernity.

17 In *The Fantastic*, Todorov distinguishes between historical and theoretical genres. The former "are the result of an observation of a literary phenomenon; theoretical genres are deduced from a theory of literature" (p. 21). A study of theoretical genre (Todorov's example is Northrop Frye's *Anatomy of Criticism*) classes literature according to variations in elements which must be common to all possible works, such as mode of enunciation or subject matter; a study of historical genre, which is what this book proposes, describes the peculiarities of an historically circumscribed body of texts. See Jerry Palmer, *Potboilers: Methods, Concepts and Case Studies in Popular Fiction*, for a fuller discussion of theoretical versus historical genre, and of various studies which exemplify both approaches (pp. 116–27).

Todorov's schema has been much criticized, with the category of theoretical genre singled out as particularly troublesome in its ahistoricity. See Christine Brooke-Rose, *A Rhetoric of the Unreal: Studies in Narrative and Structure, Especially of the Fantastic*, esp. p. 62, and Adena Rosmarin, *The Power of Genre*, pp. 23–51. I use the term transhistorical (as opposed to theoretical) genre to designate a literary mode which undergoes modification across chronological boundaries but is nevertheless distinctive, like science fiction or the Gothic in general.

18 Cited in Kathleen Spencer, "Victorian Urban Gothic: The First Modern Fantastic Literature," p. 88. Spencer identifies the late-Victorian Gothic, which historical genre she situates within the transhistorical category of the fantastic, as the "urban gothic." This genre is characterized by its gothicization of the urban setting, its close relations to detective fiction, and a concern with both contemporary science and occultism.

19 See Spencer "Victorian Urban Gothic", pp. 87–90.

20 Block, "James Sully, Evolutionist Psychology, and Late Victorian Gothic Fiction"; Lawler, "Reframing *Jekyll and Hyde*: Robert Louis Stevenson and the Strange Case of Gothic Science Fiction"; Wilt, "The Imperial Mouth: Imperialism, the Gothic, and Science Fiction." For related discussions, see Patrick Brantlinger, *Rule of Darkness: British Literature and Imperialism* (chapter 8); Sandra M. Gilbert and Susan Gubar, *No Man's Land: The Place of the Woman Writer in the Twentieth Century*, vol. II (chapter 1); John L. Greenway, "Seward's Folly: *Dracula* as a Critique of 'Normal Science'"; and John R. Reed, "The Occult in Later Victorian Fiction."

21 *The Best Supernatural Tales of Arthur Conan Doyle.* Originally published in 1900,
    McClure's Magazine.
22 Samuel Hynes argues that the boundary between *fin-de-siècle* science and
    pseudoscience was a permeable one. Writers admixed discussions of "the
    findings of biology and physics" with "matters like hypnotism and telepathy,
    as though they belonged to the same order of scientific acceptibility. And it is
    one of the striking features of end-of-the-century thought that for many
    serious investigators this was indeed true ... [I]t might well follow that a kind
    of investigation which now seems quackery would be regarded as at least
    unproven, and that serious investigation [into spiritualism], under careful
    control, would seem no less reasonable than Lodge's experiments with the
    ether" (*The Edwardian Turn of Mind*, pp. 137, 141).
23 See Robert M. Philmus' introduction to *The Island of Doctor Moreau: A
    Variorum Text*, pp. xxvi–xxx.
24 *The Complete Science Fiction Treasury of H.G. Wells*, p. 157. All other references to
    Moreau use pagination from the Signet edition.
        In a scathing review of *Moreau*, P. Chalmers Mitchell accused Wells,
    among other things, of "scaring the public unduly" by claiming a scientific
    basis for the novel. "[A] multitude of experiments on skin and bone
    grafting and on transfusion of blood shows that animal-hybrids cannot be
    made in these fashions" (*The Saturday Review* 1896, pp. 368–9). Wells
    defended himself in a letter to the editor, to which Mitchell responded with
    a further rebuttal, both letters citing various authorities on tissue grafting.
    Though their debate is quite technical, it seems to have aroused a general
    public interest; Mitchell notes sourly that "Mr. Wells might be more
    grateful for the huge advertisement my criticism seems to have given his
    book" (p. 498).
25 *Jekyll and Hyde*, however, he rejects outright for its "unclear oscillation
    between science and fantasy" (*Victorian Scientific Fiction in the UK: The Discourses
    of Knowledge and Power*, p. 94).
26 Though at other times the Gothic's citations of or references to scientific
    authorities seem more like in-jokes for the knowledgeable reader. Thus Dick
    Donovan's "The Crime of the Rue Auber" (*Stories Weird and Wonderful*,
    1889), a tale of criminal hypnosis amongst the French bourgeoisie, includes a
    character named Charcot. E. D. Fawcett's 1894 *Swallowed Alive by an
    Earthquake* (1894), which both describes imperfectly evolved "lost" races and
    considers the possibility of European devolution, features an Italian
    character named Cesare Lombardo, a name surely meant to resonate with
    that of the Italian criminal anthropologist Cesare Lombroso. In both cases,
    the text signals its awareness of its own indebtedness to the relevant scientific
    authority, but makes no explicit connections for the reader.
27 Compare a pair of similar quotes. From Hodgson's "The Haunted *Jarvee*":
    "What *is* electricity? When we've got that clear it will be time to take the next
    step [into paranormal phenomena] in a more dogmatic fashion. We are but
    speculating on the coasts of a strange country of mystery" (*Carnacki*, p. 182).

From Frank Aubrey's *King of the Dead: A Weird Romance* (1903): "In your country, people are just becoming used to the telephone and phonography; yet, by your grandfathers, such things would have been regarded as downright black magic" (p. 41).

28 Greenway discusses this scene as one which "raises a fairly subtle issue in philosophy of science and a difficult issue for Seward: how to distinguish between science and pseudoscience. Even though we [modern readers] might not take the topics Van Helsing mentions seriously, reputable scientists at the time most certainly did" ("Seward's Folly," p. 222.)

29 This comprehension is dangerously incomplete, however. Witness Van Helsing's mad wife, whom he refers to only once, in a throwaway passage, as "my poor wife dead to me, but alive by Church's law, though no wits, all gone" (p. 227).

30 Articles on criminal hypnosis and criminal anthropology appeared in such mainstream journals as *Contemporary Review*, *Forum*, *The Popular Science Monthly*, and *The Spectator*.

1. THE REVENGE OF MATTER

1 Hodgson, *Deep Waters* (reprint of *Men of Deep-Waters*, 1914). I have been unable to ascertain the original magazine publication date of "The Crew of the *Lancing*."

2 For other arguments linking monstrosity and liminality, see Noël Carroll, *The Philosophy of Horror, or Paradoxes of the Heart*; Stephen Prince, "Dread, Taboo and *The Thing*: Toward a Social Theory of the Horror Film"; Kathleen L. Spencer, "Purity and Danger: *Dracula*, the Urban Gothic, and the Late Victorian Degeneracy Crisis"; and Eric White, "The Erotics of Becoming: *Xenogenesis* and *The Thing*."

3 Cf. the conclusion of Prince's "Dread, Taboo and *The Thing*": "[T]he horror film addresses the persistent question of what must be done to remain human. By presenting the question in its negative form, by dealing with the loss of the human, the doubts informing human identity may be for the moment exorcised, and the validity and arrangement of the established social categories may be affirmed" (p. 28).

4 My argument here has benefitted from Eric White's in "The Erotics of Becoming," especially pp. 397–8.

5 *Moreau* is discussed in detail in Chapter 5.2.

6 Cf. Derrida: "This field is in effect that of *play* . . . a field of endless substitutions . . . permitted by the lack or absence of a center or origin . . ." ("Structure, Sign and Play," p. 289; emphasis in text).

7 *The Best of H. P. Lovecraft: Bloodcurdling Tales of Horror and the Macabre*, p. 193.

8 Hodgson, *Out of the Storm*. First published 1905, *The Grand Magazine*.

9 Hodgson, *Deep Waters*. First published in two parts: "From the Tideless Sea" (*The Monthly Story Magazine*, 1906), and "More News from the Homebird" (*The Blue Book Magazine*, 1907). See also "The Thing in the

Weeds" (*Deep Waters*; first published 1912, *The Storyteller*), "The Finding of the *Graiken*" (*Out of the Storm*; first published 1913, *The Red Magazine*), and "The Terror of the Water-Tank" (*Out of the Storm*; first published 1907, *The Blue Book Magazine*).

10 Pain, *Stories in the Dark*.

11 Robinson, *Under the Punkah*.

12 Hodgson, *Deep Waters*. First published 1907, *The Blue Book Magazine*.

13 Huxley, "On the Physical Basis of Life" (1869). The paper was initially delivered as a lecture in November 1868; see Huxley's footnote, p. 129.

14 Huxley proposes the phrase as a "translation" of the term protoplasm (p. 129).

15 The sexual meanings of slime are discussed in part III.

16 Jay, *Downcast Eyes: The Denigration of Vision in Twentieth-Century French Thought*, p. 286.

17 I should note that my reading of this passage in Sartre is in disagreement with Mary Douglas'. Douglas argues that for Sartre, anomalous phenomena like slime eventually serve to reify the categories they seem to call into question. "When something is firmly classed as anomalous the outline of the set in which it is not a member is clarified . . . [Sartre] makes the point that we can and do reflect with profit on our main classifications and on experiences which do not exactly fit them. In general these reflections confirm our confidence in the main classifications" (*Purity and Danger*, p. 38).

However, I cannot but read Sartre's discussion of slime as an eruption into hysterical anxiety over the ineluctibility of matter. This passage from *Being and Nothingness*, furthermore, is so well able to illustrate materialism's potential to disturb precisely because materialism has been held at bay, and seemingly mastered, in the hundreds of pages that precede it.

18 "On the Physical Basis of Life," p. 143.

19 Hodgson, *Deep Waters*. First published 1912, *The Red Magazine*.

20 Cited in John L. Greenway, "Seward's Folly," p. 228. The ellipses are Greenway's.

21 Allman works very deliberately from "On the Physical Basis of Life"; see Greenway, p. 217.

2. SYMPTOMATIC READINGS

1 Hodgson, *Deep Waters*. First published 1912, *The Red Magazine*.

2 Anomalies may of course violate multiple categories, as is the case in "The Crew of the Lancing."

3 See Freud's discussion of Hoffmann's "The Sand-Man," pp. 132–9.

4 In imagining a subjectivity which is neither discrete nor integral, Freud is of course drawing from a dense and varied range of materials generated by nineteenth-century psychology. See Henri F. Ellenberger, *The Discovery of the Unconscious: The History and Evolution of Dynamic Psychiatry* and Frank J. Sulloway, *Freud, Biologist of the Mind: Beyond the Psychoanalytic Legend*.

One important tradition in nineteenth-century psychology, in fact, identifies human subjectivity in terms we can describe as gothic: fracturable, prone to "invasion" by more potent subjectivities, and fissured as well by the *unheimlich* space of the unconscious. I am thinking of a largely forgotten chapter in the history of psychology, the *fin-de-siècle* debates over criminal hypnosis. The basic argument, joined between Jean-Martin Charcot and the Salpêtrière school on the one hand and Hippolyte Bernheim and the Nancy school on the other, was as to whether hypnotic suggestion could persuade a law-abiding subject to commit a crime. Theorizations of the unconscious had increasingly revealed the human subject's discontinuity and alienation from itself; the issue of criminal hypnosis foregrounded this loss of human self-possession, as well as positing a no-longer-discrete individual with permeable boundaries.

This largely French debate was appropriated with great enthusiasm by British Gothic novelists. Novels of criminal hypnosis explore such unsettling possibilities as whether one subjectivity might be "invaded" and taken over by another; whether an unscrupulous hypnotist might be able to induce in the subject behaviors and emotions incompatible with his or her basic nature; or whether in doing so the hypnotist merely has access to, and the ability to translate, the repressed contents of the subject's unconscious. I had planned to discuss this literature here, but the material proved so rich that I have reserved work on it for a later project.

5 Here a Freudian analysis is consistent with Sartre's, according to which the subject is compromised by its encounter with indifferentiation.

6 Pole works from Douglas' *Implicit Meanings*, which raises some of the same questions as her earlier *Purity and Danger*.

7 Showalter relates this passage to theories of multiple personality then gaining currency within *fin-de-siècle* psychology; see *Sexual Anarchy*, pp. 121–6.

8 As will occur later, in what Jacques Lacan identifies as the mirror stage; see Lacan, "The Mirror Stage as Formative of the Function of the I."

9 For Kristeva's engagement with Mary Douglas, see chapter 3 of *Powers of Horror*.

10 "The abject" in this sentence means, roughly, the object which inspires abjection. The correspondence is incomplete because the abject is not properly an object; in its anomalousness, it breaks down the distinction between the self and its objects. Elsewhere in Kristeva, "the abject" refers to the subject who has been unmade by the experience of abjection.

11 *The Best Supernatural Tales of Arthur Conan Doyle*. First published 1892, *Harper's Magazine*.

12 See Carroll's *The Philosophy of Horror* for a related discussion of the relationship between nausea and the horror text. Carroll defines Horror, a transhistorical genre which includes the *fin-de-siècle* Gothic, in terms of the affect it provokes or attempts to provoke: "shuddering, nausea, shrinking, paralysis, screaming, and revulsion" (p. 18).

13 *"Cage aux Folles*: Sensation and Gender in Wilkie Collins's *The Woman in White,"* pp. 187–8. In general, my argument in this section has benefitted from Miller's path-breaking discussion of the somatics of reading.

14 Hodgson, *"The House on the Borderland" and Other Novels.* First published in 1907. *"Glen Carrig"* has purportedly been written by a gentleman of the eighteenth century; thus the odd diction.

15 Machen, perversely, collected the most vitriolic reviews of his works in his 1924 *Precious Balms,* so we know that many of Machen's reviewers found his Gothic works absolutely disgusting. One reviewer wrote that the *The Great God Pan*'s "meaning . . . is very carefully veiled, and on the whole we are inclined to think it is quite as well that it is so, since such glimpses as we are vouchsafed of it are singularly repulsive." Another said of *The Three Imposters*: "There are some books that produce a positive physical repulsion in their reader. Mr Machen's extremely disagreeable story is one of them . . . The horror in it is palpably and very literally sickening" (*Precious Balms,* pp. 7, 18). Other reviewers, I should note, complained that Machen's obfuscating narrative style, in combination with his heightened rhetoric of the ineffable, simply produced an effect that was ludicrous.
   I am grateful to Susan Navarette for bringing this and several other works to my attention.

16 I have abridged Villiers' speech in the quotation above.

17 See Freud and Joseph Breuer, *Studies on Hysteria* (1895); and Freud, "The Aetiology of Hysteria" (1896) and *Dora: An Analysis of a Case of Hysteria* (written 1901, published 1905).

18 I am preserving the syntax but not the semantics of Freud's argument by positing that other "disturbances" than sexual ones can instantiate hysteria. While *The Great God Pan* certainly lends itself to a more faithful Freudian analysis by identifying the gothic body as female (the "disturbance" repressed is the discovery of sexual difference), I am not interested in a reading that *only* foregrounds the sexual hysteria of the Gothic. Sexual hysteria will be discussed, however, in part III.

19 In general in this study, I have given extensive analysis only to those texts that leave me slightly ill.

20 The first two reviews are by P. Chambers Mitchell and Grant Richards; the last two are unsigned.

21 The other was *The Time Machine*; see David Smith, *H. G. Wells: Desperately Mortal,* pp. 62–3.

22 Found at the back of the British Library's copy (and I assume, any first edition) of Aubrey's *King of the Dead* (1903). The advertisement culls reviews from 31 British and US journals; those cited below are from *Graphic, Vanity Fair, Spectator, Macmillan's Magazine,* and *The New York Sun.*

23 See, for example, Christopher Craft's discussion of *Dracula* in *Another Kind of Love: Male Homosocial Desire in English Discourse, 1850–1920,* especially p. 72; Spencer, "Purity and Danger"; and Robin Wood, "Introduction" to *American Nightmare: Essays on the Horror Film.*

3. EVOLUTION AND THE LOSS OF HUMAN SPECIFICITY

1 Cited in David C. Smith, *H. G. Wells*, p. 11.
2 See Peter Morton, *The Vital Science: Biology and the Literary Imagination, 1860–1900*, pp. 53–83, on what he describes as this "cheerful" version of evolutionism.
3 Norman and Jeanne MacKenzie, *H. G. Wells: A Biography*, p. 56.
4 Peter Morton characterizes Wells' work from the early 1890s as "pot-boiling." An article like "Zoological Retrogression," he says, "displays Wells's scientific imagination working at low ebb and exercising itself solely in producing fear, awe, or thrilling amusement" (*The Vital Science*, p. 106). Leaving to one side the question of the scientific value of such "pot-boilers," I will note that it is precisely their sensationalism that intrigues me.
5 First published in *Gentleman's Magazine*, 1891. Page numbers for this and the next five references are from Wells, *Early Writings in Science and Science Fiction*. I have benefitted from the careful commentary by the editors of this book, Robert Philmus and David Y. Hughes.
6 *Deep Waters*, pp. 205, 208. First published 1907, *The Story Teller*.
7 The *fin-de-siècle* Gothic also explores the idea of "survivals": that is, primitive species known to moderns only through the fossil record, which have managed to survive extinction in some unusual habitat. In Wells' "In the Avu Observatory" (1894), an astronomer battles a pterodactyl in the wilds of Borneo; and in Conan Doyle's *The Lost World* (1912), a group of explorers discovers a whole little world of prehistoric creatures, as well as a colony of ape-men, on an isolated plateau in South America. One of Machen's imposters tells a story of a race of primitive Celtic peoples, pockets of whom still survive in obscure English hill country, practicing long-forgotten magical rituals and emerging occasionally to savage the locals (*The Three Imposters*). John Buchan's "No-Man's-Land" (1898) presents a similar scenario; his abhumans are Pictish survivals in the wilds of Scotland.
8 First published 1905, *The Strand Magazine*. Page references for all Wells' stories cited herein are taken from Wells, *Twenty-eight Science Fiction Stories*.
9 First published 1896, *Weekly Sun Literary Supplement*.
10 First published 1903, *Pearson's Magazine*.
11 Conan Doyle, *Tales of Terror and Mystery*. First published 1913, *The Strand Magazine*.
12 *Darwin's Plots: Evolutionary Narrative in Darwin, George Eliot and Nineteenth-Century Fiction*, p. 123.
13 Conan Doyle, *Tales of Terror and Mystery*. First published 1910, *The Strand Magazine*.
14 Robinson, *Under the Punkah*.
15 These passages from Robinson resonate with Huxley's description of the nettle, which under the microscope is seen to pulsate with the "subtle and hidden manifestations of vegetable contractility" (Huxley, "On the Physical Basis of Life," p. 131).
16 *The Best Supernatural Tales of Arthur Conan Doyle*, pp. 301–2. First published 1880, *London Society*.

17 *The Complete Science Fiction Treasury*, p. 363.

18 Anthropophagous cephalopods may be found in Aubrey's *A Queen of Atlantis* (1899) and Hodgson's "The Thing in the Weeds," "From the Tideless Sea," "The Finding of the Graiken," and *The Boats of the "Glen Carrig"*. The man-eating plants of *Devil-Tree* and "The American's Tale" are likened, respectively, to octopi and squid, and Wells' blood-sucking flower in "The Flowering of the Strange Orchid" (1894) is tentacled.

19 Weatherby Chesney, *The Adventures of a Solicitor*.

20 Hodgson, *"The House on the Borderland" and Other Novels* (p. 407; my emphasis). *The Night Land* was published in 1912; Sam Gafford, working from recently discovered Hodgson letters, argues that the novel was written around 1903 ("Writing Backwards: The Novels of William Hope Hodgson").

4. ENTROPIC BODIES

1 Pick, *Faces of Degeneration: A European Disorder, c.1848 – c.1918*, p. 49.

2 I have benefitted from Peter Allan Dale's discussion of the second law of thermodynamics and its relation to Victorian biological and literary narrative models in *In Pursuit of a Scientific Culture: Science, Art, and Society in the Victorian Age*, especially chapters 9 and 10. Dale points out that any "direct connection" posited between the second law of thermodynamics and theories of human degeneration was not scientifically sound, requiring a "leap of imagination" (p. 230): these minus narratives provided by physics and biology were rendered compatible through a logic more gothic than scientific, in other words.

3 A somewhat longer version of this discussion appeared as "Hereditary Taint and Cultural Contagion: The Social Etiology of *Fin-de-Siècle* Degeneration Theory," in *Nineteenth-Century Contexts* 14.2 (1990): 193–214. The essay has been modified in other ways.

4 The only English translation of Morel's *Treatise on Degeneration* available to date is Edward Wing's excerpted version in the 1857 *Medical Circular*. The quote above is cited in Max Nordau, *Degeneration* (p. 16).

5 A more detailed summary of each generation's manifestation of degeneration may be found in Eric T. Carlson, "Medicine and Degeneration: Theory and Praxis," especially p. 122.

6 Medical science after Morel has shown how the mother's substance addiction or vitamin deficiencies may be passed on to the fetus, and how the infant may contract venereal disease while passing through the birth canal. Lamarckian evolutionism helped account for this seeming hereditary connection during a period when diseases like rickets, pellagra, and syphilis were still fairly mysterious in their workings. Within Morel's etiology of degeneration, venereal disease or inadequate diet induced a brain lesion, which was then passed on to the offspring through the "seed."

7 Cited in Eugene S. Talbot, *Degeneracy: Its Causes, Signs, and Results*, p. 78.

8 For a discussion of monogeny and polygeny, see Stephen Jay Gould, *The*

Mismeasure of Man, pp. 39–42. Morel distinguishes between humans' and other species' natural adaptation to particular climates (which may take the form of "reversion," and thus be confused with degeneration) and "true" degeneration "springing from an unhealthy origin" in the *Treatise*, pp. 150–1, 161, 173, and 219–21.

9 For a discussion of theories which linked venereal disease with degenerative sexuality, see Sander L. Gilman, "Sexology, Psychoanalysis, and Degeneration"; Robert A. Nye, *Crime, Madness, and Politics in Modern France: The Medical Concept of National Decline*, pp. 158–70; and Elaine Showalter, "Syphilis, Sexuality, and the Fiction of the Fin de Siècle."

10 See, for example, Wing's commentary on alcoholism in his translation of Morel's *Treatise*, p. 218.

11 Cited in Max Nordau, *Degeneration*, p. 16. See also the Wing translation of Morel, p. 137.

12 Even Morel, with his more limited model of degeneration, hinted at an etiology of degeneration including social infection as well as infectious heredity: he wrote that the very proximity of these "brutalized beings" (second-generation degenerates) with "no discrimination of good or evil" contaminated "the sane part of the population" (*Treatise*, p. 109).

13 *Outcast London: A Study in the Relationships Between Classes in Victorian Society*, chapter 6.

14 Cantlie, esp. pp. 8–13. J. Milner Fothergill speculated that diet, specifically the substitution of tea and white bread for the old diet of milk, brown bread, and homebrewed ale, was the primary cause of modern urban degeneration (*The Town Dweller: His Needs and Wants*, pp. 5–6). Excessive tea-drinking, with its "pernicious effects upon the nervous system," even led to alcoholism: "The brain is rendered unstable and excitable, hence the craving for alcohol" (pp. 7–8). Other causes included overcrowding, long working hours (especially for female laborers), and poor sanitation, as well as lack of ozone. John Edward Morgan listed the three most prominent causes of urban "enervation" as "vitiated air, constitutional syphilis, and the abuse of alcohol" (*The Danger of the Deterioration of Race from the Too Rapid Increase of Great Cities*, p. 25).

15 Cited in Stedman Jones, *Outcast London*, p. 127.

16 Fothergill's description of a typical urban degenerate is as follows: "His osseous system is not only small and slight, but it consists of defective material . . . He has ricketty limbs. His chest is apt to be deformed and the ribs bent in. While the back-bone is frequently curved, and the pelvis takes a misshapen form. Diseases of the epiphyses of the long bones is common amidst town dwellers . . . It is not unusual to see a weakly creature minus a limb which has been removed in consequence of bone disease" (*The Town Dweller*, p. 112). The characteristic urban deformities Fothergill describes seem mostly attributable to rickets, lending credibility, after all, to Cantlie's theory that lack of "ozone" was at the root of the problem (sunlight is now known to be a source of Vitamin D).

17 "Additional confirmation of [the prevalence of urban degeneration] will be found in the large number of military recruits who fail to come up to that standard of bodily fitness which the medical referees are instructed to insist upon. I have been informed by an officer specially associated with the superintendence of this service that in some of the manufacturing districts four out of every five men sent up by the sergeants for medical inspection are rejected on the ground of physical disqualification" (Morgan, *The Danger of the Deterioration of Race*, p. 7).

For a discussion of national fears about the unfitness of the British army and the 1904 Committee on Physical Deterioration formed in response to those fears, see Samuel Hynes, *The Edwardian Turn of Mind*, pp. 22–34; Nye, *Crime, Madness and Politics*, pp. 332–4; Dorothy and Roy Porter, "What Was Social Medicine? An Historiographical Essay," p. 99; and Stedman Jones, *Outcast London*, p. 78.

18 See Gilman, "Sexology," pp. 196–7; and Nancy Stepan, "Biological Degeneration: Races and Proper Places." Stepan's article provides an excellent analysis of degenerationism in relation to theories of racial hierarchy and the dangers of miscegenation.

19 Morel lamented that the "debasement" of the populations of Europe and the United States had manifested itself in an "incessant progression . . . not only of mental alienation but of all those abnormal states which are in special affinity with physical and moral evil in mankind" (*Treatise*, p. 123).

20 Nye makes a similar argument in *Crime, Madness, and Politics*, p. 144. His book in general provides a detailed and compelling analysis of the ways in which degeneration theory helped both construct and allay a variety of cultural anxieties in *fin-de-siècle* France.

21 See Gilman, pp. 193–9; and George Stocking, *Victorian Anthropology*, pp. 197–208.

22 Krafft-Ebing states that "every expression of [the sexual instinct] that does not correspond with the purpose of nature– i.e., propagation– must be regarded as perverse" (*Psychopathia Sexualis*, p. 108). This seems to include not only masturbation, sadomasochism, and homosexual activity, but also "normal" intercourse lasting longer than ten minutes (p. 382). Krafft-Ebing also considers oral sex unnatural, and argues that a man's desire to administer cunnilingus denotes his masochism. In his section on "Koprolagnia," cunnilingus is listed along with other masochistic desires, like wishing to consume the urine or feces or lick the feet of the object of desire, as an example of the "impulse to disgusting acts" (pp. 212–20).

23 "The differentiation of the sexes and the development of sexual types is evidently the result of an infinite succession of intermediary stages of evolution. The primary stage undoubtedly was bisexuality, such as still exists in the lowest classes of animal life and also during the first months of fetal existence in man. The type of the present stage of evolution is monosexuality; that is to say, a congruous development of the secondary bodily and psychical sexual characteristics belonging to the respective sexual glands" (Krafft-Ebing, *Psychopathia Sexualis*, p. 72). Sulloway discusses a number of

nineteenth-century sexologists' speculations on the relations between homosexuality or bisexuality and atavism in *Freud, Biologist of the Mind*; see especially pp. 159, 281, and 292–6.

    For a discussion of degenerative sexuality in a somewhat different context, see Birkin, *Consuming Desire*, chapters 4 and 5. Birkin locates Krafft-Ebing's analysis within the "second phase" of *fin-de-siècle* sexology – distinguished from an earlier phase, in which degenerative sexuality was perceived as morbid rather than atavistic, and a later, in which it was simply regarded as atypical (pp. 109–10).

24 For a discussion of the cultural instrumentality of neurasthenia in *fin-de-siècle* America, see Tom Lutz, *American Nervousness, 1903: An Anecdotal History*, especially chapter 1. My work has here and elsewhere benefitted from a number of conversations with Lutz about nineteenth-century social medicine.

25 For a discussion of Lombroso's and Nordau's theories of criminal aesthetics, particularly in relation to the trials of Oscar Wilde, see Regenia Gagnier, *Idylls of the Marketplace: Oscar Wilde and the Victorian Public*, pp. 147–53.

26 Despite, however, the immense popular success of *Degeneration*, which ran through numerous editions and translations, the book was received skeptically and reviewed scornfully by the medical community. William James called it a "pathological book on a pathological subject," claiming that Nordau, thanks to the indiscriminate nature of his own terms, could be classed as "a degenerate of the worst sort" ("Degeneration and Genius," p. 289); and E. C. Spitzka, denouncing the book as an "aberration of science," scoffed that "as a lunatic is apt to regard himself as the only sane being in his environment, so Nordau sees nothing but degeneration and disease outside of his own personality" (review of Max Nordau's *Degeneration*, pp. 112, 114). A *Chicago Tribune* review assessed *Degeneration* at perhaps its true worth: "A most absorbing book . . . likely to replace *Trilby*" – that is, George du Maurier's sensational 1894 novel of criminal hypnosis and demonic seduction – "as a subject of popular discussion" (cited in Richard D. Walter, "What Became of the Degenerate? A Brief History of a Concept," p. 426).

27 The subject of case 136, "K.," (a masturbator and sometime homosexual) was given this advice: "energetic combat with homosexual desires, society of ladies, eventually coitus with condom. Wedlock, when suited, as his station in life demanded it." K. returned in four months virtually cured. "He hoped to marry at an early date, and anticipated much happiness from the married state" (p. 379).

28 For a similar argument, see Pick, *Faces of Degeneration*, especially pp. 11, 106.

29 See my discussion of Richard Marsh's *The Beetle* (chapter 6).

30 Conan Doyle, *The Conan Doyle Stories* (first published in 1894, in Conan Doyle's collection *Round the Red Lamp*); de la Mare, *Eight Tales*; Pain, *Stories in the Dark*.

    For a discussion of *Jekyll and Hyde* and *Dracula* as texts which thematize degeneration, see Stephen D. Arata, "The Occidental Tourist: *Dracula* and the Anxiety of Reverse Colonialism"; Block, "James Sully"; Donald Lawler, "Reframing *Jekyll and Hyde*"; and Pick, *Faces of Degeneration*, chapter 6.

31 Shiel, *The Pale Ape and Other Pulses*, p. 200. "Huguenin's Wife" was first published in 1895, *The Pall Mall Magazine*.

32 Shiel, *The Pale Ape and Other Pulses* (1911). I have been unable to ascertain the original magazine publication date of this story.

33 Bernard Bergonzi describes the novel as "a romantic and pessimistic variant of orthodox Marxist thought: the implications of the class-war are accepted, but the possibility of the successful proletarian revolution establishing a classless society is rigidly excluded" ("*The Time Machine*: An Ironic Myth," p. 47).

34 There is some critical controversy as to the extent of Wells' familiarity with degeneration theory; see Morton, *The Vital Science*, n. 40, p. 116.

5. CHAOTIC BODIES

1 Compare Hodgson's *The House on the Borderland* and *The Night Land*, both of which deploy entropic plotting.

2 Compare George Levine's discussion of Darwinism and chance. "Darwin's laws . . . were based on what would have seemed a very strange combination of the random and the orderly . . . [T]o imagine a system in which disorder, dysteleology, and mindlessness are constitutive, and, indeed, the source of all value, is to turn the Western tradition, with its faith that all value inheres in order, design, and intelligence, on its head." Thus, "Darwin's world required a new sort of imagination, even, perhaps, a new sort of politics" (*Darwin and the Novelists: Patterns of Science in Victorian Fiction*, pp. 93, 94).

3 See, for example, *Origin of Species* pp. 82–83, 93, 259–62.

4 Compare the famous concluding paragraph of *The Descent of Man*: "Man may be excused for feeling some pride at having risen, though not through his own exertions, to the very summit of the organic scale; and the fact of his having thus risen, instead of having been aboriginally placed there, may give him hope for a still higher destiny in the distant future. But we are not here concerned with hopes or fears, only with the truth as far as our reason permits us to discover it; and I have given the evidence to the best of my ability. We must, however, acknowledge, as it seems to me, that man with all his noble qualities, with sympathy which feels for the most debased, with benevolence which extends not only to other men but to the humblest living creature, with his god-like intellect which has penetrated into the movements and constitution of the solar system – with all these exalted powers – Man still bears in his bodily frame the indelible stamp of his lowly origin" (p. 920).

5 Peter Morton makes a similar point about the post-Darwinian human body: "no longer a sophisticated product of engineering design by a Divine Craftsman, the body had to be viewed instead as a ramshackle structure where make do and mend is the only guiding inspiration; a body tacked together, like Frankenstein's monster, from a variety of ill-fitting animal parts" (*The Vital Science: Biology and the Literary Imagination, 1860–1900*, p. 108).

6 Cesare Lombroso, "Preface" to Gina Lombroso-Ferrero, *Criminal Man According to the Classification of Cesare Lombroso*, pp. xxiv–xxv. Lombroso-Ferrero's *Criminal Man* is a translation of the fifth edition of her father's *L'Uomo Delinquente*, first published in 1876.

7 Darwin discusses the possibility of human and non-human species reversion briefly and without particular affect in both *Origin of Species* and *The Descent of Man*; see, for example, *Origin*, p. 94, and *Descent*, p. 512.

8 In discussing criminal anthropology, I have chosen to concentrate on Lombroso rather than his colleagues (including Enrico Ferri, Raffaele Garofalo, Hans Gross, Hans Kurella, Antonio Marro, Maurice Parmelee, and Madame Tarnovskii) first, because Lombroso is considered the founder of the science, and his was the name most associated with criminal anthropology in the late nineteenth century; and second, because his work was accessible to the British public. A number of Lombroso's articles were published in British journals in the 1890s: "Illustrative Studies in Criminal Anthropology" (in three parts), *Monist* 1 (1891); "Atavism and Evolutionism," *Contemporary Review* 68 (1895); "Criminal Anthropology Applied to Pedagogy," *Monist* 6 (1895); "Criminal Anthropology: Its Origin and Application," *The Forum* 20 (1895). This last article is useful as a complete overview of Lombroso's work up to 1895. The English translation of *The Man of Genius* appeared in 1891; *The Female Offender*, 1895; *Criminal Man*, 1911; *Crime: Its Causes and Remedies*, 1911.

   Similarly, although Lombroso also wrote about criminality in relation to epilepsy, alcoholism, and "moral insanity," as well proposing various judicial and penal reforms to be based on his work, I will focus primarily on his theory of atavism because of its debt to evolutionary biology – this theory would have been inconceivable before Darwin – and because this was of all his theories the one that engendered the most contemporary interest and controversy.

   For discussions and summaries of Lombroso by contemporaries, see Havelock Ellis, *The Criminal* (1890) and Hans Kurella, *Cesare Lombroso: A Modern Man of Science* (1911). For a discussion of Lombroso's impact within *fin-de-siècle* Europe, see Gould, *The Mismeasure of Man* (pp. 132–8) and Pick, *Faces of Degeneration* (pp. 109–52), as well as Kurella's laudatory work. Pick in particular is useful in placing criminal anthropology within the more widespread European discourses on degenerationism; he also provides a thorough contextualization of Lombroso within *fin-de-siècle* Italy and its social troubles.

9 Lombroso studied the European, mostly Italian, criminal; like most nineteenth-century physical scientists he worked in terms of a racial hierarchy that identified Caucasians as unquestionably superior.

10 Lombroso-Ferrero (p. 8), also the source of the next six page references.

11 Lombroso's theory of the atavist was virtually ignored after 1920. However, *The Encyclopaedia of the Social Sciences* praises him for his positivism, the *Concise Encyclopedia of Crime and Criminals* for his "scientific integrity." *The Encyclopedia*

of Crime and Justice claims that Lombroso "was a master of observation, scrupulously honest in his work."

Even contemporaries of Lombroso who doubted the theory of criminal atavism credited him with an exemplary practice of the "modern" scientific method. There were, however, a few dissenters to this view. Ellis cites a Dr. Napoleone Colajanni, who "compares Lombroso's indiscriminate collection of facts to the Abbot's famous order at the sacking of Beziers: 'Kill them all; God will know his own'" (*The Criminal*, p. 42).

For a thorough critique of the nineteenth-century anthropometrical sciences, including criminal anthropology, see Gould, *The Mismeasure of Man*. Gould, working from the original data sets of the anthropometrists, particularly the craniometrists, attempts to show how unconscious bias (as well as the occasional conscious fraud) influenced the anthropometrists in their very collection of data, as well as in its analysis. "In reanalyzing these classical data sets, I have continually located *a priori* prejudice, leading scientists to invalid conclusions from adequate data, or distorting the evidence of data itself" (p. 27).

In my discussion of Lombroso I have perhaps deliberately foregrounded the outrageousness of certain arguments, but I should emphasize that this was not difficult to do. Criminal anthropology was, however, a legitimate and influential science in its own time; see Pick, *Faces of Degeneration*, pp. 120, 145. Ellis claims that "the influence of *L'Uomo Delinquente* . . . seems to have been immediate, and almost recalls that of *The Origin of Species*" (*The Criminal*, p. 41).

12 To give him his due, Lombroso found primitivism in Europe as well. In "Atavism and Evolution," he discusses a number of superstitions and survivals of primitive traditions within Europe, and writes that the "march of mankind proceeds by continual action and reaction; no people, however lofty its position, can boast too much over the lowest savage" (p. 49).

13 See Gould, *The Mismeasure of Man* (pp. 30–112) for a full discussion and critique of nineteenth-century anthropometry.

14 All of these qualities find their fullest expression in the phrase "the word of an Englishman," the meaning of which, Kidd notes proudly, is understood and respected even among the indigenous populations of South America and Egypt (*Social Evolution*, p. 349).

15 For a history of the theory of recapitulation, and of its effects on social practices, see Gould, *Ontogeny and Phylogeny*.

16 Furthermore, Lombroso and Ferrero argue, the physical abnormalities that characterize the female born criminal would have been largely eliminated by the process of sexual selection. Primitive man "not only refused to *marry* a deformed criminal, but ate her, while, on the other hand, preserving for his enjoyment the handsome woman who gratified his peculiar instincts" (*The Female Offender* p. 109; emphasis in text).

17 The female genius is even more rare than the female born criminal, but she is equally anomalous, and equally unfeminine. "Woman of genius are rare

exceptions in the world . . . Even the few who emerge have something virile about them. As Goncourt said, there are no women of genius; the women of genius are all men" (Lombroso, *The Man of Genius*, pp. 137–8).

18 See Roger Cooter, *The Cultural Meaning of Popular Sciences: Phrenology and the Organization of Consent in Nineteenth-Century Britain*; John Graham, *Lavater's Essays on Physiognomy: A Study in the History of Ideas*; and Graham Tytler, *Physiognomy in the European Novel*.

19 "The impression left to us by our fathers and transmitted to our children has become unconscious knowledge, like that of the little birds born and reared in our houses, who strike their wings and beaks in fright against their cages when they see pass above them birds of prey known only to their ancestors" ("Criminal Anthropology," p. 39).

20 Robert M. Philmus notes that Wells changed the location of the island, originally somewhere in the South Seas, from his earlier draft. "Wells now puts it in the vicinity of the Galapagos, the principal scene of Darwin's researches and hence a site at which 'biology invades history' " (*The Island of Dr. Moreau: A Variorum Text*, p. xxvi).

21 Though none of Wells' articles treat Lombroso's work at any length, they show a familiarity with criminal anthropology. For example, "Human Evolution, An Artificial Process" discusses atavism (p. 214), and Wells briefly considers Lombroso's theory of the female offender in his 1894 "The Province of Pain" (Wells, *Early Writings*, p. 196).
   I am less concerned to prove Lombroso's influence on Wells than to note similar modelings for abhumanness in both Gothic fiction and "gothic" science.

22 His quest is to construct a "true" human, but he always fails.

23 Ipecac is a drug used to induce vomiting. Montgomery remarks that "when there's much of a sea without any wind [the *Ipecacuanha*] certainly acts according [to its name]" (p. 7). This perverse detail of the ship's name provides another hint that Wells, as his reviewers feared, set out quite deliberately to nauseate his reader.
   See also Robert M. Philmus, "The Satiric Ambivalence of *The Island of Doctor Moreau* (p. 6), on the significance of the name *Ipecacuanha*.

24 Prendick is unable even to mention the word cannibalism, referring to it only as "the thing we all had in mind" (p. 4). Here, as in *The Time Machine*, the prospect of cannibalism instantiates textual hysteria.

25 Philmus also considers this passage in the Variorum *Moreau*, but discounts its significance. "Presumably the genius he is alluding to is Oscar Wilde. But even if *Moreau* had not been well under way at the time of Wilde's 'downfall', that writer surely bears no comparison with Moreau apart from being a victim of ostracism" (p. xliii).
   The first draft of *Moreau* was completed in 1894, before Wilde's trials. In this first draft, however (reproduced in the Variorum *Moreau*), Montgomery is a negligible and not particularly developed character; his "shabby vices" and effeminacy were added in the second draft, after the trials.

26 Philmus lists other possible sources for the name; see the Variorum *Moreau*, pp. xli–xliii.

27 For a discussion of *Morbid Psychology* and a reproduction of J.-J. Moreau's "family tree," see George Frederick Drinka, *The Birth of Neurosis: Myth, Malady, and the Victorians*, pp. 53–6.

28 "Not to claw bark of trees, *that* is the law. Are we not men?" Prendick writes that "sometimes I would give way to wild outbursts of rage, and hack and splinter some unlucky tree in my intolerable vexation" (p. 132).

6. UNCANNY FEMALE INTERIORS

1 *Tales of Horror and the Supernatural*, p. 160.

2 This trope of the deadliness of the female's embrace appears in any number of *fin-de-siècle* Gothic texts, but nowhere to more remarkable effect than in Richard Marsh's *The Goddess: A Demon* (1900). The novel features a "Hindoo" idol whose sudden transformation reveals her lovely, duplicitous body to be made entirely of knives. The Goddess skewers her male victim and humps him to death, literally tearing him to shreds during a horrible parody of sexual intercourse:

As Lawrence sprang forward, the figure rose to its feet, and in an instant was alive. It opened its arms; from its finger-tips came knives. Stepping forward it gripped Lawrence with its steel-clad hands . . . From every part of its frame gleaming blades had sprung; against this *cheval-de-frise* it pressed him again and again, twirling him round and round, moving him up and down, so that the weapons pierced and hacked back and front. Even from its eyes, mouth, and nostrils had sprung knives . . . A sharp-pointed blade, which proceeded from its stomach, had pierced [Lawrence] through and through . . . Down he came, with his assailant sticking to him like a limpet. Pinning him on the floor, it continued its extraordinary contortions, lacerating its victim with every movement in a hundred different places. (pp. 291–2)

3 Or as Huguenin bizarrely describes her, Andromeda becomes "*The feathered Cheetah!*" (p. 207; emphasis in text).

Bram Dijkstra discusses the *fin-de-siècle* convention of representing sphinxes whose femininity is signalled by their naked and voluptuous breasts as well as their female faces in *Idols of Perversity: Fantasies of Feminine Evil in Fin-de-Siècle Culture*, pp. 325–32. These buxom sphinxes, he speculates, point towards hysterical male anxieties about the mother (and by extension, women in general) at the *fin de siècle*: the sphinx's full breasts promise nourishment, but once she has lured her male victim within her grasp, this female monster instead drains and destroys him. Dijkstra also discusses *fin-de-siècle* representations of the lamia and Medusa on pp. 309–11 and 333–51.

The pictorial evidence through which Dijkstra argues a *fin-de-siècle* obsession with monstrous femininity is both extraordinary, and extraordinarily convincing. Other critics who track this obsession include Nina Auerbach, *Woman and the Demon: The Life of a Victorian Myth*; Gilbert and Gubar, *No Man's*

Land, vol. 2: *Sexchanges*, chapter 1; and Showalter, *Sexual Anarchy*. While representations of monstrous femininity can be found throughout the Victorian period, these critics argue, they appear with more frequency and intensity, bespeaking a more hysterical anxiety about women's place within the culture, at the end of the century.

4 A now classic articulation of this position is Sherry B. Ortner's "Is Female to Male as Nature is to Culture?"

5 See, for instance, Grant Allen's anti-feminist polemic from the 1890 *Forum*, "Woman's Intuition." "From the very nature of her bodily organization," Allen writes, "woman is emotionally more resonant than man. Her frame is made up of sounding-boards" (p. 334). As a result, "the intellectual quality in which woman is strongest is undoubtedly the intellectual quality nearest allied to the emotions; namely, intuition" (p. 335). Grant's piece is a celebration of this womanly "resonance," but E. D. Cope's article "On the Material Relations of Sex in Human Society," published in *The Monist* that same year, identifies female affectivity as an evolutionary liability. Women's "mental disabilities are: first, inferior power of mental co-ordination; and secondly, greater emotional sensibility, which interferes more or less with rational action" (p. 39).

6 See also Janet Oppenheim's discussion of the "medical assumption that biology dominated women's lives" (p. 181) in *"Shattered Nerves": Doctors, Patients, and Depression in Victorian England*, chapter 6. The female nervous system "derived its traits ... both from the limitations of the woman's brain" – less highly evolved than the man's – "and from the excesses of her reproductive organs ... At puberty and menopause, during pregnancy, childbirth, and lactation, not to mention her monthly uterine upheavals, a woman was at great risk, for all these biological events demanded heavy payments of nerve force" (pp. 187–8).

7 Donovan, *Tales of Terror* (1899), p. 9.

8 Sexual agency did not necessarily entail libidinal excesses; many New Women advocated sexual chastity for women and men alike.

For discussions of *fin-de-siècle* feminism, see A. R. Cunningham, "The 'New Woman Fiction' of the 1890s"; Linda Dowling, "The Decadent and the New Woman in the 1890s"; Showalter, *Sexual Anarchy*, especially chapter 3; and Judith R. Walkowitz, *City of Dreadful Delight: Narratives of Sexual Danger in Late-Victorian London*, especially chapters 2 and 5.

Grant Allen was one late-Victorian intellectual who feared that the advance of feminism at the *fin de siècle* necessitated a loss of distinction between the sexes. He argued that the object of the "lady lecturers," "anti-feminine old maids," and "recalcitrant mannish women of our age" was "not to defend and uphold womanhood as such, but on the contrary to turn women, if possible, into feeble, second-rate copies of men" ("Woman's Intuition," p. 333).

9 Critics who pursue the connection between the phenomenon of the New Woman and the *fin-de-siècle* Gothic's representations of female monstrosity

include Dijkstra, *Idols of Perversity*; Gilbert and Gubar, *No Man's Land* vol. 1, chapter 1; and Carol A. Senf, *"Dracula*: Stoker's Response to the New Woman."

10 Thus the title of Phyllis A. Roth's "Suddenly Sexual Women in Bram Stoker's *Dracula*." Auerbach also documents "the ease with which the Victorian angel becomes demonic" in chapter 3 of *Woman and the Demon*.

11 My discussion of *The Beetle* has been modified from an earlier essay, "'The Inner Chambers of All Nameless Sin': *The Beetle*, Gothic Female Sexuality, and Oriental Barbarism," in Lloyd Davis, ed., *Virginal Sexuality and Textuality in Victorian Literature* (Albany: State University of New York Press, 1993).

12 For an argument which works similarly to explicate the intertwined meanings of gothic sexuality and gothic raciality at the *fin de siècle*, see Judith Halberstam, "Technologies of Monstrosity: Bram Stoker's *Dracula*."

13 For a helpful overview of British colonial relations with Egypt, see Peter Mansfield, *The British in Egypt*; and Ronald Robinson, John Gallagher, and Alice Denny, *Africa and the Victorians: The Climax of Imperialism*, chapters 8–10.

14 For a similar argument about *Dracula*, see Arata, "The Occidental Tourist." Patrick Brantlinger also discusses the late-Victorian phenomenon of Gothic novels of inverse colonialism, or "invasion fantasies," in chapter 8 of his *Rule of Darkness*.

15 Marjorie does recover after two years of institutionalization. Besides memory-loss, the only remaining symptom of her trauma is beetle-phobia, a symptom shared by her husband Paul Lessingham.

7. ABJECTED MASCULINITIES

1 *The Best Supernatural Tales of Arthur Conan Doyle*, p. 255. First published 1886, *Cassell's Saturday Journal*.

2 Compare my discussion of criminal anthropology in chapter 5.1.

3 Compare Christopher Craft's discussion of the scene where *Dracula*'s Harker is nearly seduced by the three vampire women: "virile Jonathan Harker enjoys a 'feminine' passivity and awaits a delicious penetration from a woman whose demonism is figured as the power to penetrate" (*Another Kind of Love*, p. 73).

4 In both *Jekyll and Hyde* and *The Picture of Dorian Gray*, male "depravity" includes the possibility of both homosexual and heterosexual relations.

5 Compare Dick Donovan's "The Woman with the 'Oily Eyes'" or Conan Doyle's "John Barrington Cowles." Each story features a villainess who is bodily abhuman, sexually perverse, and a criminal hypnotist. Male objects of her vampiric lust are demasculinized by their essentially passive relation to a predatory female. Furthermore, here as in other stories of criminal hypnosis featuring a female hypnotist and a male subject, loss of volition and integral subjectivity through hypnotic suggestion is figured as a loss of essential masculinity.

6 "To decapitate = to castrate. The terror of Medusa['s decapitated head] is thus a terror of castration that is linked to the sight of something. Numerous analyses have made us familar with the occasion for this: it occurs when a boy, who has hitherto been unwilling to believe the threat of castration, catches sight of the female genitals, probably those of an adult, surrounded by hair, and essentially those of the mother." ("Medusa's Head," p. 212)

7 Freud's argument here is very consistent with that of other late-Victorian sociomedical figures.

8 Charles Bernheimer points out that the "many symbolic meanings of 'phallus' and 'phallic' in contemporary culture all evoke an image of the erect organ, this being the form in which male sexuality most effectively asserts power, dominance, potency, and so forth" ("Penile Reference in Phallic Theory," p. 119).

9 For further consideration of this point, see Arata, "The Occidental Tourist"; Craft, *Another Kind of Love*; and John Stevenson, "A Vampire in the Mirror: The Sexuality of *Dracula*."

10 See Craft, *Another Kind of Love*, chapter 3, and Stephen Heath, "Psychopathia Sexualis: Stevenson's *Strange Case*," for readings of the *fin-de-siècle* Gothic within the specific context of contemporary sexology.

11 See Ed Cohen, *Talk on the Wilde Side: Toward a Genealogy of a Discourse on Male Sexualities*; Michel Foucault, *The History of Sexuality. vol.* I; and Jeffrey Weeks, *Sex, Politics and Society: The Regulation of Sexuality Since 1800* and *Sexuality and its Discontents: Meanings, Myths and Modern Sexualities*.

12 James R. Kincaid puts the case even more strongly when he argues that a sexologist like Krafft-Ebing "tended to suggest with his ever-expanding categories [of sexual perversion] not mastery of a subject but a sense of pure bliss in its inexhaustible fertility, its capacity to produce abnormalities that would defeat any neat classifications" (*Child-Loving: The Erotic Child and Victorian Culture*, p. 144).

13 See, respectively, Janice Doane and Devon Hodges, "Demonic Disturbances of Sexual Identity: The Strange Case of Dr. Jekyll and Mr/s Hyde," and Jerrold E. Hogle, "The Struggle for a Dichotomy: Abjection in Jekyll and his Interpreters"; Heath, "Psychopathia Sexualis," and William Veeder, "Children of the Night: Stevenson and Patriarchy"; and Wayne Koestenbaum, *Double Talk: The Erotics of Male Literary Collaboration*, pp. 145–51, and Showalter, *Sexual Anarchy*, pp. 107–27.

14 I will limit myself to three references from the many fine critical pieces exploring sexuality in *Dracula*: Roth, "Suddenly Sexual Women"; Stevenson, "A Vampire in the Mirror"; and Craft, *Another Kind of Love*.

8. NARRATIVE CHAOS

1 Marsh, *The Seen and the Unseen*.

2 Within Gothic plotting, such a tendency is not necessarily incompatible with the entropic tendency towards bodily disorganization. *Moreau* is one instance of a novel in which bodies are liable to both loss of complexity and

intricate morphic refiguration; another is Hodgson's *The Night Land*, which projects itself many millenia into the future to imagine the heat-death of the sun and the "utter twilight of the world" (p. 377). This transfigured earth, despite its frigid inhospitality, is swarming with abominations, including a wide range of degenerate abhumans, "mighty and lost races of terrible creatures, half men and half beast" (p. 328): crab-men (p. 353), elephantine men (p. 395), wolf-men (p. 492), tusked pig-men (p. 499), and a number of others.

3 See, for instance, Robert M. Philmus, "The Satiric Ambivalence of *The Island of Doctor Moreau.*"

4 The Gothic picaresque may resist closure even when it provides a definitive ending. The shipwrecked mariners of *The Boats of the "Glen Carrig"* eventually escape the horrors of the Sargasso Sea and return to England, but the narrator asserts that they did not "discover more than the merest tithe of the mysteries which that great continent of weed holds in its silence" (p. 82). The novel, in other words, could have continued indefinitely.

Compare Hodgson's "From the Tideless Sea," purportedly written by a man trapped in a derelict hulk with his wife and child somewhere in the Sargasso Sea. He composes accounts of their encounters with the abominations found in the Sargasso weed, and sends these off in watertight containers. His second, third, and fourth manuscripts are not found by any ship, and thus only the first and fifth are shared with the reader. Like *The Boats of the "Glen Carrig"*, then, "From the Tideless Sea" has only demonstrated the "merest tithe" of the horrors of the Sargasso; the author could have written sixth and seventh manuscripts and so on. The theme of gothic nature, the story indicates, could be elaborated endlessly.

5 Degeneration theory had foreclosed that possibility by identifying modern urban life as the key source of bodily contamination and thence human retrogression.

6 *City of Dreadful Delight*, p. 17.

7 The theorists of urban degeneration, discussed in chapter 4, should be considered within the tradition of "social exploration" as well.

8 Peter Keating, ed., *Into Unknown England 1866–1913: Selections from the Social Explorers*, p. 65. Keating also excerpts Booth and Mearns, discussed below.

9 Most notably Peter Stallybrass and Allon White, *The Politics and Poetics of Transgression.*

10 See, for instance, the introduction to Booth's *In Darkest England.*

11 These instances of the gothicization of the city could be multiplied indefinitely. While I would not go so far as Kathleen Spencer, who argues that the *fin-de-siècle* Gothic deploys the urban setting so consistently that it ought to be termed the "Victorian Urban Gothic," I would agree that the metropolis is one preoccupation of the genre. See Spencer, "Victorian Urban Gothic."

12 These interpolated stories are discussed briefly above, in chapter 1 (p. 34) and chapter 3 (p. 63).

13 Robert Louis Stevenson and Fanny Van de Grift Stevenson, *The Dynamiter, or More New Arabian Nights*, pp. 17, 23.
14 See Barbara Arnett Melchiori, *Terrorism in the Late Victorian Novel.*
15 In which Florence Dombey can be kidnapped by "good Mrs. Brown," or Lucy Snowe followed and harassed on the streets at night.
16 For an argument that places Machen squarely within the decadent and symbolist tradition, despite critical – and Machen's own – disclaimers to the contrary, see Jill Tedford Owens, "Arthur Machen's Supernaturalism: The Decadent Variety." Machen moved in aestheticist circles for a brief period of his life, publishing *The Great God Pan and The Inmost Light*, with a cover design by Aubrey Beardsley, at the Bodley Head. Owen relates that "Machen knew Oscar Wilde and Lord Alfred Douglas; he dined with Wilde on several occasions and when critics characterized Machen's stories as 'disgusting', 'revolting', 'loathsome', and 'demoniac', Wilde congratulated him on the furor he had caused" (Owens, p. 117).

Works cited

Allen, Grant. "Woman's Intuition." *Forum* 9 (1890): 333–40.
Arata, Stephen D. "The Occidental Tourist: *Dracula* and the Anxiety of Reverse Colonialism." *Victorian Studies* 33.4 (1990): 621–45.
Armstrong, Nancy. *Desire and Domestic Fiction: A Political History of the Novel.* New York: Oxford University Press, 1987.
Aubrey, Frank. *The Devil-Tree of El Dorado: A Romance of British Guiana.* London: Hutchinson and Co., 1896.
   A Queen of Atlantis: A Romance of the Caribbean Sea. London: Hutchinson and Co., 1899.
   King of the Dead: A Weird Romance. London: John MacQueen, 1903.
Auerbach, Nina. *Woman and the Demon: The Life of a Victorian Myth.* Cambridge, MA: Harvard University Press, 1982.
Beard, George M. *American Nervousness: Its Causes and Consequences.* New York: Arno Press, 1972.
Beer, Gillian. *Darwin's Plots: Evolutionary Narrative in Darwin, George Eliot and Nineteenth-Century Fiction.* London: Ark, 1983.
Bergonzi, Bernard. "*The Time Machine*: An Ironic Myth." Ed. Bernard Bergonzi. *H. G. Wells: A Collection of Critical Essays.* Englewood Cliffs, NJ: Prentice-Hall, 1976.
Bernheimer, Charles. "Penile Reference in Phallic Theory." *differences: A Journal of Feminist Cultural Studies* 4.1 (1992): 116–32.
Birkin, Lawrence. *Consuming Desire: Sexual Science and the Emergence of a Culture of Abundance, 1871–1914.* Ithaca: Cornell University Press, 1988.
Block, Ed Jr. "James Sully, Evolutionist Psychology, and Late Victorian Gothic Fiction." *Victorian Studies* 25.4 (1982): 443–67.
Boothby, Guy. *Pharos the Egyptian.* London: Ward, Lock & Co., 1899.
Brantlinger, Patrick. *Rule of Darkness: British Literature and Imperialism, 1830–1914.* Ithaca: Cornell University Press, 1988.
Brooke-Rose, Christine. *A Rhetoric of the Unreal: Studies in Narrative and Structure, Especially of the Fantastic.* Cambridge University Press, 1981.
Buchan, John. *The Watcher at the Threshold and Other Tales.* Edinburgh: Thomas Nelson and Sons, 1902.
Cantlie, James. *Degeneration Amongst Londoners.* New York: Garland, 1985.

Carlson, Eric T. "Medicine and Degeneration: Theory and Praxis." Eds. J. Edward Chamberlin and Sander L. Gilman. *Degeneration: The Dark Side of Progress*. New York: Columbia University Press, 1985.

Carroll, Noël. *The Philosophy of Horror, or Paradoxes of the Heart*. New York: Routledge, 1990.

Chesney, Weatherby. *The Adventures of a Solicitor*. London: James Bowden, 1898.

Cixous, Hélène and Clément, Catherine. *The Newly Born Woman*. Trans. Betsy Wing. Minneapolis: University of Minnesota Press, 1986.

Cohen, Ed. *Talk on the Wilde Side: Toward a Genealogy of a Discourse on Male Sexualities*. New York: Routledge, 1993.

Conan Doyle, Arthur. *Tales of Terror and Mystery*. New York: Doubleday and Company, 1977.

The Best Supernatural Tales of Arthur Conan Doyle. New York: Dover, 1979.

The Conan Doyle Stories. Leicester: Galley, 1986.

Conway, Hugh [pseud. of Frederick John Fargus]. *Carriston's Gift*. Arrowsmith's Bristol Library, vol. XII. Bristol: J. W. Arrowsmith, 1886.

Cope, E. D. "On the Material Relations of Sex in Human Society." *The Monist* I (1890): 38–47.

Cooter, Roger. *The Cultural Meaning of Popular Sciences: Phrenology and the Organization of Consent in Nineteenth-Century Britain*. Cambridge University Press, 1968.

Craft, Christopher. *Another Kind of Love: Male Homosocial Desire in English Discourse, 1850–1920*. Berkeley: University of California Press, 1994.

Cunningham, A. R. "The 'New Woman Fiction' of the 1890s." *Victorian Studies* 17 (1973): 177–86.

Dale, Peter Allan. *In Pursuit of a Scientific Culture: Science, Art, and Society in the Victorian Age*. Madison: University of Wisconsin Press, 1989.

Darwin, Charles. *The Origin of Species* and *The Descent of Man*. New York: Modern Library, n.d.

De la Mare, Walter. "A: B: O." *Eight Tales*. Sauk City, WI: Arkham House, 1971.

Derrida, Jacques. "Structure, Sign, and Play in the Discourse of the Human Sciences." *Writing and Difference*. New York: Routledge, 1978.

Dijkstra, Bram. *Idols of Perversity: Fantasies of Feminine Evil in Fin-de-siècle Culture*. New York: Oxford University Press, 1986.

Doane, Janice and Hodges, Devon. "Demonic Disturbances of Sexual Identity: The Strange Case of Dr. Jekyll and Mr/s Hyde." *Novel: A Forum on Fiction* 23 (1989): 63–74.

Donovan, Dick [pseud. of J. E. Muddock]. *Stories Weird and Wonderful*. London: Chatto and Windus, 1889.

Tales of Terror. London: Chatto and Windus, 1899.

Douglas, Mary. *Purity and Danger: An Analysis of the Concepts of Pollution and Taboo*. London: Routledge and Kegan Paul, 1966.

Dowling, Linda. "The Decadent and the New Woman in the 1890s." *Nineteenth-Century Fiction* 33 (1979): 434–53.

Drinka, George Frederick. *The Birth of Neurosis: Myth, Malady, and the Victorians.* New York: Simon and Schuster, 1984.

Eagleton, Terry. *Marxism and Literary Criticism.* Berkeley and Los Angeles: University of California Press, 1976.

Ellenberger, Henri F. *The Discovery of the Unconscious: The History and Evolution of Dynamic Psychiatry.* New York: Basic, 1970.

Ellis, Havelock. *The Criminal.* Fifth edn. London: Walter Scott, 1914.

Fawcett, E. D. *Swallowed Alive by an Earthquake.* London: Edward Arnold, 1894.

Fothergill, J. Milner. *The Town Dweller: His Needs and Wants.* New York: Garland, 1985.

Foucault, Michel. *The Order of Things: An Archaeology of the Human Sciences.* New York: Vintage, 1973.

The History of Sexuality. Volume I: An Introduction. Trans. Robert Hurley. New York: Vintage, 1978.

Freud, Sigmund. "The 'Uncanny'." *On Creativity and the Unconscious.* New York: Harper and Row, 1958.

"The Aetiology of Hysteria." *Early Psychoanalytic Writings.* New York: Collier, 1963.

Dora: An Analysis of a Case of Hysteria. New York: Collier, 1963.

"Medusa's Head." *Sexuality and the Psychology of Love.* Ed. Philip Rieff. New York: Collier, 1963.

and Breuer, Joseph. *Studies on Hysteria.* New York: Basic, n.d.

Gafford, Sam. "Writing Backwards: The Novels of William Hope Hodgson." *Studies in Weird Fiction* 11 (1992): 12–15.

Gagnier, Regenia. *Idylls of the Marketplace: Oscar Wilde and the Victorian Public.* Stanford University Press, 1986.

"Evolution and Information, or Eroticism and Everyday Life, in *Dracula* and Late Victorian Aestheticism." Ed. Regina Barreca. *Sex and Death in Victorian Literature.* Bloomington: Indiana University Press, 1990.

Subjectivities: A History of Self-Representation in Britain, 1832–1920. New York: Oxford University Press, 1991.

Gilbert, Sandra M. and Gubar, Susan. *No Man's Land: The Place of the Woman Writer in the Twentieth Century*, vol. II: *Sexchanges.* New Haven: Yale University Press, 1989.

Gilman, Sander L. "Sexology, Psychoanalysis, and Degeneration." *Difference and Pathology: Stereotypes of Sexuality, Race, and Madness.* Ithaca: Cornell University Press, 1985.

Gould, Stephen Jay. *Ontogeny and Phylogeny.* Cambridge, The Belknap Press, 1977.

The Mismeasure of Man. New York: W. W. Norton and Company, 1981.

Goux, Jean-Joseph. "The Phallus: Masculine Identity and the 'Exchange of Women'." *differences: A Journal of Feminist Cultural Studies* 4.1 (1992): 40–75.

Graham, John. *Lavater's Essays on Physiognomy: A Study in the History of Ideas.* Berne: Peter Lang, 1979.

Greenway, John L. "Seward's Folly: *Dracula* as a Critique of 'Normal Science'." *Stanford Literature Review* 3 (1986): 213–30.

Halberstam, Judith. "Technologies of Monstrosity: Bram Stoker's *Dracula*." *Victorian Studies* 36.3 (1993): 333–52.

Haggerty, George E. *Gothic Fiction/Gothic Form*. University Park: Pennsylvania State University Press, 1989.

Haraway, Donna J. "A Cyborg Manifesto: Science, Technology, and Socialist-Feminism in the Late Twentieth Century." *Simians, Cyborgs, and Women: The Reinvention of Nature*. New York: Routledge, 1991.

Heath, Stephen. "Psychopathia Sexualis: Stevenson's *Strange Case*." *Critical Quarterly* 28 (1986): 93–108.

Hekma, Gert. "'A Female Soul in a Male Body': Sexual Inversion as Gender Inversion in Nineteenth-Century Sexology." Ed. Gilbert Herdt. *Third Sex, Third Gender: Beyond Sexual Dimorphism in Culture and History*. New York: Zone, 1994.

Herdt, Gilbert, ed. *Third Sex, Third Gender: Beyond Sexual Dimorphism in Culture and History*. New York: Zone, 1994.

Hocking, Joseph. *The Weapons of Mystery*, London: George Routledge and Sons, 1890.

Hodgson, William Hope. *"The House on the Borderland" and Other Novels*. Sauk City, WI: Arkham House, 1946.

Carnacki the Ghost-Finder. Sauk City, WI: Mycroft and Moran, 1947.

Deep Waters. Sauk City, WI: Arkham House, 1967.

Out of the Storm: Uncollected Fantasies by William Hope Hodgson. Ed. Sam Moskowitz. West Kingston, RI: Donald M. Grant, 1975.

Hogle, Jerrold E. "The Struggle for a Dichotomy: Abjection in Jekyll and his Interpreters." Eds. William Veeder and Gordon Hirsch. *Dr. Jekyll and Mr. Hyde after One Hundred Years*. University of Chicago Press, 1988.

Huxley, T. H. "On the Physical Basis of Life." *The Fortnightly Review* N.S. 26 (1869): 129–45.

Hynes, Samuel. *The Edwardian Turn of Mind*. Princeton University Press, 1968.

Jackson, Rosemary. *Fantasy: The Literature of Subversion*. London: Methuen, 1981.

James, William. "Degeneration and Genius." *Psychological Review* 2 (1895): 287–94.

Jay, Martin. *Downcast Eyes: The Denigration of Vision in Twentieth-Century French Thought*. Berkeley: University of California Press, 1994.

Keating, Peter, ed. *Into Unknown England 1866–1913: Selections from the Social Explorers*. Manchester University Press, 1976.

Kidd, Benjamin. *Social Evolution*. New York: Macmillan and Company, 1895.

The Control of the Tropics. New York: Macmillan and Company, 1898.

Kincaid, James R. *Child-Loving: The Erotic Child in Victorian Culture*. New York: Routledge, 1992.

Koestenbaum, Wayne. *Double Talk: The Erotics of Male Literary Collaboration*. New York: Routledge, 1989.

Krafft-Ebing, Richard von. *Psychopathia Sexualis: A Medico-Forensic Study*. Trans. Harry E. Wedeck. New York: G. P. Putnam's Sons, 1965.

Kristeva, Julia. *Powers of Horror: An Essay on Abjection*. Trans. Leon S. Roudiez. New York: Columbia University Press, 1982.

Kurella, Hans. *Cesare Lombroso: A Modern Man of Science.* Trans. M. Eden Paul. London: Rebman Limited, 1911.

Lacan, Jacques. "The Mirror Stage as Formative of the Function of the I." *Écrits: A Selection.* New York: W. W. Norton and Company, 1977.

Lawler, Donald. "Reframing *Jekyll and Hyde*: Robert Louis Stevenson and the Strange Case of Gothic Science Fiction." Eds. William Veeder and Gordon Hirsch. *Dr. Jekyll and Mr. Hyde after One Hundred Years.* University of Chicago Press, 1988.

Le Fanu, J. S. *Best Ghost Stories of J. S. Le Fanu.* New York: Dover, 1964.

Levine, George. *Darwin and the Novelists: Patterns of Science in Victorian Fiction.* Cambridge, MA: Harvard University Press, 1988.

Lombroso, Cesare. "Illustrative Studies in Criminal Anthropology." Parts 1–3. *Monist* 1 (1891): 177–85, 186–96, 336–43.

The Man of Genius. London: Walter Scott, 1891.

"Atavism and Evolutionism." *Contemporary Review* 68 (1895): 42–9.

"Criminal Anthropology Applied to Pedagogy." *Monist* 6 (1895): 50–59.

"Criminal Anthropology: Its Origin and Application." *The Forum* 20 (1895): 33–49.

and Ferrero, William. *The Female Offender.* New York: Philosophical Library, 1958.

Lombroso-Ferrero, Gina. *Criminal Man According to the Classification of Cesare Lombroso.* Montclair, NJ: Patterson Smith, 1972.

Lovecraft, H. P. *The Best of H. P. Lovecraft: Bloodcurdling Tales of Horror and the Macabre.* New York: Ballantine, 1982.

Lutz, Tom. *American Nervousness, 1903: An Anecdotal History.* Ithaca: Cornell University Press, 1991.

Machen, Arthur. *The Great God Pan. The House of Souls.* New York: Alfred A. Knopf, 1922.

Precious Balms. London: Spurr and Swift, 1924.

Tales of Horror and the Supernatural. New York: Alfred A. Knopf, 1948.

The Three Imposters. Ed. Martin Secker. *The Eighteen-Nineties: A Period Anthology in Prose and Verse.* London: Richards, 1948.

MacKenzie, Norman and Jeanne. *H. G. Wells: A Biography.* New York: Simon and Schuster, 1973.

Mansfield, Peter. *The British in Egypt.* New York: Holt, Rinehart and Winston, 1971.

Marsh, Richard. *The Goddess: A Demon.* London: White and Co., 1900.

Marvels and Mysteries. London: Methuen and Co., 1900.

The Seen and the Unseen. London: Methuen and Co., 1900.

The Beetle. Eds. Graham Greene and Hugh Greene. *Victorian Villainies.* New York: Penguin Viking, 1984.

Martindale, Colin. "Degeneration, Disinhibition, and Genius." *Journal of the History of the Behavioral Sciences* 7 (1971): 177–82.

Melchiori, Barbara Arnett. *Terrorism in the Late Victorian Novel.* London: Croom Helm, 1985.

Miller, D. A. "*Cage aux Folles*: Sensation and Gender in Wilkie Collins's *The*

Woman in White." Ed. Elaine Showalter. *Speaking of Gender.* New York: Routledge, 1989.

Mitchell, P. Chalmers. "Mr. Wells's *Dr. Moreau." The Saturday Review* 81 (1896): 368–9.

Reply to Letter of H. G. Wells. *The Saturday Review* 82 (1896): 498.

Morel, B. A. "An Analysis of a Treatise on the Degenerations, Physical, Intellectual, and Moral, of the Human Race, and the Causes which Produce their Unhealthy Varieties." Trans. Edwin Wing. *The Medical Circular* 10 (1857): 122–3, 136–7, 150–1, 161, 173, 187, 207–8, 219–21, 232–3, 254–5, 267–8; and 11 (1857): 14, 37, 49–50, 61–2, 73–4, 109, 133–4, 146, 182, 193, 205, 218, 229–30, 241, 277–8, 302–3.

Morgan, John Edward. *The Danger of the Deterioration of Race from the Too Rapid Increase of Great Cities.* New York: Garland, 1985.

Morton, Peter. *The Vital Science: Biology and the Literary Imagination, 1860–1900.* London: George Allen and Unwin, 1984.

Nordau, Max. *Degeneration.* Trans. from the 2nd German edn. New York: D. Appleton and Company, 1895.

Norris, Margot. *Beasts of the Modern Imagination: Darwin, Nietzsche, Kafka, Ernst, and Lawrence.* Baltimore: Johns Hopkins University Press, 1985.

Nye, Robert A. *Crime, Madness, and Politics in Modern France: The Medical Concept of National Decline.* Princeton University Press, 1984.

Oppenheim, Janet. *"Shattered Nerves": Doctors, Patients, and Depression in Victorian England.* New York: Oxford University Press, 1991.

Ortner, Sherry B. "Is Male to Female as Nature is to Culture?" Eds. Michelle Zimbalist Rosaldo and Louise Lamphere. *Woman, Culture, and Society.* Stanford University Press, 1974.

Owens, Jill Tedford. "Arthur Machen's Supernaturalism: The Decadent Variety." *University of Mississippi Studies in English* 8 (1990): 117–26.

Pain, Barry. *Stories in the Dark.* London: Grant Richards, 1901.

Palmer, Jerry. *Potboilers: Methods, Concepts and Case Studies in Popular Fiction.* London: Routledge, 1991.

Philmus, Robert M. "The Satiric Ambivalence of *The Island of Doctor Moreau." Science-Fiction Studies* 8.1 (1981): 2–11.

ed., H. G. Wells, *The Island of Doctor Moreau: A Variorum Text.* Athens: The University of Georgia Press, 1993.

Pick, Daniel. *Faces of Degeneration: A European Disorder, c.1848 – c.1918.* Cambridge University Press, 1989.

Pole, David. "Disgust and Other Forms of Aversion." *Aesthetics, Form and Emotion.* London: Duckworth, 1983.

Poovey, Mary. *Uneven Developments: The Ideological Work of Gender in Mid-Victorian England.* University of Chicago Press, 1988.

Porter, Dorothy and Roy. "What Was Social Medicine? An Historiographical Essay." *Journal of Historical Sociology* 1 (1988): 90–106.

Prince, Stephen. "Dread, Taboo and *The Thing*: Toward a Social Theory of the Horror Film." *Wide Angle* 10.3 (1988): 19–29.

Radcliffe, Ann. "On the Supernatural in Poetry." *The New Monthly Magazine and Literary Review* 16 (1826): 145–52.

The Mysteries of Udolpho. London: Oxford University Press, 1970.

Reed, John R. "The Occult in Later Victorian Fiction." Ed. Peter B. Messent. *Literature of the Occult.* Englewood Cliffs, NJ: Prentice Hall, Inc., 1981.

Richards, Grant. Rev. of *The Island of Dr. Moreau,* by H. G. Wells. *The Academy* 49 (1896): 443–4.

Robinson, Phil[ip Stewart]. *Under the Punkah.* London: Sampson, Low, Marston, Searle, and Rivington, 1881.

Robinson, Ronald, Gallagher, John and Denny, Alice. *Africa and the Victorians: The Climax of Imperialism.* Garden City, NY: Anchor, 1971.

Rosmarin, Adena. *The Power of Genre.* Minneapolis: University of Minnesota Press, 1985.

Roth, Judith. "Suddenly Sexual Women in Bram Stoker's *Dracula.*" *Literature and Psychology* 27 (1977): 113–21.

Said, Edward. *Orientalism.* New York: Vintage, 1978.

Sartre, Jean-Paul. *Being and Nothingness.* Trans. Hazel E. Barnes. New York: Washington Square, 1966.

Senf, Carol A. "*Dracula*: Stoker's Response to the New Woman." *Victorian Studies* 26.1 (Autumn 1982): 33–49.

Shiel, M. P. *The Pale Ape and Other Pulses.* London: T. Werner Laurie, n.d.

Showalter, Elaine. *The Female Malady: Women, Madness, and English Culture, 1830–1980.* New York: Penguin, 1985.

"Syphilis, Sexuality, and the Fiction of the Fin de Siècle." Ed. Ruth Bernard Yeazell. *Sex, Politics, and Science in the Nineteenth-Century Novel: Selected Paper from the English Institute, 1983–84.* Baltimore: Johns Hopkins University Press, 1986.

Sexual Anarchy: Gender and Culture at the Fin de Siècle. New York: Penguin, 1990.

Smith, David C. *H. G. Wells: Desperately Mortal.* New Haven: Yale University Press, 1986.

Spencer, Herbert. *Descriptive Sociology,* III: *Lowest Races, Negrito Races, and Malayo-Polynesian Races.* New York: D. Appleton and Company, 1874.

The Principles of Sociology. Vol. I. New York: D. Appleton and Company, 1898.

Spencer, Kathleen L. "Victorian Urban Gothic: The First Modern Fantastic Literature." Eds. George E. Slusser and Eric S. Rabkin. *Intersections: Fantasy and Science Fiction.* Carbondale: Southern Illinois University Press, 1987.

"Purity and Danger: *Dracula,* the Urban Gothic, and the Late Victorian Degeneracy Crisis." *ELH* 59.1 (1992): 197–225.

Spitzka, E. C. Review of Max Nordau's *Degeneration. American Journal of Insanity* 52 (1896): 106–17.

Stallybrass, Peter and White, Allon. *The Politics and Poetics of Transgression.* Ithaca: Cornell University Press, 1986.

Stedman Jones, Gareth. *Outcast London: A Study in the Relationships Between Classes in Victorian Society.* New York: Pantheon, 1971.

Stepan, Nancy. "Biological Degeneration: Races and Proper Places." Eds. J. Edward Chamberlin and Sander L. Gilman. *Degeneration: The Dark Side of Progress.* New York: Columbia University Press, 1985.

Stevenson, John. "A Vampire in the Mirror: The Sexuality of *Dracula.*" *PMLA* 103 (1988): 139–49.

Stevenson, Robert Louis. *Dr. Jekyll and Mr. Hyde.* New York: Signet, 1987.

and Stevenson, Fanny Van de Grift. *The Dynamiter, or More New Arabian Nights.* Cleveland: The World Syndicate Publishing Co., n.d.

Stocking, George. *Victorian Anthropology.* New York: The Free Press, 1987.

Stoker, Bram. *The Lair of the White Worm.* New York: Zebra, 1978.

Dracula. Ed. Maurice Hindle. New York: Penguin, 1993.

Sulloway, Frank J. *Freud, Biologist of the Mind: Beyond the Psychoanalytic Legend.* New York: Basic, 1979.

Suvin, Darko. *Victorian Science Fiction in the UK: The Discourses of Knowledge and Power.* Boston: G. K. Hall and Co., 1983.

Talbot, Eugene S. *Degeneracy: Its Causes, Signs, and Results.* London: Walter Scott, 1898.

Todorov, Tzvetan. *The Fantastic: A Structural Approach to a Literary Genre.* Ithaca: Cornell University Press, 1975.

Tytler, Graham. *Physiognomy in the European Novel: Faces and Fortunes.* Princeton University Press, 1982.

Veeder, William. "Children of the Night: Stevenson and Patriarchy." Eds. William Veeder and Gordon Hirsch. *Dr. Jekyll and Mr. Hyde after One Hundred Years.* University of Chicago Press, 1988.

Walkowitz, Judith R. *City of Dreadful Delight: Narratives of Sexual Danger in Late-Victorian London.* University of Chicago Press, 1992.

Walter, Richard D. "What Became of the Degenerate? A Brief History of a Concept." *Journal of the History of Medicine and the Allied Sciences* 11 (1956): 422–9.

Weeks, Jeffrey. *Sex, Politics and Society: The Regulation of Sexuality Since 1800.* London and New York: Longman, 1981.

Sexuality and its Discontents: Meanings, Myths and Modern Sexualities. London and New York: Routledge and Kegan Paul, 1985.

Wells, H. G. Letter. *The Saturday Review* 82 (1896): 497.

Twenty-eight Science Fiction Stories. New York: Dover, 1952.

Early Writings in Science and Science Fiction. Eds. Robert Philmus and David Y. Hughes. Berkeley: University of California Press, 1975.

The Complete Science Fiction Treasury of H. G. Wells. New York: Avenel, 1978.

The Time Machine. New York: Bantam, 1982.

The Island of Dr. Moreau. New York: Signet, 1988. (Reviews in *Athenaeum* 3576 (1896): 615–16; *The Critic* o.s. 29 (1896): 55–6.)

White, Eric. "The End of Metanarratives in Evolutionary Biology." *Modern Language Quarterly* 51.1 (1990): 63–81.

"The Erotics of Becoming: *Xenogenesis* and *The Thing.*" *Science-Fiction Studies* 20.3 (1993): 394–408.

Wicke, Jennifer. "Vampiric Typewriting: *Dracula* and its Media." *ELH* 59 (1992): 469–93.

Wilde, Oscar. *The Picture of Dorian Gray*. New York: Penguin, 1985.

Wilt, Judith. "The Imperial Mouth: Imperialism, the Gothic and Science Fiction." *Journal of Popular Culture* 14 (1981): 618–28.

Wood, Robin. "Introduction." *American Nightmare: Essays on the Horror Film*. Eds. Andrew Britton *et al*. Toronto: Festival of Festivals, 1979. 7–28.

Index

CAMBRIDGE STUDIES IN NINETEENTH-CENTURY
LITERATURE AND CULTURE

General editors

Gillian Beer, *University of Cambridge*
Catherine Gallagher, *University of California*, Berkeley

Titles published

4517068R00123

Printed in Great Britain
by Amazon.co.uk, Ltd.,
Marston Gate.